# Mundane Methods

Manchester University Press

# Mundane Methods

## Innovative ways to research the everyday

Edited by Helen Holmes and
Sarah Marie Hall

Manchester University Press

Published by Manchester University Press
Altrincham Street, Manchester M1 7JA

www.manchesteruniversitypress.co.uk

British Library Cataloguing-in-Publication Data

A catalogue record for this book is available from the British Library

ISBN    978 1 5261 3970 2    hardback
ISBN    978 1 5261 3971 9    paperback

First published 2020

Typeset
by Toppan Best-set Premedia Limited
Printed in Great Britain
by TJ International Ltd, Padstow

# Contents

# List of figures

# List of contributors

**Les Back** is Professor of Sociology at Goldsmiths, University of London. Key themes in his work include developing collaborative forms of research writing and new styles of research craft. These issues are developed his books *The Art of Listening* (Oxford: Berg, 2007) and, with Shamser Sinha, *Migrant City* (Abingdon: Routledge, 2018).

**Thomas Birtchnell** is Senior Lecturer in the School of Geography and Sustainable Communities, University of Wollongong. A confluence of interest in his work is critical techno-futures and sustainable development with a regional focus on South Asia. His latest book, co-authored with John Urry, is *A New Industrial Future? 3D Printing and the Reconfiguration of Production, Distribution, and Consumption* (London: Routledge, 2016).

**Megan Blake** is a Senior Lecturer in Human Geography, University of Sheffield. She has an established international reputation for her research focusing on 1) surplus food chains and practices of redistribution; 2) community organisations, social innovation and practices of resilience; and 3) social inequalities. She is the creator of Food Ladders, a multi-scaled and asset-based approach that uses food to increase everyday food security, connect communities and increase local resilience by reducing vulnerability. Her film, *More Than Just Food*, illustrates the ways that community-based food ladders can change places.

**Lynne Chapman** is a freelance reportage-sketcher, recording events and research, currently working with universities in England and Australia. She is author of *Sketching People* (Kent: Search Press/Barrons, 2016) and co-authored (with Sue Heath and the Morgan Centre Sketchers) 'Observational sketching as method' (*International Journal of Social Research Methodology*, 21 (6): 713–728, 2018). Lynne is also an award-winning children's book illustrator, an Urban Sketchers Correspondent and founder of Urban Sketchers Yorkshire.

**Rebecca Collins** is Senior Lecturer in Human Geography at the University of Chester. Her research focuses on the intersection of youth geographies, material cultures and everyday (un)sustainabilities. She is particularly interested in the cultural production of waste and excess.

**Simon Cook** is a Senior Lecturer in the Faculty of Health, Education and Life Sciences at Birmingham City University and a PhD candidate in the Department of Geography at Royal Holloway, University of London. His research concerns the everyday practices of daily life: the ways in which they happen, how they change, and what they can tell us about societies and spaces. This is currently manifest in a project exploring the rise of run commuting.

**Sarah Marie Hall** is Senior Lecturer in Human Geography at the University of Manchester. Her research focuses on the everyday impacts of economic and political change, particularly as they intersect with gender and other forms of social inequality. She is the author of *Everyday Life in Austerity: Family, Friends and Intimate Relations* (Basingstoke: Palgrave Macmillan, 2019).

**Theresa Harada** has a PhD in Human Geography and works as an ethnographer at the Australian Centre for Culture, Environment, Society and Space, University of Wollongong. Her interests include mobilities, energy efficiency and sustainable practices, and innovative social science methods.

**Sue Heath** is a Professor of Sociology and co-directs the Morgan Centre for Research into Everyday Lives at the University of Manchester. In addition to her methodological interests, she has published widely in the fields of youth studies, housing and intergenerational relations. Her most recent book is *Shared Housing, Shared Lives: Everyday Experiences Across the Lifecourse* (Abingdon: Routledge, 2018).

**Helen Holmes** is a Lecturer in Sociology at the Sustainable Consumption Institute/Sociology Department, University of Manchester. Her work explores materiality and consumption focusing on the lived everyday relationships we have with objects. Recent projects include a three-year fellowship investigating contemporary forms of thrift and a current study exploring lost property and the potency of absent objects. She has published in leading journals including: *Sociology*; *Sociological Review*; *Work, Employment and Society*; and *Geoforum*.

**Dawn Lyon** is Reader in Sociology in the School of Social Policy, Sociology and Social Research at the University of Kent. She has published in the fields of the sociology of work, time, gender, migration, youth studies, and visual and sensory sociology. She is particularly interested in the rhythms of work and everyday life. Her book, *What is Rhythmanalysis?*, was published by Bloomsbury Academic in 2018.

**Kate McLean** is a designer working at the intersection of human-perceived smellscapes, cartography and the communication of 'eye-invisible' sensed data. She leads international public smell walks, translating the resulting data using digital design, watercolour, animation, scent diffusion and sculpture into smellscape mappings. She is Programme Director for Graphic Design at Canterbury Christ Church University.

**Susanna Mills** is a public health specialty registrar and National Institute for Health Research Clinical Lecturer at Newcastle University. She is a medical doctor by background and her PhD focused on home food preparation. Her current main research interests are public health nutrition and the intersection with food sustainability.

**Chris Perkins** is Reader in Geography at the University of Manchester. His interests lie at the interface between mapping technologies and social and cultural practices, with ongoing research into performative aspects of contemporary mapping behaviour and play, alongside an emerging interest in island studies. His most recent book is *Time for Mapping: Cartographic Temporalities* (Manchester: Manchester University Press, 2018).

**Laura Pottinger** holds a PhD in Human Geography from the University of Manchester. Her research explores consumption, alternative economies, and everyday forms of social and environmental activism, with a focus on food, gardens and young people's politics.

**Christian Reynolds** is a Knowledge Exchange Research Fellow at the Department of Geography, University of Sheffield. Christian's research examines the economic and environmental impacts of food consumption, with focus upon food waste, and sustainable, healthy and affordable diets. He is a co-editor with Lazell, Soma and Spring of the upcoming *Routledge Handbook on Food Waste*, https://orcid.org/0000-0002-1073-7394.

**Morag Rose** is a Lecturer in Human Geography at the University of Liverpool. She is also a walking artist and founder of psychogeographical collective The LRM (Loiterers Resistance Movement). Her research interests include public space, walking as a creative, political and cultural act, community mapping, gender and the built environment, and the geographies of Dr Who.

**Alison Slater** is a Senior Lecturer in Design History at Manchester Metropolitan University. Her research focuses on encounters with dress, particularly working-class and everyday dress, using oral history and material culture approaches. She is interested in the relationships between objects and identity, and history and memory, particularly experiences that sit outside traditional historical and archival records, using primary research to gather new insights.

**Lyndsey Stoodley** is a PhD candidate in the School of Geography and Planning at Cardiff University. Her research interests include environmentalism in surfing communities, artificial waves and water more broadly. She is the co-founder of the Institute for Women Surfers Europe, and enjoys surfing small waves on big boards.

**Becky Tipper** has a PhD in Sociology from the University of Manchester, where she also spent several years as a researcher. She now works outside academia but maintains interests in the sociology of human–animal relations, ethnography, and the use of fiction and creative writing in social research.

**Gordon Waitt** is Professor of Geography in the School of Geography and Sustainable Communities, University of Wollongong. He has a research interest in the everyday and seemingly mundane objects. He combines mixed-qualitative research methods with embodied theoretical approaches to address questions of social, mobility, energy and environmental justice. His recent work focuses on household sustainability, liveability, fuel poverty and mobilities. He works and lives in Dharawal Country.

**Karin Widerberg** is a Professor of Sociology at the Department of Sociology and Human Geography, University of Oslo. Time, work and work-life, the body, family life and sexual violence are her research fields. Methodology, however, is a key issue in all her writings, and exploring qualitative approaches such as Institutional Ethnography and Memory Work, is a main concern and activity. Her most recent book is *In the Heart of the Welfare State: An Invitation to Institutional Ethnography* (Oslo: Cappelen Damm, 2015).

**Samantha Wilkinson** is a Senior Lecturer in Childhood and Youth Studies at Manchester Metropolitan University. She has a background in Human Geography, and has conducted research into diverse topics, including young people's alcohol consumption experiences, home care for people with dementia, Airbnb, and hair and identity.

**Sophie Woodward** is a Senior Lecturer in Sociology at the University of Manchester. She carries out research into material culture, materiality, everyday lives and consumption. She is carrying out research into dormant things (things people keep but are not using). She is the author of several books on fashion and clothing as well as on creative methods – *Material Methods: Researching and Thinking with Things* (London: Sage, 2019) – and feminist theory – *Birth and Death: Experience, Ethics, Politics* (Abingdon: Routledge, 2019 with Kath Woodward).

**Wendy Wrieden** is Principal Research Associate at the Institute of Health and Society, Newcastle University. She is a Registered Nutritionist (Public Health) and has led research projects concerned with dietary interventions, surveys and dietary assessment methodology, including a project to monitor the Scottish diet. Her research interests include working with community organisations in social and policy aspects of nutrition, qualitative research and food choice.

# Foreword: making the mundane remarkable

## Les Back

A few years ago I was invited to participate in BBC Radio 4's *Thinking Allowed* edition on studying everyday life. It's my favourite radio show and Laurie Taylor – the show's host – has a special talent for bringing the best out of his guests. Not that the conversations are easy or without challenge because Laurie also has an equal flair for the deceptively simple question. That is, a question that seems straightforward on first hearing, but then the more you think about it the more elusive an adequate answer becomes. Laurie asked me: 'given everyday life is all around us why don't more sociologists study it?' Mmm …

I want to start here because I think my answer chimes with the contents of this wonderful collection that takes mundane everyday things seriously. Is one reason why sociologists are hesitant to train their minds on the everyday or quotidian trivialities because we run the risk of being made fun of: 'You are writing an article about Christmas lights or the social behaviour in cafés or caffs? That's like being paid for sunbathing!' I have a sneaking suspicion that some of the researchers in this book have been subject to similar indignities. But as anthropologist Clifford Geertz once commented, one of the 'psychological fringe benefits' of anthropological research is that it teaches us what it feels like to 'be thought of as a fool … and how to endure it' (Geertz, 2000: 30). Maybe we shy away from the banal to avoid the accusation of seeming trivial or commonplace.

Strangely, it is the humdrum nature of our subject matter that makes it so difficult to study. The second reason why everyday life is not studied more is because it is incredibly hard to do. Social scientists depend on the specular aspects of society's problems to justify the significances of our mission. Focusing on society's bad news gives us a sense of purpose and importance somehow. Georges Perec, the eccentric bard of the mundane, sums this up so well when he writes: 'railway trains only begin to exist when they are derailed, and the more passengers that are killed, the more they exist' (Perec, 1997: 209).

Perec had an extraordinary life and was part of post-war French alternative literary culture. He was a Polish Jew and his father was killed fighting the Nazis and his mother was taken and murdered in Auschwitz. He was orphaned by the spectacular murderous power of the fascist machine. His uncle and aunt took the place of his parents and raised him. I wonder in a way if his ear for what he referred to as 'banal facts, passed over in silence' provided an anchor for him through those dark times (Perec, 1997: 174).

He never finished his degree in history at the Sorbonne but worked as an archivist in a science laboratory up until just before the end of his life. He characterised his writing as part 'sociological ... looking at the ordinary and the everyday', part autobiographical, part ludic or playful, and part novelistic (Perec, 2009: 3–4). He had an extraordinary attentiveness to things. He manages to enchant the mundane through noticing detail and its significance. I see the same quality in Erving Goffman (1956) or the brilliantly attentive Rachel Hurdley (2015) or Sophie Woodward (2015).

Perec wrote a little book, *An Attempt at Exhausting a Place in Paris*, which I think is the best realisation of Clifford Geertz's notion of thick description (Geertz, 1973). At the beginning of the book Perec introduces Place Saint Sulpice, the subject for his weekend study, and lists the existing public knowledge about it. Then comments: 'My intention in the pages that follow was to describe the rest ... that which has no importance: *that which happens when nothing happens* other than the weather, people, cars, and clouds' (Perec, 2010: 3). What a brilliant invitation to the study of everyday life but equally what a difficult challenge. It makes me think of Jennifer Mason's wonderful project on the weather in Hebden Bridge that states with tender confidence that 'weather is woven into every aspect of social life' (Mason, 2016: 2).

Perec does not really give us many clues with regard to how he does his work. How do we write something interesting when nothing seems to be happening? 'I find my direction by following my nose', he comments (Perec, 2009: 5). It is hard, very hard, to practise endotic (as opposed to exotic) sociology – spectacular social problems somehow seem to offer us better clues. It makes us think though about attentiveness as a vocation – a matter of training our senses and then sifting imaginatively what we find for significance, like panning for gold on the mundane surface of life.

For fifty years the qualitative research imagination was held hostage by the tape recorder. To do qualitative research meant to conduct interviews, transcribe them and present the idiomatic voices of our participants in anonymous block quotations. I have written elsewhere about my own love affair with the tape recorder as both a research companion and a device. In the digital age this has all changed: we are thinking, working and inquiring in a very different informational environment. We are encountering unprecedented opportunities to work differently as a result and communicate and circulate the fruits of our work in new ways combined with the old established conventions. Indeed, it seems that some of our old conventions are being made new again in this environment, from drawing to Polaroid photographs to fieldnotes.

Despite the constraints placed on our research environment by the institutional structures for measuring value in an increasingly commercialised university environment, we are on the cusp of what I want to claim is a renaissance in qualitative research. I think the book you are holding in your hands now might be read as evidence in support of this claim; the skills we need to practise endotic sociology are demonstrated within its chapters.

I cannot think of a better metaphor for the work we do as researchers than C. Wright Mills's suggestion that social research is a craft. Carol Smart – co-editor of a beautiful book called *The Craft of Knowledge* (Smart, Hockey and James, 2014) – commented that craft is also interesting because it is not necessarily tied to professionalised forms of expertise. She wrote to me in an email:

> I think craft has strong feminine meanings. OK I know many crafts are/were male preserves but so were many associated with women e.g. sewing, knitting, cooking. My reading is that men abandoned the association with craft as more kudos and income was linked to professionalisation (eg medics versus midwives). Women were denied access to professions and so their association with 'mere' craft led to a diminution notion of the status of craft. Craft has been seen as rather humble and undervalued – hence feminine (or working class). (Carol Smart, personal correspondence, 21 July 2014)

Perhaps what is interesting about craft is the idea that knowledge is about doing and making things with words but not only with words. People are documenting and sharing their lives through their smartphones at an unprecedented frequency and quantity. There is almost no version of culture now that exists independently of the melding of lives on-screen and off-screen.

Research is not only a matter of sitting down and talking but also involves getting up on our feet or going out on a mobility scooter, as some chapters in this book explore. Talking to people, moving alongside them, can often produce a different quality of conversation, as Maggie O'Neill's fantastic work on the everyday landscapes of migrants reveals (e.g. O'Neill and Perivolaris, 2014).

Culture here would be written within, but also beyond, words. Texts collaged alongside pages that also become screens including moving images, still photography, drawing, soundscapes and music. Suzanne Hall's wonderful fieldwork that plots the threads of globalised networks on a single south London street is a good example (Hall, 2012). I am also thinking of the ways in which drawing here is not just representational device but also a mode of discovery and analysis. Rachel Hurdley, who writes brilliantly about design and office spaces and the things people bring to work to make them habitable, uses sketching as a way to discover, to look closely and outline the shape of significance (Hurdley, 2015). What is striking in the Lynne Chapman drawings included in this volume (see Heath and Chapman, this collection) is the impression that this is exactly what she does as she sketches. Attentive film practice is another example of how the mundane can be made remarkable. Jennifer Mason and visual anthropologist Lorenzo Ferrarini do this successfully in their extraordinary film on *Living the Weather* (see Mason, 2016 for the accompanying book), and Jennifer's work on social atmospheres I think is so much in the spirit of Perec at the same time achieving something beyond it.

Teaching research methods is often the most unloved part of any social science degree programme. It is the orphaned part of the curriculum. Yet, it should be the most exciting part of what students learn and what we teach. There is much in the pages of this book that gives fresh resources for teaching the craft of research.

In order to embrace the opportunities that lie before us, we need to be bold and license experimentation of the kind being done by the authors in this volume. Shaking off those fears of being made fun of for taking seriously the seemingly trivial, scholars of everyday life are faced with the difficult task of finding ways *to make the mundane remarkable*. This collection brings together some of the best examples of scholarly work that does precisely this. The result is a kind of re-enchantment of the things we so often take for granted and the mundane aspects of social life can be celebrated and read with a new sense of wonder.

## Bibliography

Geertz, C. (1973) *The Interpretation of Cultures: Selected Essays*, New York: Basic Books.

Geertz, C. (2000) *Available Light: Anthropological Reflections on Philosophical Topics*, Princeton, New Jersey: Princeton University Press.

Goffman, E. (1956) *The Presentation of Self in Everyday Life*, Edinburgh: University of Edinburgh, Social Sciences Research Centre.

Hall, S. (2012) *City, Citizen and Street: The Measure of the Ordinary*, London: Routledge.

Hurdley, R. (2015) 'Pretty pants and office pants: making home, identity and belonging in a workplace', in E. Casey and Y. Taylor (eds) *Intimacies, Critical Consumption and Diverse Economies*, Basingstoke: Palgrave Macmillan, 173–196.

Mason, J. (ed.) (2016) *Living the Weather: Voices from the Calder Valley*, Manchester: Morgan Centre for Research into Everyday Lives, University of Manchester.

O'Neill, M. and Perivolaris, J. (2014) 'A sense of belonging: walking with Thaer through migration, memories and space', *Crossings: Journal of Migration & Culture*, 5 (2&3): 327–338.

Perec, G. (1997) *Species of Spaces and Other Pieces*, London: Penguin Books.

Perec, G. (2009) *Thoughts of Sorts*, Boston: Verba Mundi Book.

Perec, G. (2010) *An Attempt at Exhausting a Place in Paris*, Cambridge, MA: Wakefield Press.

Silverman, D. (2013) *A Very Short, Fairly Interesting and Reasonably Cheap Book About Qualitative Research*, London: Sage.

Smart, C., Hockey, J. and James, A. (eds) (2014) *The Craft of Knowledge: Experiences of Living with Data*, Basingstoke: Palgrave Macmillan.

Woodward, S. (2015) 'The hidden lives of domestic things: accumulations in cupboards, lofts, and shelves', in E. Casey and Y. Taylor (eds) *Intimacies, Critical Consumption and Diverse Economies*, Basingstoke: Palgrave Macmillan, 216–232.

# 1

# Introduction: mundane methods and the extra-ordinary everyday

## Sarah Marie Hall and Helen Holmes

## Researching the everyday

Researching the everyday is more important and significant now than ever before: beyond a fad or cultural currency, understanding the mundane is key to critical and conceptual social science. But what is the everyday, and how do we research it? These questions have long perplexed social and cultural theorists. While no firm consensus has ever been reached, what scholars do agree on is that there is no 'one' everyday — that everyday lives are multiple, messy and full of methodological possibilities. Though, as Cloke, Crang and Goodwin (2014: 926) note, the everyday is 'a notoriously difficult term to define, ... we can generalise that it is an arena of social life that includes repetitive daily cycles and routines that we learn but eventually take for granted'. This academic interest in everyday life, while not an especially new phenomenon, can contemporaneously be traced back to the 'cultural turn' within the social sciences, from around the early 1970s, when engagements between cultural studies and philosophical traditions were raising questions about 'how we make sense of the world around us' (Clayton, 2013: 1).

As a result, scholarly interest in everyday life has grown considerably since 2010, with the ordinary and mundane now at the fore of social science research. Where previously interested in the spectacular and the extraordinary, social science has turned away from a focus on grand structures and functions to pay attention to the grounded, the experiential and the 'blindingly obvious' (Woodward and Miller, 2007: 335). In trying to make sense of the everyday, it is common for authors (and we are no exception!) to pepper their work with synonyms like 'mundane, familiar and unremarkable' (Scott, 2009: 2), and to draw attention to the habitual, rhythmic and banal; 'the things that people do on a day-to-day basis' (Holloway and Hubbard, 2001: 1). This can, at times, give the impression that the everyday is limited to the realms of the prosaic and parochial, and can have the effect of making the everyday seem (for some) an unexciting avenue for research.

It would be a misunderstanding, however, to assume this – or that a conceptual or empirical focus on the everyday provides a narrowing of scale or practice: that which is close, localised, observable. Rather, the everyday can be a window into 'the ongoing problematic of the relationship between the local and the global, in the context of global flows of capital, information and people that have produced a heightened interconnectedness of different parts of the world' (Dyck, 2005: 234). Moreover, researching the everyday is not an unproblematic endeavour, and by raising concerns about the practice and performance of knowledge and power, ethical considerations also surface (Rose, 1993). Furthermore, positionality and reflexivity play an important role, where everyday life and academic life collide (Hall, 2014).

So, instead of limiting our understanding of human societies and cultures, the lens of the everyday offers possibilities, both big and small. In addition to offering micro-, meso- or macro-level analysis, 'theoretical perspectives that inform our understanding of everyday life ... cut across the disciplines of the social sciences, from psychology to philosophy and sociology' (Scott, 2009: 10). We adopt a similar approach within this collection, exploring social science as broadly defined and recognise, like Aitken and Valentine (2005: 8), that 'disciplinary boundaries are not cast in stone; they are fuzzy and chameleon-like, changing before our eyes as we focus deeper'. Everyday life, as a result, is an exciting and expanding field incorporating a wide range of interdisciplinary scholars, attempting to engage with the vivacity of the (extra)ordinary everyday. In doing so, scholars tune into recent theoretical and methodological advances in the fields of new materialism, sensory and embodied approaches and the ever growing mobilities turn, while also paying homage to longer histories, such as the influence of feminist methods – of the humble interview and intimacy of Memory Work. By exploring the minutiae of daily experiences and ways of making sense of the world we inhabit, such work also highlights their cultural, ethical, social and political significance.

## Methods for exploring everyday life

While research on the everyday is rapidly growing (Back, 2015; Pink, 2012; Rinkinen, Jalas and Shove, 2015), methodological approaches for studying the mundane seemingly lag behind. As Back (2007: 8) notes, 'we need to find more considered ways to engage with the ordinary yet remarkable things found in everyday life.' Social scientists, it seems, are no longer content with research designs comprising only traditional methods such as interviews, focus group or observation, and there is a real need to expand the empirical toolkit. This is not to argue against using the traditional interview, or other staples in the researcher's toolkit (see also Les Back's foreword in this collection), but rather to think about ways in which we can broaden our methods and techniques to fully encounter everyday life in all its sensory, multifarious glory.

To date minimal literature or resources exist which explore methodological approaches for studying the everyday. While such methods are undoubtedly occurring in varying disciplines and involve a multitude of settings and subjects, the practicalities of how one may undertake such research are seldom documented. Exceptions to this include the methods-based texts of Mason and Dale (2011) and Back and Puwar (2010), whose ground-breaking work has opened up the arena for research into the everyday, renewing and invigorating social science research. In doing so, Mason and Dale (2011) present a range of mixed, creative methods for studying the fields of personal life and relationships; places and mobilities, and socio-cultural change: from working creatively with longitudinal survey data; to considering socio-technical methods; to innovative approaches to mapping. Similarly, Back and Puwar's *Live Methods* (2010) engages with the experimental and serendipitous nature of research on the everyday, exploring 'storying', 'art'-based and digital approaches to sociology. Sarah Pink's (2013) work has also been an influential voice on visual methods, dealing with all aspects of the visual methods, including photographs, video and also digital media; focusing on the practicalities of conducting such methods, as well as considering theoretical and analytical perspectives. Buscher, Urry and Witchger (2010) apply a similar focus to advance mobile methods for social science research. In their key text, *Mobile Methods* they draw upon the interdisciplinary work of scholars in the field of mobilities to discuss the challenges and opportunities of researching movement.

Aside from the more contemporary inroads into methodological approaches to studying the everyday, we must also credit two key qualitative methods texts which we believe have provided the foundations for such innovative work. These include, but are no means limited to, Mason's (2017) comprehensive guide to conducting qualitative research, a go-to guide for social science undergraduates; and Cook and Crang's (2007) practical toolkit for conducting all aspects of ethnographic research. These hands-on texts have paved the way for bottom-up, grounded approaches to research; a prerequisite for conducting research on the everyday.

With this in mind, we should also mention the influence of feminist perspectives on methods for studying the everyday. Work such as that of Roberts (1981), Bell and Roberts (1984) and the Women and Geography Study Group (1997) implicitly explores the everyday through its focus on the experiences, narratives and stories of research. Such work encourages us to consider the reflexivity and positionality of ourselves, and the ethics of our own research practices (Davies, 2008). This now essential component of qualitative research is vital to studies on the mundane and everyday. Reflexivity urges us to pay attention to how we as researchers are active participants in the construction of knowledge and to listen closely to the multiple voices of other parties and experiences (Panelli, 2004). Indeed, as this collection illustrates, those voices and experiences come from a range of arenas – including animal, material and non-human worlds.

These key texts offer the foundations from which *Mundane Methods* begins – enabling us to bring together an innovative and original set of chapters which make a distinctive methodological contribution to research on the everyday. This collection is purely qualitative in approach, providing a non-positivist understanding and interpreting, rather than measuring, the everyday world. We provide flexible, hands-on methods for studying the messy, slippery and multiple dispositions of the mundane. This is not to undervalue the significance of the empirical material given in this collection in any way. Rather, this book aims to approach the everyday both as an object of study and as a method of inquiry, weaving them together to offer chapters which are both appealing in terms of their empirics but also innovative in terms of their methods. In this way the collection differs from other methods textbooks, bringing methods to life while also demystifying them.

## About the collection

The aims of this collection are twofold. First, and primarily, it is to provide students and scholars at all career stages with a methodological toolkit for studying the mundane and the everyday, including practical, hands-on information about using such methods in different research fields. Such instructive advice is particularly lacking in current methodological literature on the everyday and also within teaching resources. This collection bridges this lacuna. Secondly, and as a result, the collection will showcase examples of some of the most innovative, fresh and interesting contemporary social science research on the everyday, with a view to providing research inspiration to other scholars.

The collection is structured into three key themes: materials and memories; senses and emotions; and mobilities and motion. We discuss each of these in more detail below before introducing the chapters. However, it must be stressed that each theme also interweaves encounters, relationships, practices, spaces, temporalities, imaginaries and much more. In sum, and as the collection illustrates, research on the everyday will always overspill any categories or classifications we assign.

## Introducing the themes

### Materials and memories

The material turn within social science prompted a focus on the materials and objects of everyday life. Following calls for the 'rematerialisation' of social and cultural studies (Jackson, 2004: 172), a new body of scholarship emerged devoted to the material culture of everyday life. In the main this was about rejecting previous scholarly focus on 'spectacular consumption' and commodities as cultural markers, and rather replacing such 'symbol over substance' (Gregson and Crewe, 1998: 40) approaches with those which centre on how the fibres, textures, patterns and forms (Miller, 2005) of the objects and materials around us structure our everyday lives and interactions. Such work has focused on 'ordinary' forms of consumption (Gronow, 2001), such as second-hand shopping (Clarke, 2001; Gregson and Crewe, 2003; Tranberg-Hansen, 2005), food consumption (Miller, 1997, 2002) and networks of household reciprocity (Hall, 2016; Holmes, 2018a). 'Follow the thing' has been one such methodological approach for studying everyday materiality – following an object or commodity from its raw material through to its disposal or re-use (Cook et al., 2004; Evans, 2018; Norris, 2005). Other work on material culture has engaged with the embodied and sensory capacities of materials and objects, drawing on the relationships that cultures and individuals form with objects.

Studies on memory explore the experiences and stories of participants, revealing how memory practices are beholden to social contexts and are laden with values and norms (Misztal, 2003). Collective memory has been of particular interest to social scientists, illuminating mnemonic communities whereby memory is a means of creating shared understandings of history and identity (McNay, 2009). In particular, work on memory has explored its importance to family identity, acting as a central component in family practice (Morgan, 2011). Approaches for studying memory include drawing on biographical accounts, diaries and stories to reveal the work of memory in everyday life (Widerberg, 2011).

Other work unites materiality with memory. Studies such as those by Hallam and Hockey (2001) on death, Finch and Mason (2000) on inheritance and Holmes (2018b) on the material affinities of kinship unite materiality with memory to reveal how objects are used to memorialise loved ones passed. Similarly, work on the home has explored the importance of objects in creating 'private museums of memory' (Hecht, 2001: 123), whereby furnishings, objects, smells and atmospheres are a means of sensory place making, enabling inhabitants to construct and display narratives about their identity and family (Hurdley, 2006; Widerberg, 2010). Other studies have explored how material objects can represent memories of past places and people (Waters, 1999).

With this collection we build on and consolidate this work on materiality and memory. Opening up the theme on materiality and memory is Sophie Woodward. Exploring the mundane objects people collect, Woodward reveals how a combination of innovative material methods, involving collection audits, object mapping and object biographies, can reveal the mundane materialities of collections. Clothing as a collection is similarly drawn upon in the following chapter by Alison Slater, who uses the textile metaphor of pleats and folds to explore the memories of dress. Using oral testimony, the clothing memories of women living in the North West of England during the Second World War are unfolded. Karin Widerberg is next, detailing her methods for studying memory and the mundane. This includes a set of techniques used to elicit the memories and experiences of participants, the researcher and research-subjects and how these can be developed through analysis and writing. Material methods are further explored in the following two chapters. Helen Holmes draws on her work on everyday thrift to examine the role of the object interview in revealing how mundane objects structure the everyday; offering practical guidance on how to conduct such interviews, while Sarah Marie Hall and colleagues explore material transformation through a cook-along method involving talking, doing and observing.

## Senses and emotions

Senses and emotions have been examined by many philosophers, though for a long while Cartesianism (from the work of seventeenth-century philosopher, Rene Descartes) dominated Western philosophy, positing 'mind/body dualism' as pivotal to understanding lived experience. According to Descartes, the mind was the core of human possibility, intelligence, spirituality and personality, whereas the body was simply a machine, a fleshy envelope, subordinate to the mind (Bordo, 1993). So it goes, 'all of the social sciences [have] been built upon a particular conception of the mind and the body which sees them as separate, apart and acting on each other' (Johnson, 1989: 134, cited in Longhurst, 1997), rather than considering their interrelationality.

These ideas have, since the 1970s, been critically addressed across the social sciences disciplines, as part of the cultural and reflexive turns, and with wider social shift around feminist politics and the body (e.g. abortion, contraception and sexual violence). This ran concurrent with a 'welling up' of curiosity about the social implications of emotions (Davidson and Milligan, 2004: 523), and recognition of their 'power to transform the shape of our lives, expanding or contracting our horizons' (Davidson, Bondi and Smith, 2007: 1).

What emerged was an attuned interest in not how the body and mind sit apart, but how they co-exist and converse. Emotions and senses became seen as inextricable, since emotions can be understood as 'how we feel – as well as think – *through* "the body"', with 'tangible effects on our surroundings' (Davidson and Milligan, 2004: 523–524). Emotions shape our everyday experiences and perceptions of social environment, and likewise our spatial surroundings can become a surface for emotional, psychological and affective qualities. Notwithstanding, qualities valued in the empirical exploration of senses and emotion are typically intersubjectivity, relationality and experience.

Furthermore, a sense of and feelings about 'being-in-the-world' are commonly referenced as key elements of everyday life (Davidson and Milligan, 2004; Holloway and Hubbard, 2001), relating directly to this theme of senses and emotions. Interestingly, and in this context, it is worth mentioning that the term 'empirical' (as in empirical research) comes from the Greek word 'empeiria', meaning 'experience'. Our interactions with and understanding of the social world are constructed through our senses; sight, hearing, smell, taste, touch. Each sense offers nuanced, characteristic ways of capturing information about our social environment, and at different bodily scales and proximities.

Senses and emotions are not only 'out there' to be documented but are also tools for research. Moreover, empirical research also requires the active involvement of the researcher, being in and of the research process. While it is fair to say that 'the researcher's choice of method will reflect their ontological position (what they believe counts as valid knowledge)' (Scott, 2009: 186), the materiality, sensory, corporeal, fleshy nature of fieldwork is ever present (Longhurst, Ho and Johnston, 2008), even if it is not considered fundamental to the data collected. Social studies on senses and emotions routinely adopt methods that involve deeper personal emersion and reflection, that is, techniques that connect with one's own sensory and subjective – and reflexive – experiences. And so, with a growth of research around embodiment and emotion, researchers have recognised the need to research with and through all the senses; that words can only tell a partial story.

With this in mind, the chapters for this section include Sue Heath and Lynne Chapman, writing on sketching as method for capturing those elements less likely to be represented, or even possible to represent, within social research. Likewise, Dawn Lyon writes on using the body as a tool for research, but this time to look at rhythm and ways to capture rhythm using audio-visual techniques. The theme of capturing and articulating emotions and senses is continued with Becky Tipper's piece researching everyday human–animal relations through ethnographic eavesdropping, calling for more reflexive practices to truly master the art of listening piece on eavesdropping on animals, calling for more reflexive practices to truly master the art of listening. Chris Perkins and Kate McLean's chapter also pushes the boundaries of sensory methods with a focus on smell mapping, mustering together senses, emotions and temporalities to make sense of the everyday. Closing this theme is Rebecca Collins on using auto-ethnography in life drawing classes as a means of delving into everyday sensory and emotional states of 'reflexive-thinking-being'.

## Mobilities and motion

Thirdly, everyday life is also a site of mobility and motion, across time, society and space. Suffice to say, the new mobilities paradigm brought forth questions about how social lives are characterised by movements as well as moorings (Hannam, Sheller and Urry, 2006); and how mobility and motion together get at a broad array of actions, subjects and possibilities of the everyday. With revitalised thinking about both mobility and motion, and cutting across disciplinary divides, the new mobilities paradigm sought to uncover the interdependence of mobilities, and the ways in which mobility and motion lead directly onto understanding social relationships, materials, economies and politics – across an array of quotidian spaces (Sheller and Urry, 2006). Urry's (2003) contention that mobility and motion can be a lens for appreciating the networked nature of social life is in many ways closely connected to Massey's (1991) ideas around time–space compression in a hyper-linked world of ever growing and faster movement. As Adey (2017: 1) explains, 'we simply cannot ignore that the world is moving. Maybe, the world is moving a bit more than it did before too. We might even say that mobility is ubiquitous; it is something we do and experience almost all of the time.'

The ubiquity of mobility and motion has especially captured the recent imaginations of social researchers. In particular, 'mundane mobilities' is a budding area for social researchers interested in how mobilities are a 'commonplace and regular occurrence … enmeshed with the familiar worlds we inhabit, constituting part of the unreflexive, habitual practice of everyday life' (Binnie et al., 2007: 165). Examples of research on mundane mobilities and movements include tourism, holidays, dance, cycling and journeying (see Edensor, 2007; Hall and Holdsworth, 2016; Jayne and Leung, 2015; Moran, 2005; McIlvenny, 2015), to name but a few. In relation to this, another growing and connected area of research relates to intimate mobilities. As Holdsworth (2013) posits, while research on mobilities might focus on exceptionalities of distant travel and movement (such as work on tourism, for instance), everyday life is littered with intimate mobilities, bound up with the forming or dissolving of intimate relations.

Despite this, few of these works centre the method within their work, and typically use traditional techniques – such as observations, photography and interviews – to collate data on motion and mobility, rather than pushing at empirical boundaries. Notable exceptions include recent work on sound walks (e.g. Butler, 2007) and videos of family car journeys and passengering (e.g. Laurier et al., 2008), thought to add sophisticated, real, embodied and nuanced understanding to experiences of place. On this note, the chapters within this section take methodologies of mobility and motion as their key premise, weaving together traditional as well as perhaps less oft considered forms of movement.

This includes Simon Cook's use of jogging, or rather 'jographies', including a mixture of run-along interviews and mobile video ethnography. Wandering and derives form the basis of Morag Rose's chapter on playful, ludic, and creative ways of exploring everyday walking, while Thomas Birtchnell, Theresa Harada and Gordon Waitt centre their discussion on the electric mobility scooter to rethink ideas of everyday movement and mobility, and how they can be researched and approached. With embodied, immersive methods, Lyndsey Stoodley introduces surfing techniques and techniques to explore surfing, sea and self. Back on land, and closing the collection, Samantha Wilkinson writes on walking, dancing, taxi-ing and bus journeying with young people on nights out, as well as mobile phones within and as method.

## Using the collection

With these wide-ranging examples and exploratory flavours, taken together our collection presents readers with a plethora of practical approaches for studying the everyday. Filled with exercises, tips and examples to guide users through each method, alongside interdisciplinary approaches from a range of scholars at various career stages, the collection is as much a hands-on, jargon-free, how-to guide as it is a key text on methodological reflections and academic debates. Ultimately, we hope to spark empirical experiments for our readers; illustrating that you do not need to reinvent the wheel in order to innovate methodologically – but perhaps you can take the vehicle in more exciting directions!

## References

Adey, P. (2017) *Mobility* (2nd edn), London: Routledge.

Aitken, S. and Valentine, G. (eds) (2005) *Approaches to Human Geography Philosophies, Theories, People and Practices*, London: Sage.

Back, L. (2007) *The Art of Listening*, Oxford: Berg.

Back, L. (2015) 'Why everyday life matters: class, community and making life liveable', *Sociology*, 49 (5): 820–836.

Back, L. and Puwar, K. (2010) *Live Methods*, London: Wiley-Blackwell.

Bell, C. and Roberts, H. (1984) *Social Researching: Politics, Problems, Practice*, London: Routledge and Kegan Paul.

Binnie, J., Edensor, T., Holloway, J., Millington, S. and Young, C. (2007) 'Mundane mobilities, banal travels', *Social & Cultural Geography*, 8 (2): 165–174.

Bordo, S. (1993) *Unbearable Weight: Feminism, Western Culture, and the Body*, Berkeley, CA: University of California Press.

Buscher, M., Urry, J. and Witchger, K. (2010) *Mobile Methods*, London: Routledge.

Butler, T. (2007) 'Memoryscape: how audio walks can deepen our sense of place by integrating art, oral history and cultural geography', *Geography Compass*, 1: 350–372.

Clarke, A. (2001) 'The practice of the normative: the making of mothers, children and homes in North London', http://discovery.ucl.ac.uk/1317584/1/252292.pdf (accessed 15 June 2015).

Clayton, J. (2013) 'Geography and everyday life', *Oxford Bibliographies: Geography*, Oxford: Oxford University Press.

Cloke, P., Crang, P. and Goodwin, M. (2014) *Introducing Human Geography* (3rd edn), London: Routledge.

Cook, I. et al. (2004) 'Follow the thing: papaya', *Antipode*, 36 (4): 642–664.

Cook, I. and Crang, M. (2007) *Doing Ethnographies*, London: Sage.

Davidson, J. and Milligan, C. (2004) 'Embodying emotion sensing space: introducing emotional geographies', *Social & Cultural Geography*, 5 (4): 523–532.

Davidson, J., Bondi, L. and Smith, M. (eds) (2007) *Emotional Geographies*, London: Ashgate.

Davies, C. A. (2008) *Reflexive Ethnography: A Guide to Researching Selves and Others*, London: Routledge.

Dyck, I. (2005) 'Feminist geography, the 'everyday', and local–global relations: hidden spaces of place-making', *Canadian Geographer*, 49 (3): 233–243.

Edensor, T. (2007) 'Mundane mobilities, performances and spaces of tourism', *Social & Cultural Geography*, 8 (2): 199–215.

Evans, D. (2018) 'Rethinking material cultures of sustainability: commodity consumption, cultural biographies and following the thing', *Transactions of the Institute of British Geographers*, 43: 110–121.

Finch, J. and Mason, J. (2000) *Passing On: Kinship and Inheritance in England*, London: Routledge.

Gregson, N. and Crewe, L. (1998) 'Tales of the unexpected: exploring car boot sales as marginal spaces of contemporary consumption', *Transactions of the Institute of British Geographers*, 23: 39–53.

Gregson, N. and Crewe, L. (2003) *Second-Hand Cultures*, Oxford: Berg.

Gronow, J. (2001) *Ordinary Consumption*, New York: Routledge.

Hall, S. M. (2014) 'Ethics of ethnography with families: a geographical perspective', *Environment & Planning A*, 46 (9): 2175–2194.

Hall, S. M. (2016) 'Everyday family experiences of the financial crisis: getting by in the recent economic recession', *Journal of Economic Geography*, 16 (2): 305–330.

Hall, S. M. and Holdsworth, C. (2016) 'Family practices, holiday and the everyday', *Mobilities*, 11 (2): 284–302.

Hallam, E. and Hockey, J. (2001) *Death, Memory and Material Culture*, Oxford: Berg.

Hannam, K., Sheller, M. and Urry, J. (2006) 'Editorial: mobilities, immobilities and moorings', *Mobilities*, 1 (1): 1–22.

Hecht, A. (2001) 'Home sweet home: tangible memories of an uprooted childhood', in D. Miller (ed.) *Home Possessions*, Oxford: Berg, 123–148.

Holdsworth, C. (2013) *Family and Intimate Mobilities*, Basingstoke: Palgrave Macmillan.

Holloway, L. and Hubbard, P. (2001) *People and Place: The Extraordinary Geographies of Everyday Life*, London: Pearson Education.

Holmes, H. (2018a) 'From alternative to ordinary: the challenges and possibilities of everyday provisioning models', *Geoforum*, 88: 138–147.

Holmes, H. (2018b) 'Material affinities: doing family through the practices of passing on', *Sociology*, 53 (1): 174–191.

Hurdley, R. (2006) 'Dismantling mantelpieces: narrating identities and materialising culture in the home', *Sociology*, 40: 717–733.

Jackson, P. (2004) 'Local consumption in a globalizing world', *Transactions of the Institute of British Geographers*, 29: 165–178.

Jayne, M. and Leung, H. H. (2015) 'Embodying Chinese urbanism: towards a research agenda', *Area*, 46 (3): 256–267.

Johnson, L. C. (1989) 'Embodying geography – some implications of considering the sexed body in space', *New Zealand Geographical Society: Proceedings of the 15th New Zealand Geography Conference*, Dunedin, August, 134–138.

Laurier, E., Lorimer, H., Brown, B., Jones, O., Juhlin, O., Noble, A., Perry, M., Pica, D., Sormani, P., Strebel, I., Swan, L., Taylor, A., Watts, L. and Weilenmann, A. (2008) 'Driving and "passengering": notes on the ordinary organization of car travel', *Mobilities*, 3 (1): 1–23.

Longhurst, R. (1997) '(Dis)embodied geographies', *Progress in Human Geography*, 21 (4): 486–501.

Longhurst, R., Ho, E. and Johnston, L. (2008) 'Using "the body" as an "instrument of research": kimch'i and pavlova', *Area*, 40 (2): 208–217.

Mason, J. (2017) *Qualitative Researching* (3rd edn), London: Sage.

Mason, J. and Dale, A. (2011) *Understanding Social Research: Thinking Creatively About Method*, London: Sage.

Massey, D. (1991) 'A global sense of place', *Marxism Today*, June: 24–29.

McIlvenny, P. (2015) 'The joy of biking together: sharing everyday experiences of vélomobility', *Mobilities*, 10 (1): 55–82.

McNay, M. (2009) 'Absent memory, family secrets, narrative inheritance', *Qualitative Inquiry*, 15 (7): 1178–1188.

Miller, D. (1997) 'Coca-cola: a black sweet drink from Trinidad', in D. Miller (ed.) *Material Cultures*, London: UCL Press, 169–188.

Miller, D. (2002) 'Making love in supermarkets', in B. Highmore (ed.) *The Everyday Life Reader*, London: Routledge, 339–345.

Miller, D. (2005) 'Introduction', in S. Kuchler and D. Miller (eds) *Clothing as Material Culture*, Oxford: Berg, 1–19.

Misztal, B. (2003) *Theories of Social Remembering*, Milton Keynes: Open University Press.

Moran, J. (2005) *Reading the Everyday*, London: Routledge.

Morgan, D. (2011) *Rethinking Family Practices*, Basingstoke: Palgrave Macmillan.

Norris, L. (2005) 'Cloth that lies: the secrets of recycling in India', in S. Kuchler and D. Miller (eds) *Clothing as Material Culture*, Oxford: Berg, 83–105.

Panelli, R. (2004) *Social Geographies: From Difference to Action*, London: Sage.

Pink, S. (2012) *Situating Everyday Life*, London: Sage.

Pink, S. (2013) *Doing Visual Ethnography* (3rd edn), London: Sage.

Rinkinen, J., Jalas, M. and Shove, E. (2015) 'Object relations in accounts of everyday life', *Sociology*, 49 (5): 870–885.

Roberts, H. (1981) *Doing Feminist Research*, London: Routledge.

Rose, G. (1993) *Feminism & Geography: The Limits of Geographical Knowledge*, London: Polity Press.

Scott, S. (2009) *Making Sense of Everyday Life*, Cambridge: Polity.

Sheller, M. and Urry, J. (2006) 'The new mobilities paradigm', *Environment and Planning A*, 38: 207–226.

Tranberg-Hansen, S. (2005) 'From thrift to fashion: materiality and aesthetics in dress practices in Zambia', in S. Kuchler and D. Miller (eds) *Clothing as Material Culture*, Oxford: Berg, 106–120.

Urry, J. (2003) *Global Complexity*, Cambridge: Polity.

Waters, C. (1999) 'Representations of everyday life: L. S. Lowry and the landscape of memory in postwar Britain', *Representations*, 65 (Winter): 121–150.

Widerberg, K. (2010) 'In the homes of others: exploring new sites and methods when investigating the doings of gender, class and ethnicity', *Sociology*, 44 (6): 1181–1196.

Widerberg, K. (2011) 'Memory work: exploring family life and expanding the scope of family research', *Journal of Comparative Family Studies*, 42 (3): 329–337.

Women and Geography Study Group (1997) *Feminist Geographies: Explorations in Diversity and Difference*, Harlow: Longman.

Woodward, S. and Miller, M. (2007) 'A manifesto for the study of denim', *Social Anthropology*, 15 (5): 335–351.

# Part I

## Materials and memories

# 2

# Opening up material collections: adored, forgotten about, potent and mundane objects

Sophie Woodward

## Introduction

Material collections have been understood as a form of 'special' consumption, consisting of items separated off from use (Belk, 1995); if we approach them instead through the lens of the mundane, houses and other everyday spaces are full of collections of objects which include the used and the unused, the special and the forgotten about (Woodward and Greasley, 2015). A wardrobe is a case in point – containing cherished items like a wedding dress, habitual items we wear all the time like a pair of jeans, and items that never make it out of the wardrobe as they are forgotten about. Instead of thinking about everyday collections – like wardrobes, drawers, attics, CD collections – as just being an empirical focus of research, in this chapter I will suggest that opening up material collections is a methodological approach that allows new ways of understanding everyday life and consumption. While there is existing empirical work on collections (Parrott, 2011), they have not really been considered as a methodological approach. Thinking about collections as a methodological approach enables us to understand the complexities of everyday consumption, as we are able to explore the relationship between the unused, the cherished and the habitually used. While individual objects may have particularly strong resonances, this is an approach that centres relationships in multiple ways: between things (how individual items in a collection acquire meanings from others), between things and spaces (items stuffed at the back of a drawer) and between people through things (keeping or disposing of things mediates our relationships).

Thinking about 'opening up collections' as a methodological approach involves situating this approach in the theoretical perspectives that frame it, as well as the methods that constitute it. The approach is one that explores how focusing upon the *relationships between things* can be a route into thinking about the relationships between people and draws from theoretical understandings of the effects that things can have (such as Miller, 2005), as well as theories of assemblages (such as Bennett, 2009). This chapter will introduce these positions and the implications they have for how we might approach everyday collections. I will draw upon a range of examples from my own research – wardrobes, cupboards, garages (Woodward, 2007, 2015) – as well as other studies including music collections (Greasley, 2008), mantlepieces (Hurdley, 2006) and whole houses (Arnold et al., 2012; DeSilvey, 2006). Exploring material collections can use just one method (such as collection audits – interviewing people about their things) but is more commonly a mixed-methods approach. The methods that are adapted to this methodology include: object/collection interviews, object mapping, ethnographic observations, visual methods such as photographs and drawing, and follow-the-thing methods (see also Holmes, this collection). Although there are many challenges – not least due to how we can adapt methods to effectively understand the relationships we have with things – the methodology is one that is replete with possibilities for developing an understanding of everyday lives that incorporates the forgotten about, the accidental, the habitual and the cherished.

## Researching material collections: a background

A methodological focus upon collections has a number of distinct disciplinary trajectories, such as archaeology, museology and the social sciences. In the case of archaeology (and to a degree museology) finding ways to understand a range of objects in spatial proximity is a necessity arising out of what is encountered in the research. An absence of living people to talk to or observe means that methods for understanding how things accumulate in spaces have been well developed. Although excavation has been the dominant trope of archaeology, a parallel methodological development that is of particular resonance here is methods to explore surface assemblages as well as the practices through which things accumulate in those spaces (Joyce and Pollard, 2010). As social scientists tend to carry out research in contemporary contexts, they have access to people's verbal accounts of practices and everyday lives rather than having to interpret these from material remains. As a consequence, methods which centre people's verbal accounts have dominated. Theoretical developments within the field of material culture studies (see Miller, 2005) have pointed to the ways in which objects are mutually constitutive of our everyday lives and relationships. Things have properties and thing-power (Bennett, 2009) that affect how we are able to connect to other people (Woodward, 2015). When this is taken in tandem with the ways in which our relationships to things are often habitual and non-verbalised, we need methods that allow us to understand these material relationships, as well as harness them in our research. Objects are not just things to research, but also to research with (see Woodward, 2019). The method that this chapter outlines is one which seeks to use the collection as a methodological possibility to generate different kinds of data, such as: verbal (getting people to talk about it), visual (taking photographs, doing drawings, object maps) or observational (notes or videos of people interacting with the collection).

What is a collection? When we think about 'collectors' it is easy to envisage what this might entail – often a group of the same category of objects (like stamps) separated off from daily use. However, I am here suggesting that we can think about collections as they include everyday objects. Many collections include both the separated off, as well as the mundane and everyday; for example, in Hurdley's research (2006) mantlepieces may include special items as well as objects that end up there – such as items put out of the way of children's reach. We could think about a photo-album as a kind of collection; in Rose's research on the practices of family photography (Rose, 2010) she discusses the practices of photographing as well as printing, sorting and putting in an album. These albums may spend most of the time unused sitting at the back of a drawer or on a shelf, but are then occasionally taken out, looked at and perhaps reordered, expanded upon and shown to others.

Collections may be of very different scales; for example, Arnold et al. (2012) used multiple methods (mapping, photography, house history questionnaires, video-tours, observations) to comprehensively document the possessions of houses in the contemporary US. The house as a whole can be seen as a whole collection, as well as smaller-scale gatherings of objects, such as in particular spaces, like the things stuck to the front of a fridge by magnets. While this would certainly not be considered a collection in any conventional way, the medical prescriptions, invites, children's art and phone numbers that gather on the fridge are central to how daily life is organised. DeSilvey's research on a derelict homestead in Montana (2006) explores the totality of residual material culture and challenges how we think about the collection, as many of the objects she encounters are decaying or falling apart. Faced with the challenge of how to inventory these things, she rejects categorisations of similar things together, and instead sees the ways in which objects have ended up in spaces together as allowing insights into everyday life. As the objects are decaying through becoming rusty, being covered in mould or nibbled at by mice, DeSilvey's understanding of objects in collections is widened out to incorporate environmental elements as well as just the things themselves.

Shifting our understanding of what a collection is, I argue, is central to developing this as a method for exploring the complexities of everyday life. Collections can be reframed as everyday by defining them as assemblages (see Woodward and Greasley, 2015). In Bennett's formulation (Bennett, 2009), assemblages include many different elements – objects, materials, humans and non-humans. So, for example, a fridge door assemblage would include stickers, magnets, cards, drawings, dust, spilled substances. People are part of the assemblage, as there is no clear separation between us and these material elements. As we interact with these things, through sorting out, or as things change (a card rips or becomes weathered down), the assemblage changes. As a whole, the collection has agency, as the mass of things on the fridge makes us feel we need to get organised, or things start to fall off the fridge. Individual things connect to other things which affects the meanings they have – a CD relegated to the attic is less likely to be regularly listened to than one in a pile by the CD player. The methodological implications of this are that, in order to fully understand everyday practices of consumption and use, we need to develop methods that look at how things are organised in particular spaces, how they have come to be there and how people interact with the assemblages.

Thinking about collections in this way allows us to widen the remit of what we can empirically think of as a collection. Within sociology, collections have been approached as special and by definition as separated off from everyday consumption or usage patterns (see Belk, 1995); while this may be true of certain kinds of collections, it fails to develop the potential for a methodological approach which focuses upon collections of goods within everyday life. Empirical projects have emerged which take the everyday collection as their focus, such as wardrobes (see Klepp and Bjerk, 2014; Woodward, 2007), bins (Robinson et al., 2015) and music collections (Greasley, 2008). Taken together these highlight the possibilities for looking at the collection as it broadens our understanding of everyday consumption to include the forgotten about, the unwanted and things we are ambivalent about, as well as the potent (the cherished or the feared). Many of these approaches arose out of an empirical interest in particular fields or topics, and as a consequence the possibilities of this approach have not been fully explored methodologically (see Woodward and Greasley, 2015 for discussion of the empirical and theoretical potentials of this approach), which is what this chapter aims to do.

## Delving into collections: using the method in my research

I have used this methodological approach in a number of different projects, starting with research into women's wardrobes in the contemporary UK (see Woodward, 2007 for a full account). The research arose from an interest in developing a grounded account of women's relationship to clothing that did not reduce the meanings of clothing to the externally defined fashion system. Centring wardrobes was a route into looking at the everyday material relationships people had to their clothing as they engaged with their body shapes, multiple roles they had to occupy in their lives and their relationships to others. Looking at wardrobes included looking at clothing women did not wear and, as such, this approach opened up a way of thinking about clothing in terms of biographical shifts in people's identities, as well as shame, insecurity and anxiety.

The broad orientation for the wardrobe study was ethnography; the research started with a wardrobe interview, which involved auditing all of the clothing that women owned. I asked them to talk through each item in the wardrobe as I also took photographs of them; I also photographed the individual spaces in which things were kept. The photographs allowed an understanding of what was in there and how it was organised, and the verbal accounts from women gave the stories of specific items of clothing. Taking photographs gave me an additional resource as I was able to revisit the items of clothing when I was doing the analysis and to think about them as objects: how they were kept, what the patterns of wear were on objects. Photographs certainly do not directly represent the item of clothing or allow access to all material elements of it (not least because photos are static) but proved useful in allowing me to engage with at least the colours, fabrics and condition of the clothing. In addition, straight after the interviews I also did rough sketches/maps of the spaces where things were kept. This was often a quick sketch of where a wardrobe was in a room, or where wardrobes were in relationship to each other, or a quick sketch of the overall wardrobe and the 'types' of things in different spaces in case I did not get photographs of them or it was unclear from the interviews.

Following this, I asked women to fill in clothes diaries. These formed the basis of the second interview, which allowed me to think about the wardrobe as dynamic, and as it related to everyday practices. The clothes diaries were handwritten, and participants were asked to fill them out over a two-week period. I asked them to write down what they put on in the morning as well as anything they tried on but did not end up wearing. I also asked them to make some notes on what they did that day. If they changed clothes in the course of the day, I also asked them to note this down in the same way as the morning act of dressing. In addition, I did follow-up wardrobe interviews, as well as some observations of how women made clothing selections. As wardrobes are changing – in terms of how they are organised as well as new items being acquired and disposed of – revisiting the wardrobe allowed for a sense of this dynamism. Looking at how women selected outfits, both through the diaries and through observations, allowed me insights into the relationships between individual items. It is possible to focus upon both the whole wardrobe as an assemblage and as smaller clusters (see also Skjold, 2014), or groupings of clothing as smaller assemblages. Smaller assemblages can be spatial – such as a drawer for sports clothes – or can be seen through how people put clothing together (so, for example, the relationship between different items in the wardrobe that are 'always worn together' even though a top may be in a different section from a skirt). Given that wardrobes are rarely ordered around outfits this method is a particularly useful approach to think about clothing but requires an understanding of the wardrobe as a whole.

An additional research project for which I have used the 'opening up the collection' approach is my ongoing Dormant Things project (see Woodward, 2015), which in some ways develops the approach in the research I carried out into wardrobes. It focuses upon things that accumulate within domestic spaces but that are not currently being used, which I have termed 'dormant things'. The house as a totality is seen as an assemblage of things, and I also focus upon the smaller spaces within the home where things accumulate, such as attics, garages, shelves, drawers and tables, among others. The research centres houses, spaces and the things that have accumulated in them, rather than people and their possessions. Qualitative methods have tended to be people centred (Nordstrom, 2013); however, the 'material turn' (Bennett and Joyce, 2013) has theoretically de-centred people, as humans and non-humans (including materials and environmental factors) are understood to be co-constituted in material and relations. The implications of this shift are that we need methods that do not always centre people; the Dormant Things project, while drawing upon what people say, attempts to centre things in the sampling strategy, the methods and the analysis (also see Holmes, this collection and Slater, this collection). Sampling involved selecting types of houses (old with storage spaces such as cellars; new with limited storage, flats) while incorporating a range of living arrangements within these (such as people living alone or several people together). The emphasis is upon the house and its things.

The empirical research started with a 'household' audit, which was asking people to show me around their home and all of the spaces with things that were not being used. I took photographs of spaces, and after the audit I drew a map of the house and its spaces to give a feel for how spaces connected. In addition to seeing the house as a whole as a kind of collection, I got people to show me each of the smaller spaces and in addition to showing them to me they talked me through the things in there. In follow-up visits, the emphasis was upon in-depth audits of spaces. Participants were able to choose any space to show me, such as a drawer or a cupboard, and we went through each item more slowly. In both the initial and the follow-up visit, the rooting through these spaces was participant led (although

I prompted and asked questions before and afterwards). This meant that I was able to use the power of the collections and the individual objects to impact upon how people responded.

So, for example, on one occasion a participant had got down a box of 'old stuff' – things that had been moved from her parents' house when she first moved in with her now husband. I asked her if we could go through it to see what was in it. She rummaged through, pulling items out and telling me about them. Many items she had no idea were in there, and in some cases caught her by surprise as she was clearly affected by them as they reminded her of a time in her childhood, or of her parents. Theories of material culture suggest that things affect us through their materiality; they are potent (see Bennett, 2009) and evocative, such as reminding us of a former time. This method of using material collections is one that harnesses the power of things, and sees how they provoke and affect people as a way in which people's responses are generated. It is a way of getting away from pre-rehearsed narratives or generalised discourses.

Taking photographs of spaces and the things in them makes the phase of analysis easier as you are able to think about which things are placed together, as well as to try to engage with the material details of things. Unless people are asked to describe objects, these details are absent from verbal accounts. I also used the method of sketching in the Dormant Things project; Lynne Chapman, an artist who did a residency in the Morgan Centre at the University of Manchester (see Heath and Chapman, 2018; Heath and Chapman, this collection), accompanied me on some of the second interviews. While we went through one of the storage spaces, Lynne sketched the space and the things in it as well as including some of the words that people used. This allowed a combination of the visual and the verbal and managed to capture the resonances that these things had in everyday life in a way that the photographs did not.

The approach is one that could be used more broadly, particularly within the field of consumption but also in the study of everyday lives. First, it could be developed to look at specific genres of material culture, such as clothes, food, CDs, books and so on, by considering a particular form of material culture as a kind of 'collection'. This approach opens up the possibilities for comparative approaches between different genres of material culture (see Woodward and Greasley, 2015 for a comparison of clothing and music as an example).

Secondly, given that this approach foregrounds the relationships *between* things, then it could be developed for projects focused explicitly upon these material relationships as they mediate the relationships between people. So, for example, this could be achieved by focusing upon particular types of things (such as inherited objects) or types of relationships (such as friends as they share things like clothing). Thirdly, collections-based approaches could be used to think about the temporalities of everyday life. The approach outlined in this chapter suggests that collections contain not only things that are currently used, but as they are dynamic and temporally emerging they also include the old, unused, habitually used, rarely used and the dormant (see Woodward, 2007). It opens up a space for empirically engaging with how everyday consumption practices are temporally complex. Finally, the approach is one that lends itself to small-scale as well as larger-scale projects, as a whole house can be seen as a collection (see Woodward, 2015), as well as much smaller spaces such as a fridge door (see Arnold et al., 2012).

## Top tips for engaging with collections

Doing research by looking at and getting people to talk about their collections often produces unexpected and telling insights. However, given that there is not much written about the method and as an approach within the social sciences it is still in its infancy, there is a reliance upon the skill of the researcher. This skill in part comes from how prepared you are, as well as experience of using the method. If you are trying to do it for the first time, then I would suggest piloting your methods, as having some sense of what will happen is helpful (even though of course this always depends upon different people). As with many other qualitative methods there is always an element of 'thinking on your feet'; on one occasion I arrived for a wardrobe interview, only for the participant to tell me she wanted to do the interview outside as it was sunny (even though the wardrobe was inside). The interview involved her in the garden talking about her clothes; I asked her to describe items, as she ended up going to get a few things. She also showed me the wardrobe to photograph on the way out; and so, although it wasn't the interview I had planned, by adapting to what the participant wanted I still gained some interesting insights into her clothing (not least as a way to interrogate her sense of what was in the wardrobe).

Despite this example, it is a method that has to really be done in situ to be effective – such as in a garage or living room where things are kept, as you look at and get people to talk about things in relationship to where they are usually kept. While this may seem like a challenge – in getting people to be willing to let you into private spaces often unseen even by a person's close family – I never found that people who volunteered to take part in the research were unwilling to let me do an interview in front of the wardrobe or in the garage. There have been numerous instances in fieldwork when people have not wanted to show me specific things, either as they were too upsetting, or as they were simply seen as too mundane. An example of the latter is when people briefly showed me their pyjama drawers or home clothes but moved quickly on. In part this is due to things seeming uninteresting to participants, but also as they are uncomfortable with the scrutiny of me photographing their comfy tracksuit bottoms that are only ever worn at home.

In addition, you may find that people often have full and detailed stories about 'special' items, and the challenge is to make sure you retain a focus upon the mundane and everyday items too. One thing which characterises the mundane is that we often do not see or are unaware of it, and in using mundane methods like collection-based interviews we are placing these unseen aspects of life under scrutiny. In addition, in contrast to 'special' items, people have a routine and little considered relationship with these mundane items. Methods like asking people to talk about them give people cause to reflect upon them, but also raises the importance of having methods which do not just centre the verbal as we also observe the things themselves and what people do with them.

The approach is one that involves dealing with huge amounts of things (for example, one desk drawer can contain hundreds of things) and also generates huge amounts of interesting data to be analysed. The rich, potentially excessive data is one of the strengths of the method; however, this is also a challenge, as it can feel overwhelming when you are faced with so many things to deal with in an interview setting as well as when you come to analyse your data. You may feel that you cannot get people to talk about everything, or that when someone starts to talk about something, they move swiftly on to another item. When I did the wardrobe research, I had a list of questions I wanted to think about for each item in the wardrobe (how it got there, specific memories attached to it, when it is worn, how often). I soon had to abandon the idea of getting all this information at the first interview (not least due to the time this would take). I managed this by doing return visits as it was part of an ethnography. However, it is also important to accept that if you are getting people to talk about, or take images of, such a large number of things, you may not get detailed data for every single item. This does not mean that your data will not be rich, insightful and unexpected.

The challenge of time is an important one to consider: do you need comprehensive data? It may be that you want to get a sense of the collection as a whole while getting more depth on specific items, or it may be that you want to get a comprehensive sense of everything (Arnold et al., 2012) and sacrifice getting in-depth narratives for multiple objects. Every time I have used the method, I have done return visits to at least some of my participants. This approach produces both an amazing breadth of data as well as rich and deep data. So, for example, in the wardrobe interviews, an initial visit may result in two hundred photographs for one person as well as some brief accounts of each of the items of clothing to which these correspond. At the same time, an item of clothing that people encounter and have forgotten about at the back of the wardrobe may be an occasion for reflection and produce an extensive narrative about relationships to other people or relationships to a former self or aspect of the self. In addition to this, you have many different types of data; for each research encounter you may have photographs, audio recordings, transcripts and maps/sketches of where things are in the house/wardrobe. It is a neglected area of research, and as a consequence you will be making people (participants and readers of your research) think about things they may never have thought about before. Participants encounter things they did not even know they had, as they respond therefore not in pre-prepared discourses and answers, but in ways that surprise even them.

## Conclusions

If you were to look through the literature on research methods, you would not find a definition or discussion of 'opening up collections' as a method (although see Woodward, 2019 for a discussion of assemblages as methods). Although collections have been an empirical focus, there has been little acknowledgement of them as a

---

## Box 2.1: Training, tools and equipment

Given that opening up collections is an approach rather than a prescribed set of methods, the tools and training necessary are dependent upon the specific methods that you choose to carry out.

### Training

If this is the first time you have carried out an object-based method, then piloting the method is essential. Although there are few, if any, training possibilities in object-based methods, you may be able to go on a training course in creative methods, including visual methods (as these are often a key component of this method). In lieu of training in object-based methods you can ask others who have used the method for advice, and make sure you read up on the possibilities of the method (see Woodward, 2019). There are also well-developed literatures on connected methods (such as Rose, 2016) that can be adapted.

### Equipment

The tools needed depend on the particular methods you adopt, but may include: an audio recorder (for interviews); a digital camera (to capture images of objects that are talked about, as well as to photograph whole spaces); a video camera if you are videoing the collection audit; notepad and paper for sketching out where things are (I use mine to do quick maps of the objects within a room); and a note pad with small pen attached for each participant (if you are asking them to complete diaries).

---

methodological possibility (although see Klepp and Bjerk, 2014 for a discussion of wardrobe methods more specifically). Although collections are simultaneously empirical, theoretical and methodological, this chapter has sought to focus upon the methodological potential of the approach. It draws upon theoretical positions that highlight the potency of things in relationship to each other and the ways our lives are co-constituted by things, as they help make us and our relationships. Material collections as an approach to empirical research is one that foregrounds the materiality of things and how they can affect us, as well as the relationalities of things. In particular it draws upon the potency of things in people's lives, as objects have the power to affect us, through their materiality as well as their histories; encountering objects in a collection interview is an occasion for the past, memories, the future and feelings about other people to assert themselves.

These collections can be formal, deliberate collections, accidental ones (like a pile of stuff on a counter); they can be large scale or small scale. The collection of things and people's responses to and uses of them are the basis for generating data. It is an approach that can draw upon many methods; some of the possibilities discussed in this chapter include ethnography, observations of use, object or collection interviews, diaries, photographs, sketching, and space and object mapping. These are not exhaustive – the key thing to remember when thinking about which specific methods you employ is do they allow you to understand any of the following:

- the relations between things in spaces;
- how these relations are dynamic as things change and through how people interact with them;
- how things in the collection affect people;
- how people reflect upon and talk about things?

These are the core focuses of a collection-based methodological approach.

I have used this approach in two research projects and intend to use it again in research into everyday relationships. It is an approach that opens up the hidden, unseen and unexpected dimensions of everyday life and relationships. Things in collections and the responses they generate often surprise participants and can produce findings that are both unexpected and make you think differently about a topic. Even if you are not interested in collections per se, or even in material culture, a methodological approach like this can reframe how you see everyday lives. It allows an understanding of the everyday that encompasses the habitual and routine, as well as the cherished.

---

### Box 2.2: Further reading

DeSilvey, C. (2007) 'Art and archive: memory-work on a Montana homestead', *Journal of Historical Geography*, 33 (4): 878–900.

Klepp, I. and Bjerk, M. (2014) 'A methodological approach to the materiality of clothing: wardrobe studies', *International Journal of Social Research Methodology*, 17 (4): 373–386.

Woodward, S. and Greasley, A. (2015) 'Personal collections as material assemblages: a comparison of wardrobes and music collections', *Journal of Consumer Culture*, 17 (3): 659–676.

# References

Arnold, J., Graesch, A., Ragazzini, E. and Ochs, E. (2012) *Life at Home in the Twenty-First Century*, Los Angeles: Cotsen Institute of Archaeology Press.

Belk, R. (1995) *Collecting in a Consumer Society*, New York: Routledge.

Bennett, J. (2009) *Vibrant Matter: A Political Ecology of Things*, Durham, NC: Duke University Press.

Bennett, T. and Joyce, P. (eds) (2013) *Material Powers: Cultural Studies, History and the Material Turn*, London: Routledge.

DeSilvey, C. (2006) 'Observed decay: telling stories with mutable things', *Journal of Material Culture*, 11 (3): 318–388.

Greasley, A. (2008) *Engagement with music in everyday life: an in-depth study of adults' musical preferences and listening behaviours*. PhD thesis, University of Keele, Department of Psychology.

Heath, S., the Morgan Centre Sketchers (Chapman, L. and 2018) 'Observational sketching as method', *International Journal of Social Research Methodology*, 21 (6): 713–728.

Hurdley, R. (2006) 'Dismantling Mantelpieces: narrating identities and materializing culture in the home', *Sociology*, 40: 717–733.

Joyce, R. and Pollard, J. (2010) 'Archaeological assemblages and practices of deposition', in D. Hicks and M. Beaudry (eds) *Oxford Handbook of Material Culture Studies*, Oxford: Oxford University Press, 291–309.

Klepp, I. and Bjerk, M. (2014) 'A methodological approach to the materiality of clothing: wardrobe studies', *International Journal of Social Research Methodology*, 17 (4): 373–386.

Miller, D. (ed.) (2005) *Materiality*, Durham, NC: Duke University Press.

Nordstrom, S. (2013) 'Object-interviews: folding, unfolding, and refolding perceptions of objects', *International Journal of Qualitative Methods*, 12 (1): 237–257.

Parrott, F. (2011) 'Death, memory and collecting: creating the conditions for ancestralisation in South London households', in S. Byrne, A. Clarke, R. Harrison and R. Torrence (eds) *Unpacking the Collection: Networks of Material and Social Agency in the Museum*, London: Springer, 289–305.

Robinson, G., Riley, M., Metcalfe, A., Barr, S. and Tudor, T. (2015) 'Exploring 'pro-environmental actions through discarded materials in the home', *Unmaking Waste 2015 Conference Proceedings*, University of Adelaide, 533–541.

Rose, G. (2010) *Doing Family Photography: The Domestic, the Public and the Politics of Sentiment*, London: Routledge.

Rose, G. (2016) *Visual Methodologies* (4th edn), London: Sage.

Skjold, E. (2014) *The Daily Selection*. PhD thesis, Design School Kolding and Doctoral School of Organisation and Management Studies at Copenhagen Business School.

Woodward, S. (2007) *Why Women Wear What They Wear*, Oxford: Berg.

Woodward, S. (2015) 'Hidden lives of dormant things: cupboards, lofts and shelves', in E. Casey and Y. Taylor (eds) *Intimacies: Critical Consumption and Diverse Economies*, Basingstoke: Palgrave Macmillan, 216–232.

Woodward, S. (2019) *Material Methods: Researching and Thinking with Things*, London: Sage.

Woodward, S. and Greasley, A. (2015) 'Personal collections as material assemblages: a comparison of wardrobes and music collections', *Journal of Consumer Culture*, 17 (3): 659–676.

# 3

# Listening to dress: unfolding oral history methods

Alison Slater

## Introduction

In textile construction, folds bring two parts of a fabric together and pleats secure or set folds more permanently using stitching or heat setting. There are different types of pleats, which can be functional or decorative (or both) and add an extra dimension to a flat piece of cloth. In 2005, Martin Ball used these textile metaphors to explain how history is written: 'thinking of history as fabric gives it a sense of physical materiality, as ... something that can be folded, to bring together times and places that are otherwise separate and apart ... to make a story' (Ball, 2005: 158). Ball suggests that in selecting their evidence and writing their accounts of the past, historians choose which points to bring together, what to conceal and what to reveal, and in doing so 'each one pleats the fabric of history' (Ball, 2005: 158). This chapter applies these ideas to memories of clothing collected using oral history methods, where recollections of the past are related through interviews between a historian-researcher and an interviewee with first-hand experience of the period.[1] In oral testimonies, the pleats and folds that Ball describes are multiplied as both the historian-researcher and the interviewee influence the story that is told, and what the resulting narrative reveals or conceals. The historian-researcher sets the parameters of their study, frames their questions or schedule of discussion, and selects appropriate participants. The interviewee volunteers to take part, can guide the conversation and has control over what they choose to include or leave out. Their oral testimony is also dependent on successful memory storage and retrieval.

This chapter explores oral history methods through the study of dress history, using accounts from my doctoral research (Slater, 2011). It shows how oral testimonies, collected through interviews with women who lived in the North West of England during the Second World War, can unpack – or unfold – what their clothing memories say about their lives at that time. Ball's (2005) analogy of the folds and pleats of history writing are particularly relevant for memories of dress, which set personal experiences against a wider context of social life and social history. Our clothing practices and how we remember them are woven into our everyday lives, our changing sense of self and our sense of belonging to wider groups of people, both at the time when garments were worn and at the time they are remembered. By 'Listening to Dress', to how narratives are told, what is said and what is left unspoken, we can understand how interviewees fold and pleat their own life histories. The chapter also provides practical advice for other researchers using oral history methods.

## Undertaking an oral history of dress

Oral history has featured in dress history accounts since the late 1980s. A germinal chapter was Taylor's (2002: 242) 'Approaches using oral history', which purported that 'since clothing is such a fundamental factor within everyday life and human experience, memories of dress should be able to make significant contributions to the field of oral history'. Indeed, oral historians, including Elizabeth Roberts (1984), whose research covered my period and geographical area, have recognised the value of recollections of dress within broader accounts of everyday life. However, there remains an underlying resistance to the use of oral history within dress history and fashion studies, potentially because both sit on the edge of traditional areas of academic inquiry (Biddle-Perry, 2005). Although it is acknowledged that first-hand accounts about wearing clothes can 'provide new perspectives, which challenge and contradict previous historical and cultural assumptions', oral history remains underused among dress and fashion historians (Biddle-Perry, 2005: 89; Taylor, 2013). In order to write an oral history of dress, researchers must therefore draw upon established oral history methods and apply these to the study of dress history and/ or fashion studies. My study was methodologically guided by texts by oral historians (Lummis, 1987; Ritchie, 2003; Thompson, 2000), and social and psychological research informed an analysis of how memory influenced the accounts of dress that were collected through the interviews. Following Lummis (1987: 26–27), I use the term 'oral evidence' to describe the oral testimonies given in interviews and consider 'oral history' to be the post-interview contextualisation of the interviewees' narratives.

Oral historians recognise that the interview is an active process between two people, depending on mutual notions of trust and respect (Lummis, 1987; Thompson, 2000). In oral history research, interviewees are usually self-selecting and volunteer to take part. Potential participants may be found by advertising and/or word of mouth. In my study, 'snow-balling' became an important method for recruiting participants, as interviewees went on to recommend friends who might want to take part. The number of interviewees required for sufficient information to be gathered depends on the research project and the timescale for data collection (Thompson, 2000); for my doctoral research, I interviewed eleven women between January and October 2009.

As in any social survey, the interviewees should be asked to provide background details that contextualise their oral evidence, including biographical information relating to both the past and present. As clothing varies according to sub-cultural affiliation (including age, gender, geographical location and economic circumstance), I collected background contextual information relating to these factors, but it was recorded in writing prior to the interview to ensure anonymity in the audio recording (Slater, 2011). Some oral historians, including myself, use standardised interview questions to compare responses from different interviewees. Others have a schedule of topics to discuss. Where questions are used, the type of question asked should be considered. Ideally, a combination of open and closed questions should be used to allow the interviewee to share anything they feel is relevant. For example, in one question my participants were asked 'what were your favourite items of clothing during rationing?', followed by 'what made them special to you?' (Slater, 2011). The framing of the questions, and the tone in which they are asked, should be considered to prevent leading or manipulating the interviewee towards an answer (Lummis, 1987; Ritchie, 2003; Thompson, 2000). The length of an interview should be guided by the interviewee. It is advised that no single interview lasts longer than two hours; some interviewees may want to talk for a longer period of time but the interviewer should be aware of signs of tiredness.

Interviews for oral history collect social evidence through interpersonal dynamics. Oral historians accept that no single account will ever be complete and that accounts given on different occasions and to different interviewers may vary. It is the responsibility of the interviewer to ensure that their interviewees can speak freely around the topics covered (Lummis, 1987; Ritchie, 2003; Thompson, 2000). Some interviewees may feel they have nothing extraordinary to share or that their lives have not been particularly interesting and may need reassurance that their experiences are important (as exemplified in the title of Lomas, 2000). The interviewer should respect the interviewee's sensitivities and privacy but encourage the expression of personal thoughts and feelings. The extent to which ideas can be challenged depends on each interviewee, but 'part of that respect lies in treating them as a person capable of debate and discussion and not as an old oracle whose message cannot be queried' (Lummis, 1987: 68–69). Lummis (1987: 15) asserts that oral historians should strive to record 'the best account that it is possible to achieve by self-conscious methodology'. Such an approach allows interviewees to articulate the complex realities of their accumulated life experiences, leading to discoveries that may not be found through other methods.

One of the issues in oral history relates to the aspects of oral evidence consciously or unconsciously controlled by the interviewee, namely to what is spoken and what is left unsaid or forgotten. Oral evidence is grounded in autobiographical memories, which are personally experienced events consciously remembered from previously stored information (Coser, 1992; Tulving, 1983). However, autobiographical memories are influenced by wider social and cultural factors (Ross and Wang, 2010; Sangster, 1994). For example, experiences (and therefore memories) of dress are influenced by social class, economic circumstance, gender, geographical location and occupation in addition to individual preferences. Therefore, in research that relies upon autobiographical memory, the phenomenon of 'collective memory' must also be considered. For further work on collective memory see also the chapter by Widerberg in this collection.

According to Halbwachs (1925 in Coser, 1992), autobiographical memory can only be expressed through collective memory, which is a socially constructed notion of the past shared by a group of people with something in common. Halbwachs (1925) explains that because collective memory stems from a single system of ideas belonging to a social group, 'the framework of collective memory confines and binds our most intimate remembrances to each other' (cited in Coser, 1992: 53). Collective memory helps a group define and explain their present through 'how it remembers (or wants to remember) the past' (Ritchie, 2003: 36). The sharing of memories is essential in order for social cultures to survive (Coser, 1992). As Campbell (2008: 42) asserts, 'we remember with and in response to other people ... we share memory and sharing shapes memory'. However, like Campbell, 'I refuse to be alarmed by this' and I acknowledge 'the social power that authority over the past secures' (2008: 42). In choosing this method, some of this authority is given to the interviewees, who can choose what to put on the record depending on what they feel is important and relevant. The researcher-historian should then ensure the interviewees' words guide their analysis.

Sound recording preserves the oral evidence, the spoken word, verbatim. Many oral historians then transcribe their interviews to assist with the analysis of findings.[2] However, the process of transcription adds a layer of interpretation and can remove something of the essence of the original spoken account. In writing, narratives, informal phrases and punctuation are more formalised and verbal expression or changes in tone of voice are harder to capture than in speech. To ensure accurate transcription, notes need to be taken during the interview of any non-verbal gestures and any elements of human emotion (laughter, tears, etc.) in order for these to be edited into the transcription at the appropriate point. Pauses and interruptions should also be noted as these can change the flow or direction of the account given. A commitment to accuracy in transcription, with repeated reviews of the transcriptions while listening to the oral recording, ensures a true reflection of the interview in order to provide the most honest written account possible as a basis for future analysis (Lummis, 1987).

Once the interview has been transcribed, the findings should be mapped onto other sources of evidence, including the contextual information gathered about the interviewee. Following Lummis (1987), it is the comparison with existing documentation and literature, both contemporary to the period and secondary sources, that transforms oral evidence into oral history.

## Listening to memories of wartime dress

The everyday experiences of dress in the lives of working-class women, and those living in Northern counties of England, are under-represented in existing literature and in museum collections. These institutions tend to prioritise higher-quality and fashionable examples and, as a result of the circumstances of their wearers, working-class garments have traditionally been reused to the point of discard. My doctoral research used oral history methods to investigate memories of dress from eleven working-class women who lived in the geographical region to the north of Manchester, England, in the Second World War, to bring to light the experiences and memories of a social milieu that is often omitted from the official collective record (Slater, 2011).[3]

The period of my research had a clear beginning and ending, framed within the outbreak of the Second World War on 1 September 1939 and the announcement of Victory in Europe on 8 May 1945. These dates offer a useful chronological framework in establishing all histories of the Second World War, but dating working-class dress is more complicated. While fashionable styles come and go, everyday dress evolves at a slower pace and changes in working-class dress are even slower. Unless an interviewee is able to contextualise their own narratives against a specific historical event, or extraordinary moment in their own life, memories of interwar, wartime and post-war working-class dress are interwoven. However, this in itself became an important finding as it showed that working-class women had different experiences from their middle- and upper-class counterparts (Slater, 2011). My interviewees offered alternative accounts to the common themes of wartime dress, suggesting that the British government's restrictions on dress to support the war effort, including clothing rationing (June 1941 to March 1949), the Utility clothing scheme (1941) and Make Do and Mend (1942), had less impact on working-class families than their social and economic circumstances (Slater, 2011).

Alongside the investigation of working-class wartime dress, my research questioned the role of memory and reflection in oral evidence. The fallibility of human memory is problematic in oral history research. Sometimes interviewees fail to remember or memories may be muddled, re-contextualised, dramatised or deliberately described to fit their current character (Lummis, 1987; Ritchie, 2003; Samuel and Thompson, 1990). However, Lummis argues that 'there is a solid base of factual information ... which remains constant' (1987: 130). This aligns with psychological research (Bernstein and Loftus, 2009). Furthermore, my interviewees were fully aware of the fallibility of their autobiographical memories. They highlighted their uncertainties about potential errors in their recollections, and questioned and interpreted their own memories as they were related (Ritchie, 2003).

Lummis argues that the spatial and temporal distance between the past and present in interviews for oral history offers room for 'sanctioning', which acknowledges differences between the values of 'then' and 'now' (1987: 54). As Lummis predicted, my interviewees also sanctioned their own narratives when they wanted to clarify a change in viewpoint or circumstance. For example, JS described the brown colour of the coat she had dyed: 'I nearly said "n— brown" that's what we used to call it but you can't say that now.' While the term is now considered a racist slur, its use was common in Britain in the second quarter of the twentieth century as a colour name. Although JS felt able to report this, she sanctioned her account by acknowledging the societal change since the period. Sanctioned narratives such as this can also raise ethical issues for the historian-researcher. I have edited, or sanctioned, the citation of the racist term here, but after consideration it was stated in full in the original transcript and my PhD thesis to be true to JS's account. This is an example of the moral battle between the historian-researcher's responsibility to accurately record and discuss the interviewee's own words while adhering to current attitudes that differ from those of the past.

Social constraints rather than failures in memory can have the greatest effect on the advantages and disadvantages of using oral evidence (Lummis, 1987). However, social attitudes of the period may have a more significant effect on reportage than present attitudes. In wartime Britain, family secrets or activities that the local community may have disapproved of were kept private and it seems that the threat of a similar kind of disapproval was reflected in the oral evidence. My interviewees employed techniques to ensure their privacy, protecting themselves from perceived criticism or misinterpretation. This was evident in accounts about the acquisition of material, particularly fabric, that may have come from the 'black market', where money was illegally exchanged for restricted items, including clothing and food. AC described that a local woman would make dresses for her, but 'I don't know where we got the material from at all ... I'm sorry I can't tell you that'. Similarly, MH was unsure where the parachute material used to make a tennis dress for grammar school had come from but clarified that 'it would not be illegally because our parents wouldn't have countenanced that'. In a follow-up conversation with JS to discuss a plastic raincoat bought by her mother in the late 1940s, she explained: 'I don't know where she got it from – I hope it wasn't black market!' A number of the interviewees felt strongly that both the local community and the church provided a moral social grounding and reinforced judgement of morally and legally questionable acts. Although the phrasing of the examples given here suggests that these interviewees did not personally experience black market activities, it is possible, as JS suggests, that these took place but were not reported. One interviewee gave an account of having a garment made on the black market on the condition that it was anonymised.

Collective memory may play a role in the silences around behaviours or events that were morally, socially or culturally questionable. The interviewees' emphasis on respectability formed an inescapable part of their reportage. Although the desire to appear respectable in public featured strongly in both specific and generic personal memories, there was a strong collective consciousness of belonging to a respectable working-class group. Ross Poole (2008: 149) suggests that rather than simply transmitting 'information from the past to the present; [collective memory] also transmits responsibilities'. If one remembers past actions that were, or may be perceived as, questionable, the current self may be held, or hold itself, responsible and accountable for its previous actions (Poole, 2008). The current self chooses whether to report a particular memory in full, in part or to remain silent. For my interviewees, the social attitudes of their past and their identities as respectable working-class women dominated their oral evidence. It seems that in their responsibilities to keep collective memory alive (following Halbwachs, 1925 in Coser, 1992; Poole, 2008), portraying the notion of a respectable wartime identity was an important factor for them to convey to a younger interviewer.

It also seems that the interviewees held themselves responsible for accurately portraying and, because of the nature of the interview, preserving their story. While methods have been sought to judge if the memories of an individual can be believed or not, the veracity of memory cannot currently be determined beyond a clinical setting (Bernstein and Loftus, 2009). Therefore, at the time of writing, Lummis's suggestion that 'the careful historical evaluation of the information itself is probably as sound as anything that can be offered by psychologists' remains the case (Lummis, 1987: 117). Psychologists and oral historians suggest that the accuracy and therefore reliability of oral evidence is likely to be higher when recollections are set into a context of time and place or associated with a particular event (Bernstein and Loftus, 2009; Lummis, 1987; Paller, Voss and Westerberg, 2009). The reliability of oral evidence may be higher if it includes contemporary comparisons that suggest accurate recall beyond personal experience (Lummis, 1987). This was evident in my research when interviewees discussed their wartime dress within their wider experiences in society at the time, whether that was at school, as part of a family, through their changing circumstance from childhood to adulthood, or the impact (or lack of impact) of clothing rationing on their lives.

Some recollections, particularly of traumatic events where the interviewee was actually involved, were reported with intense emotion. My research supported Lummis' (1987) assertion that emotional intensity positively correlates with clarity in recall (Slater, 2011; 2014). Memories of exceptional or extra-ordinary events were more detailed and described more fluently than those that were less distinctive. For example, AC remembered her 'long blue satin dress' because her mother 'fell down a step and broke her arm', and MF had a distinct memory of the destruction of a beaded jumper when it fell off the washing line onto the stove. Other experiences were not reported in detail, including the regular activity of mending clothing. Interestingly, the interviewees suggested that mending was undertaken by others in their household and their age influenced this reportage. For example, when asked 'what did "Make Do and Mend" mean to you?', MC responded:

> I couldn't tell you.
> *Do you remember just having to 'Make Do and Mend' before the war?*
> Yeah but I couldn't tell you.
> *That's ok.*
> My mother would do it for us you see.
> (Verbatim discussion cited in Slater, 2011)

This could also account for responses where some of the younger interviewees were 'unable to say' or 'unable to remember'. The interviewees were aware that their parents did what they could to minimise the public appearance of their limited economic circumstances. While children were taught to observe moral codes, their parents may not always have practised what they taught. Younger children may have been unaware of the decisions that older family members took to provide clothing within the family. However, the limitation of childhood memories provides further evidence of the impact of collective memory on what is reported and what is left unsaid, and that the collective memory of the period overrides current concerns (Mills, 2016; Slater, 2011). In oral evidence, autobiographical memory can explain the different factors that influenced how dress was experienced by an individual, and collective memory can assist the explanation of personal experience and the reasons why individuals made particular choices in relation to dress.

The interviewees acknowledged that their recollections of wartime dress were interwoven with others: over seventy years of memory merging together, overlapping, contorting and twisting with each other. My task was to question, their task was to tell me what they 'felt' to be their true experience. Some interviewees questioned the relevance of their seemingly mundane memories against collective knowledge; as the interviewee with perhaps the worst memory stated: 'don't take much notice of me, this is just what I remember! [Laughs]' (DS). Furthermore, the retrospective nature of oral evidence and the changing contexts from the period of storage to that of recall can assist the explanation of past decisions. My interviewees seem to have taken a critical approach in narrating their recollected experiences. There seems to have been a commitment to accuracy on the part of the interviewees (as predicted by Lummis, 1987) that was verbally articulated in their oral evidence. In line with Poole's (2008) suggestion, my interviewees considered themselves to be responsible for their actions in the past and accountable for what they related, or chose not to relate, about the past in the present. Where they could not say or did not feel they could give a truthful answer, my interviewees said as much and where they recognised discrepancies in their accounts, these were also related. While they did not adopt the terms used by Ball (2005), my interviewees were consciously aware that in retelling their stories, they were folding and pleating their own histories of autobiographical and collective experiences of dress. In taking part in my study, they were also handing a responsibility over to me to share their stories while minimising further distortions in my interpretation as historian–researcher.

## Lessons learnt

This section reflects on my experiences of using oral history methods and writing up findings, both in relation to my own research and as a supervisor of postgraduate research students. There are three key lessons that I wish I had learned earlier on.

The first is that you need to get used to the sound of your own voice. While there are many sources available to give advice, nothing quite prepares you for hearing your own voice on the interview recording. You need to be prepared to listen to (and wince at) the number of times you messed up asking a question or got the tone of your voice wrong. While the advice in this chapter is based on good practice, learning to interview takes time and requires practice; learning by listening to and controlling your own voice can be as important for reflexive research as getting advice from existing sources on oral history methods.

The second thing to consider is what you will call your interviewees and how you discuss your participants when you write up your research. This may seem far away at the start of a study but thinking about how you present your interviewees is important and has impact. When I began my primary research, using initials was deemed the most appropriate method of ensuring anonymity. In adherence to ethical research guidance, I gained informed consent to use an individual's initials, which worked in my PhD thesis and I have maintained the use of initials in this chapter. But when discussing more personal accounts of my interviewees' narratives, using initials can seem a bit remote, a bit impersonal. Had I gained consent from the outset to use a first name (either their real names or an agreed pseudonym) this would have assisted the transition into different types of writing about my findings. In a 2014 article on materiality and memory in oral history narratives, I used first names to discuss the experiences of two interviewees as case studies. I did not specify if Mary and Doris were their real names or pseudonyms, but simply ensured that their names began with their first initial (see Slater, 2014).

I was concerned about the ethics involved in changing their identifiers but concluded that using names made them more personable. In future research, I will agree names with the interviewees at the time of the interview to enable them to make this decision and choose how (or who) they wanted to be identified (as).

Thirdly, it can assist the research analysis to ask your interviewees for their own definitions of the keywords in your study. For example, following other sources the respondents in my study were categorised as working class on the basis that their social and economic circumstance adhered to the criteria accepted by social historians (Roberts, 1995: 6): 1. they (or their father or husband) belonged to social classes III, IV or V according to the Registrar General's classification of occupations and were paid a weekly wage rather than monthly salary; 2. they lived in a working-class area (e.g. small terraced or council housing); 3. they consider themselves to have been working class during the Second World War, since they have responded and volunteered to take part in this survey of working-class dress. However, I did not ask them specifically about how or why they defined themselves as belonging to this socio-economic group.

One aspect that my research uncovered was the role of mothers in working-class girls' experiences of dress, particularly among families seeking to have a 'respectable' public appearance. While the occupations of fathers and/or husbands were significant in the formal organisation of social class status (as in definition 1 above), working-class mothers were found to have more impact on what their children wore and how they appeared in public. Despite a persistent lack of money, respectable working-class mothers managed their family's public appearance to ensure they presented an identity that both denied and disguised their true circumstances and demonstrated their abilities to cope in times of hardship. In this sense, the role of mothers was perhaps more significant in terms of their daughters' identities as a 'respectable' working-class girl than the occupation of their father (Slater, 2011). Asking specific questions about definitions of 'class' may have shaped my findings and my interpretations.

If you are interested in undertaking your own oral history study, the Oral History Society's (2018) website is a good place to start (see Box 3.1). The Oral History Society provides advice on undertaking legal and ethical projects, digital audio recording equipment, and also runs training sessions in collaboration with National Life Stories at

---

### Box 3.1: Training, tools and equipment

British Library (2018) 'Oral history', www.bl.uk/collection-guides/oral-
   history, (accessed 27 September 2018)
Oral History Society (2018) 'Getting started: recording equipment',
   www.ohs.org.uk/advice/getting-started/3/ (accessed 27 September
   2018)
Oral History Society (2018) 'Is your oral history legal and ethical?',
   www.ohs.org.uk/advice/ethical-and-legal/ (accessed 27 September
   2018)
Oral History Society (2018) 'Training', www.ohs.org.uk/training/
   (accessed 27 September 2018)

---

The British Library. If you are undertaking your research within a
university or other institution, you should also refer to their ethical
policies around research using human participants. Oral history
research requires the informed consent of interviewees and a consideration of current data protection legislation. Under UK Copyright
Law, the speaker of oral evidence retains the copyright for their
spoken words. They should therefore at a minimum be asked to give
informed consent for you to cite their account and any citation should
be attributed to its speaker (unless a specific request for anonymity is
given or this is part of the consent agreement).

One final point to consider is that oral history can only interview
survivors (Lummis, 1987). Oral evidence cannot be rediscovered in
an archive at a later date if it was never recorded in the first place.
For every story that is told, another will be lost. Therefore, if there
is a project that you want to undertake, or someone who you want
to ask about their past, then do not leave it too late. Oral histories of
dress are therefore, like any study reliant upon memory, limited to
the period within living memory.

## Conclusion

Oral history is one of the first research methods we learn, even if we
do not think of it in this way. We grow up hearing stories from those
around us. Oral histories shape our family histories and individual
ideas about who we think we are. Our individual and collective pasts

are woven in the pleats and folds of our ancestors' narratives (or lack of them).

While oral history is still underused in dress history (Taylor, 2013), when key conceptual principles are applied there is no reason why reflexive academic research using interviews for oral history cannot add to our understanding of everyday life among a particular group of people at a particular time. It is with the full acknowledgement of its limitations that oral history provides a valuable historical method. By taking criticisms and issues of the method on board at the start of a project, oral historians can take on the strength of reflexivity while maintaining an ever conscious awareness of the dangers in creating and interpreting their evidence, especially in the light of the perceived unreliability of oral evidence. Acknowledging the weaknesses of the oral history method does not make it less valid. In fact, the reflexivity engendered by heightened awareness of the evidential traps has led to a critical attitude towards all evidence, wherein oral evidence deserves no lesser standing in the hierarchy of historical 'truth'.

There is no unselective access to the past, either through history or memory. Memory does not have a chronology in the temporal sense of history, but both have their own agendas. Autobiographical memory in its most general sense is interwoven with collective memory; personal and collective memories inform and reflect each other. However, by grounding research into past events and experiences in the words of those who were there, and analysing their findings against contemporary and secondary sources, historian-researchers can offer oral histories that enlighten our understanding of the past within living memory.

With oral histories of dress, and particularly working-class dress, auto/biographical memory is one of the few sources of information available to the historian-researcher. Ball's (2005) suggestion that the metaphors of folds and pleats are akin to history writing is particularly valuable for dress history. The material construction of clothing and the material memories we associate with garments worn in our past are in themselves shaped by folds and pleats. Dress is a part of our everyday lives (also see Woodward, this collection). It lives with us; we carry it on our backs both in life and in memory.

Oral evidence levels the fields of dress history and fashion studies. It offers a moment in time where extraordinary examples that stand out in history can meet the ordinary, the everyday and the mundane.

## Box 3.2 Further reading

Abrams, L. (2010) *Oral History Theory*, London: Routledge.

Bornat, J. and Diamond, H. (2007) 'History and oral history: developments and debates', *Women's History Review*, 16 (1): 19–39.

Connerton, P. (1989) *How Societies Remember*, Cambridge: Cambridge University Press.

Gluck, S. B. and Patai, D. (eds) (1991) *Women's Words: The Feminist Practice of Oral History*, Abingdon: Routledge.

Hajek, A. (2014) *Oral History Methodology*, London: Sage.

Kuhn, A. (2002) *Family Secrets: Acts of Memory and Imagination* (2nd edn), London: Verso.

*Oral History* (1969–ongoing) Oral History Society and University of Essex.

*Oral History Review* (1973–ongoing) Oxford: Oxford University Press.

Perks, R. and Thompson, A. (eds) (1998) *The Oral History Reader*, London: Routledge.

Roberts, E. (1995) *Women and Families: An Oral History, 1940–1970*, Oxford: Blackwell.

Sandino, L. and Partington, M. (eds) (2013) *Oral History in the Visual Arts*, London: Bloomsbury.

We all wear clothes and all have clothing memories. By 'listening to dress' and using this 'mundane method', we can start to understand more about the broader contexts of our individual and collective embodied experiences.

## Notes

1 The term 'historian-researcher' is used here to acknowledge that an oral historian is involved in both the creation and analysis of oral evidence.

2 There is debate among oral historians regarding transcription and whether manual transcription, outsourced transcription services or computer software should be used (or even if audio recordings should be transcribed at all). For a smaller study, I recommend that the historian-researcher undertakes both the interviews and the transcription. While time-consuming, verbatim transcription can assist in the analysis process. In all cases the transcripts must reflect the oral account and should be preserved in line with current legal requirements around consent and data protection.

3 Although the collective term 'women' is used, in reality the interviewees ranged from young girls to adult females; in September 1939, the youngest interviewee was four years old and the eldest was twenty-two. The age possibilities were determined by the methodology. Interviewees were required to be old enough to remember their wartime clothing, but also physically and mentally capable of being interviewed and giving informed consent. Grouping the interviewees together as 'women' recognises that their responses reflect that the memories of their younger selves in the past are told from a mature perspective in the present.

# References

Ball, M. (2005) 'The pleating of history: weaving the threads of nationhood', *Cultural Studies Review*, 11 (1): 158–173.

Bernstein, D. M. and Loftus, E. F. (2009) 'How to tell if a particular memory is true or false', *Perspectives on Psychological Science*, 4 (4): 370–374.

Biddle-Perry, G. (2005) '"Bury me in purple lurex": promoting a new dynamic between fashion and oral historical research', *Oral History*, 33 (1): 88–92.

Campbell, S. (2008) 'The second voice', *Memory Studies*, 1 (1): 41–48.

Coser, L. (ed. and trans.) (1992) *Maurice Halbwachs: On Collective Memory*, Chicago: University of Chicago Press.

Lomas, C. (2000) '"I know nothing about fashion: there's no point interviewing me": the use and value of oral history to the fashion historian', in S. Bruzzi and P. Church Gibson (eds) *Fashion Cultures: Theories, Explorations and Analysis*, Abingdon: Routledge, 363–370.

Lummis, T. (1987) *Listening to History*, London: Century Hutchinson.

Mills, H. (2016) 'Using the person to critique the popular: women's memories of 1960s youth', *Contemporary British History*, 30 (4): 463–483.

Oral History Society (2018) 'Advice for experts and beginners', www.ohs.org.uk/advice/ (accessed 27 September 2018).

Paller, K. A., Voss, J. L. and Westerberg, C. E. (2009) 'Investigating the awareness of remembering', *Perspectives on Psychological Science*, 4 (2): 185–199.

Poole, R. (2008) 'Memory, history and the claims of the past', *Memories Studies*, 1 (2): 149–166.

Ritchie, D. (2003) *Doing Oral History: A Practical Guide* (2nd edn), Oxford: Oxford University Press.

Roberts, E. (1984) *A Woman's Place: An Oral History of Working-Class Women 1840–1940*, Basingstoke: Macmillan.

Roberts, E. (1995) *Women and Families: An Oral History, 1940–1970*, Oxford: Blackwell.

Ross, M. and Wang, Q. (2010) 'Why we remember and what we remember: culture and autobiographical memory', *Perspectives on Psychological Science*, 5 (4): 401–409.

Samuel, R. and Thompson, P. (1990) *The Myths We Live By*, Abingdon: Routledge.

Sangster, J. (1994) 'Telling our stories: feminist debates and the use of oral history', *Women's History Review*, 3 (1): 5–28.

Slater, A. (2011) *The Dress of Working-Class Women in Bolton and Oldham, Lancashire 1939 to 1945*. PhD thesis, Manchester Metropolitan University.

Slater, A. (2014) 'Wearing in memory: materiality and oral histories', *Critical Studies in Fashion and Beauty*, 5 (1): 125–139.

Taylor, L. (2002) *The Study of Dress History*, Manchester: Manchester University Press.

Taylor, L. (2013) 'Fashion and dress history: theoretical and methodological approaches', in S. Black, A. de la Haye, J. Entwistle, R. Root, A. Rocamora and H. Thomas (eds) *The Handbook of Fashion Studies*, London: Bloomsbury, 23–43.

Thompson, P. (2000) *The Voice of the Past: Oral History* (3rd edn), Oxford: Oxford University Press.

Tulving, E. (1983) *Elements in Episodic Memory*, Oxford: Clarendon Press.

# 4

# Memory Work: an approach to remembering and documenting everyday experiences

## Karin Widerberg

## Introduction

In an increasingly mediated society, the importance of discovery and questioning of the mundane becomes vital to ground actions, individually and collectively, in alternative ways. Memory Work is an approach developed to help explore the mundane by problematising the things we take for granted. Through recalling and documenting stories of memories and experiences, participants, researchers and research-subjects are invited to look for variety – in one's own stories as well as in relation to the stories of the others – regarding content as well as interpretations. A set of techniques is developed in this chapter to make this happen, in writing as well as in analysis. Focusing on the social aspects of a story does not only imply a possibility to connect different analytical levels (micro and macro) and verify concepts and theories. It also allows us to question or specify fixed or simplified categories and concepts by making other memories, experiences and understandings visible. As such it is an approach that stimulates creativity and knowledge production in research (also see Slater, this collection, for another memory-focused method).

The approach can be used in different settings and on different themes in both teaching and research, with varying degrees of collective or individual participation. Here a case of a one-day research seminar is chosen to illuminate the techniques of the approach and the kinds of knowledge that can be gained thereby. The illustration is meant to inspire further use and development of the approach so as to fit different situations and themes in teaching and research.

## Memory Work – the original approach

Memory Work was developed as a collective method by the sociologist Frigga Haug (Haug, 1987). The aim was to develop a method that would facilitate the problematisation of the things in everyday life we take for granted, especially gender, since it is this same taken-for-grantedness that contributes to making patriarchy invisible and difficult to change. But the aim was also to develop a non-positivistic research method where the division and hierarchy between researcher and research subjects were eliminated. Formulated as a feminist research method, and aiming at empowerment and liberation in both its process and results, the collective approach was underlined. Briefly, the procedures of the method were as follows.

A group of women were to decide the theme for the Memory Work. Once the theme was settled, different kinds of 'triggers', for example photos, could be used to get the memory process started. The stories were to be written as concretely and as detailed as possible, preferably about a specific event or situation. To facilitate an observing gaze and the production of detailed accounts, the use of the form of the third person was proposed when writing the story. All the stories were then to be read and analysed as if the author were absent so as to allow for all possible interpretations. Ownership of 'true' interpretations would just hamper the analytical process and must therefore be stated as an unproductive stance and accordingly strictly avoided during the workshop.

Further, the aim was not to look for personal explanations but rather to look for social explanations (social relations and patterns) of what the stories could teach us about the doings of gender (West and Zimmerman, 1987; also see Wilkinson, this collection). That is, how gender is being done in all kinds of everyday activities (getting dressed, cleaning, shopping and so forth) and relations (siblings, friends, work-mates and so forth). One way to make the gender of the story visible so as to further our understanding of how gender is done, is to exchange the female character in the story with a male, and vice versa. After a preliminary analysis, there is often a demand to rewrite the stories or even to write new ones. A theme might seem interesting to pursue in more detail, triggering new memories. But a thematic silence might also be challenged by further Memory Work on a specific topic. By rewriting the stories or writing new ones, the picture becomes richer and more varied.

Haug and her fellow sisters explored and developed the method when trying to problematise the sexualisation of the female body as a theme (Haug, 1987). Since then, the method has been used and explored with a variety of themes but also in a variety of different ways. Only a few Memory Work projects have been done with such rigour and over such a long time span as that modelled by the Haug collective. Crawford et al.'s (1992) Memory Work on the social construction of emotion and Kaufman et al.'s (2003) examination of the self in relation to the natural world are noteworthy examples. They both lasted several years and were written collectively. The vast majority of Memory Work projects are however conducted over a shorter time span and are usually not collectively authored. The role of the collective will then also vary regarding the decision of the theme and its specific formulation but also in relation to how, when and where the stories are written and analysed. Quite a few projects have also developed the approach so as to fit their theoretical or thematic interests. Davies, for example, has extended the approach to something she calls 'collective biography' (Davies, 2000, 2008) founded upon a theoretical understanding of the individual as related to the collective. I have myself tried to illuminate that the use of the approach as an individual endeavour allows for an understanding of the 'I' as not only social but also multiple (Widerberg, 1999). The approach has also been used to explore experiences and not only memories, through writing about them here and now (Davies, 2000; Widerberg et al., 2001). Doing exercises of different kinds, writing about them and then analysing the stories, is an example of an expansion of the approach so as to explore experiences in new ways (see Kaufman et al. (2008) for a further presentation and discussion of the field, as well as examples of some major Memory Work, including my own use and development of the approach).

## A case – exploring motherhood through Memory Work

In the spring of 2013 I was a guest professor at the Morgan Centre of the University of Manchester and asked to give a one-day workshop in Memory Work for their staff, including PhD scholars and masters' students. Around thirty participants, aged 25–75 (the majority in the age group 30–50), all women except for three men, were there to learn about the approach of Memory Work.

Since the focus was on the methodological approach rather than a particular theme and we only had a day at our disposal, I had decided the theme beforehand. I had chosen 'motherhood', knowing that all the participants were gender researchers and therefore likely to find such a theme interesting. Ethical considerations, in relation to the group and setting, should always guide the topic chosen and how the theme is to be presented. When approaching a theme like motherhood, 'other mothers' might be a way to start to explore an area as vast and complex as this. One's own mother/mothers might be too personal and vast as a field of experiences and memories to start with. Besides, in describing other mothers, one's own mother will lurk in the background since comparisons – as will be demonstrated in the stories presented below – are a fundamental aspect of memory making. Further, having limited time at our disposal, the topic chosen had to be formulated in such a way as to allow for short and descriptive written accounts of a particular situation.

I had previously run a similar workshop on fatherhood, but then with only male gender researchers, and successfully started out with 'My friend's father' (Widerberg, 2011). I decided to do the same here and chose 'My friend's mother' as the theme for our memory stories. When presented, it was not however met with acclamation or joyful anticipation by the participants, who actually seemed rather hesitant and even reluctant. At this stage of the process participants quite often express that they do not have any memories or anything to write about, no matter the theme in question. Since I was familiar with this very first reaction, and knew that the atmosphere would change once they started writing and reading the stories, I was confident enough to persuade them to give it a try. I knew that after some minutes of thinking the memories and stories would come to them and that the instructions I was to give them would help them get started.

Knowing from experience that the participants' resistance is often founded on doubts regarding memory and interpretation, I always say a few words about it all. I accordingly stress that writing a memory always means interpretation, since interpretation is what drives the memory forward, that is, how and what we remember. Every memory has layers of interpretation, especially if the memory is of something that happened long ago. Even so, I tell them, they should try not to analyse while writing, but give the story a chance to be told as straightforwardly as possible. Concepts, hasty analyses, immediately processing it academically – here that is more of a problem than a resource; it closes more doors than it opens, at this stage. Writing the stories anonymously, I further tell them, is not only or even primarily to facilitate the writing process; it is meant to enrich the interpretation process. The written stories are to be interpreted collectively. No one can or is then allowed to claim ownership of the story (or of the 'correct' interpretation). But once the analyses have been completed, they can, if they so wish, tell each other which story was theirs.

All the steps in the process from writing to analysing are accordingly roughly presented before we embark on the writing of stories. This is important so as to make the participants feel comfortable and safe and ready to contribute, and not feel lured into something they might regret afterwards. But they also need to understand the very reasons behind the specific instructions given, so as to make the approach work. So, after presenting the approach of Memory Work along the lines presented above, the participants were given the following instructions, handed out to them but also further explicated by me verbally.

## Memory Work instructions

Writing (30 minutes)

- Write a short story of (a situation of encountering/meeting/being with)
  ...

*My friend's mother.*

- Use 5–10 minutes to think about which story to write;
- Use 20 minutes to write the story in first person (that is, I). Write as descriptively and concretely as possible, avoid interpretation and if you write about feelings try to describe them descriptively and as embodied. Try to write as if you were there, then, in the voice and with the gaze of that age;
- On the bottom at the back of the page, write the year of your birth. **Do not write your name!**

Reading (45 minutes)

- Choose one person in the group to read all the stories (if there are many participants, two people can take turns). Number the stories as you go along, writing the number on the top of the paper.
- Choose one person to take notes, but be sure to make notes yourself.
- When reading the stories, the author shall NOT make themselves known. Do NOT show in any way that it is your story that is read. And DO NOT try to help out if the reader has problems reading your handwriting. No one shall own the (correct) interpretation! The purpose is to get all kinds of interpretation on the table. So *do not ruin the work by letting yourself be known as the storywriter!*
- Read one story, slowly.
- Read the same story again, but read 'I' as a different gender, that is she/he instead of I.
- What happens with the story when it's given a different gender? What changes, does anything not make sense? What is there to learn from such an exercise?
- All the participants take notes. But you *do not get into a full discussion* and analysis of each story – except for the gender issue. It will have to wait until all stories have been read.

Since the group was mainly made up of women, certain adaptations had to be made in relation to the amount of participants and their gender. Like other qualitative approaches, it always has to be developed so as to fit the purpose. What we had to do here was first of all to treat the stories as if they were all written by women so as not to make the male authors known. It further meant that there was no point in trying to guess the gender of the author. If the group had been more mixed however, there would have been an extra opportunity to discuss gender interpretations. It is also worth noting that the participants were asked to write the story in the first person, not the third person as suggested by Haug. This was due to my experiences from other short workshops, where I have found that the participants find it easier to start writing if they can use the form of first person. Once a story has been written, a new story in the form of the third person is however more feasible and accordingly an option for extended workshops running over several days.

We all wrote the stories – including myself – directly after my presentation, in the plenary session, so as not to create an interruption and a delay that might trigger a resistance. This also de-dramatised the writing process and illustrated that it can be done anywhere and everywhere. Writing in a big group is also helpful in the sense that the act of writing with others triggers your own writing. The atmosphere of silence and concentration when everybody is writing – and not for exams! – is also an expression of a particular kind of fellowship rarely experienced in academic settings. It feels good, as several participants expressed when briefly commenting on the act of writing as they handed over their stories. There was also a general expression that it had been much easier and more interesting to write than they had expected when being presented with the topic.

The large number of participants, however, made certain arrangements necessary. With a small group, the stories can more easily be distributed and read by each participant. Use of a laptop also allows for writing the story in three versions, just exchanging the 'I' for a 'he' and a 'she', thereby facilitating reading the stories in different gender versions. Since this was not an option here – only a few of the participants brought their own laptop – we split up into three groups with 9–10 people in each. In the groups the stories were read out loud by one person in the group, while the others listened and took notes. Each story was read out twice, the second time with the male voice telling the story. Commenting upon each story was not encouraged, due to the shortage of time, other than very brief comments as to the gender aspect of the text when given a different gender. The act of having the stories read out loud by one person – instead of having them passed around and reading them ourselves – was experienced as a bonus. One could concentrate on listening and one did not have to feel a pressure to read fast so as not to have the next in line waiting for the story in question.

When all of us gathered again, in a plenary session, the analytical process started. We opened for discussion by asking for spontaneous reactions to all the stories read in each group while I made notes on the blackboard. All kinds of reflections, also on themes other than motherhood, were encouraged. Other interesting themes were hereby made visible as topics for future Memory Work. Returning to the theme of motherhood, however, we then started a discussion of relevant themes and relations and their connections. Had we more time at our disposal, this would have been a good starting point to continue writing stories about motherhood but now more focused on a specific theme or relation.

Finally, I asked for comments regarding the exercise of changing the gender of the stories. Here we seemed to have had similar reflections in the different groups, including the one in which I took part. The stories either seemed to be gender neutral, due to gender playing a less prominent role when being a child and relating to grown-ups. Or, we did not agree with each other as to the gender stereotyping, regarding activity, emotions or reflectivity expressed in the story. An important conclusion to be drawn from such an exercise is that it is also our own preconceptions or prejudices that come to the surface, and not only some actual and empirically founded gender patterns. As such, the exercise is extremely valuable as a foundation for further analytical explorations and discussions of the doings of gender and the 'undoing of gender' (Deutsch, 2007). In other words, we need to question whether our focus on gender make us overstate its presence and importance. Memory stories should accordingly not be used as straightforward empirical evidence regarding gender patterns, but as a highly creative platform for further empirical and theoretical investigations. After having discussed the stories in more general terms, each group picked out one of its stories to be read and discussed in the plenary session. Four stories were accordingly chosen and here we allowed for comments and reflections after each of the stories had been read out loud. The analysis of these stories confirmed the issues raised in our previous discussions. So, what was then at stake in these stories?

Before focusing on the content of the stories, there is one important issue regarding levels of analysis, that the stories made us particularly aware of, that needs to be mentioned. The instructions were to try to write the story in the voice of the child entering the scene in question. But of course, our voice of today as grown-ups and academics is also always there, more or less visible. In addition to these two voices, we have the voice and gaze of us as readers (including the writer) when understanding the situation from our present knowledge and perspectives. When for example interpreting a story of a mother working full-time as a housewife as a sad story, our present gaze will likely colour the interpretation. These different levels of analysis are of course not exceptional to Memory Work, it is just that memory stories make the process of reconstruction of experiences – orally or textually – more visible and obvious. It is accordingly something we also have to bear in mind when analysing empirical statements and data.

When the time was up for such meta-analysis, as well as the analysis of the content of stories and the workshop had to come to an end, I asked permission to have a copy of the stories for further analysis and potential publication. It is my experience that such consent is most often given. The participants have seen how the stories have been used and their anonymity granted throughout the process. The very focus on social patterns and not on individual characteristics in the analytical process makes it less problematic to give such consent. Here, when consent was granted, some of the participants wanted the original copy of the story back, while others did not. But let us now finally turn to the stories!

## Telling stories – an example

The full text of an example story is presented below so as to illustrate the length and content of stories written at this workshop. When discussing these stories, reflections about motherhood, its different themes and relations, came to the surface. These are also presented below to illustrate analytical themes and variety.

### Anna's mother

'I am really enjoying playing with Anna in her big bedroom. We always play the same game: we have collected lots of matchboxes and there are small imaginary people living in them. But they are so real to me as I kit out the matchboxes with blankets and other household things that people might need. I am so engrossed in our game when Anna's mother comes in without knocking on the door. I have a small man in my hand and I feel really silly as I hurry to put him away in his matchbox.

She is looking at me and smiling. She looks really old and wears old-fashioned clothes. She is so much older than my mum. She has no chin so it looks as if her head is attached directly on her body. She offers us milk and we know we have to accept it. I don't like her milk as it is very creamy and not what I am used to. I think it must be good for me, as Anna's mum doesn't go to work. All her work is at home looking after Anna's dad who is also very old. I think she must know that the milk is good for me as her job is being a mum. My mum works and our milk is not creamy.

I take the milk and drink it, as I want her to leave so that I can play again. She watches us drink but she doesn't talk, she never talks much. In Anna's house they don't talk much as Anna's dad does not like noise. I am glad she does not ask about the game. She leaves and we play.'

## Reflection

This story expresses many of the issues raised in our discussions and found in most of the other stories. This includes the *comparison* of mothers, one's own mother to the mother of the friend. Looks, clothes and food but also ways of being are used to pin down the differences between mothers. And it is this difference, very often perceived as strange either in an exciting or threatening way, which colours the picture of the friend's mother. As such it tells us something about the normative mother, that is, one's own mother.

To investigate motherhood such stories are but a first step. From these stories a particular issue or situation can be chosen so to allow a particular focus and for more in-depth studies. New Memory Works can then be undertaken, individually or collectively, preferably combined with other qualitative approaches such as interviews, observations or analyses of texts, pictures and films. To me though, as a reader of all the texts – however varied the stories are and the atmosphere thereby expressed – I am left not primarily with an increased interest in the doings of motherhood but with a renewed interest in childhood. It is the gaze of the child, the vulnerability of her position as child that captures my interest as a reader of these stories, reminding me of my own written stories about 'other people's homes' (Widerberg, 2010). Just like in my own stories, the stories of the workshop transmit tenderness towards us kids venturing out into the world where the homes of our friends represent some of the first steps to be taken. Ending up with a new thematic focus is not rare when using Memory Work. In fact, the very purpose of the approach is to make us discover things we take for granted.

## Practical guidelines – with caution!

As described in the introductory part of this chapter, the approach has been used and developed in quite different ways to fit different theoretical and/or political interests and contexts. And yet, founded on my own experience when teaching or supervising, I also know that one needs some reassurance so as to dare to embark on an approach like this, not yet made into 'standard procedures' or 'curricula'. To attend a course and to practise the approach is, then, by far the best way to get started. That is also the reason I have tried to describe such a course in as much detail as possible, so as to illustrate how it is actually done. In addition to the instructions given for the workshop presented above, I would like to stress the following points regarding collective and individual Memory Work.

## As a collective enterprise

Depending on the estimated number of participants and time at your disposal, a *detailed plan* for the workshop/course/lecture has to be outlined. This is very important so as not to waste precious time or stretch the participants' patience, but also to make them trust that this is 'serious business'. Of course, minor changes underway must be allowed or even encouraged, but it is important to get started right away. Ask the participants to give it a chance, before discussing what and how things could have been done differently, but schedule time for such discussions. The less time you have at your disposal, the more detailed the plan needs to be. For instance:

- *A lecture (2 hours).* Teaching on a theme, you can invite the students to write a memory story in class. Formulate the task so as to make it easy to write, like 'Describe a situation when you were made aware of being a woman/man' (see Widerberg, 1998) and hand out a piece of paper for them to write on, anonymously. Tell them you will read the stories and analyse them in relation to themes from the curricula and present the results on the next occasion.
- *A half-day workshop.* Presentation of the approach and the plans for the day should not exceed thirty minutes. If writing (30 minutes) and reading the stories (30–45 minutes), along the directions given above, this still leaves an hour for discussions and thirty minutes for general discussions of the approach as such. It is tight but it works as an appetiser for the approach.

You need a *chosen theme* and *well-formulated task*. You have the ethical responsibility when choosing the theme, or themes – it might be good to have extra themes up your sleeve. Make sure you formulate the task for writing in such a way as to make it easy to write. Try it out for yourself before the event. We can learn a lot about everyday life through Memory Work on mundane topics, as for example getting dressed, vacuum cleaning, cooking, shopping for groceries and so forth (for a description of courses with such themes, see Widerberg, 2008).

If you are fortunate enough to belong to a research group where you all want to try out the approach, you will of course design it all collectively. Most of us are not however in such happy circumstances and might not have a chance to organise a workshop or give a lecture. Memory Work as an individual enterprise is then the only solution. As such, however, interesting opportunities regarding exploration can be guaranteed.

## As an individual enterprise

Before embarking on a research project, it might be quite fruitful to do a pilot project on yourself, on the theme chosen. I have done it myself, once in connection to a project on sexual harassment and again on another related to tiredness (described in Widerberg, 2008). And all Master's and PhD students are advised to do the same. Similar procedures to those described for Memory Work as a collective enterprise could be used:

- Write about specific situations/events/experiences as concretely as possible.
- Allow yourself to write many stories over a longer time span. New memories will pop up as you go along, so give it some time.
- Analyse the stories along the lines described above. The material can be used to question both the themes but also the approaches you had in mind for the project to follow. Maybe you'll have to change both your questions and how you intended to pose them to the research subjects. But it can also help you to understand their responses. All this was true for our project on sexual harassment. Both design and analysis were highly influenced by what we learned through our own Memory Work on the theme (see more about this in Widerberg, 2008).
- If you have a chance to invite fellow researchers to discuss your stories, this might be quite fruitful. If so, make use of some of the advice given above so as to allow for as open a discussion as possible. That is, look for the social, not the personal in the situations

described. And try not to own the 'true' interpretation. The stories belong to the group now!

- You do not have to present the stories in your final work but can still make use of the insights won through writing them. You just have to explicate their impact on the design and analysis.
- If you do want to present the stories in your final work, make sure how this can be done without putting yourself and your work in a vulnerable position.
- Finally, writing a piece of work with your own Memory Work as the sole empirical material is something quite different, requiring other measures. Having also done this myself (see Widerberg, 2008), it is not something I would recommend anyone to start with, however fruitful it might seem. If you are on the safe side, regarding position and reputation, you might consider it. And even then, the debates about your printed stories can be hard to handle, not only for you but also for your family. Ethical considerations here definitively include yourself as a research subject!

Finally, the fact that the researcher when doing Memory Work is always also a research subject is worth stressing here. Memory Work is not only an approach that allows you to gain new insights and knowledge but also an approach where you are put in the place of the research subject on the theme chosen. You will, in other words, experience what it feels like to answer the questions you pose others. This kind of knowledge is of course highly valuable when conducting a research project.

---

### Box 4.1: Training, tools, and equipment

Since Memory Work is an explorative approach that should be designed in relation to theme, participants, context and time at hand, general guidelines cannot and should not be assumed. That would in fact contradict the very aim of the approach. However, there are some basic tools that readers will find useful to have to hand when using this method:

- If all the participants have laptops that can be connected to a printer, this is an advantage since such texts are easier to read and can be made into three versions with a single press of a button (exchange I for a she/he).
- If the above is not the case, a single sheet of paper and pencil should be handed out.

## Concluding discussion – remembrance, memory and Memory Work

### Memories we live by

In most cultures remembrance is cultivated both individually and collectively. In families we tell and retell family memories to knit us together, to help us negotiate and shape the aims and functioning of our family unit (Smart, 2011). And we are surrounded by institutions – school, workplace, labour union, to mention just a few – that tell and retell the memories of the community, with a similar aim: to knit us together, to make us participate in the well functioning of our society. Films, books and art, but also urban and rural planning, are created to make us remember, not only our own history but also the histories of other generations and groups. Memories and remembering are accordingly about identity – about who we are as individuals, as a family and as a society – and as such, of course, they constitute a highly contested area. We know that experiences and memories of oppression, violence and sexual assaults are made to be forgotten in the family as well as in society. The issue of whose memories and what kind of memories should be highlighted is therefore a battle-ground in both research and politics. Embracing memories as a means to discuss continuity and change of and within the family institution is therefore asking for trouble. The fact that the tool, the memory, is a construction and as such a subject for social investigation in its own right before being made use of as a means to investigate continuity and social change does not make the task any easier. In this chapter I have argued that there are ways of working with memories – using Memory Work as an example that presents an alternative to the nar-rative turn and its dilemmas, producing not only other memories but maybe also other outlines of individual and collective identities.

### Memories we tell

Within social science, research memories are used to substantiate an experience (or set of experiences), to pin it down descriptively so as to make the retold experience as contextually rich as possible. The aim is to make us all – research subject, researcher and reader – engage with the experience anew. Memories are 'collected' or 'gathered' on specific themes or as a part of a life-story/(auto-) biography, through interviews, written texts, diaries and documents in which visual means (photo, film) too may serve as triggers. Memory Work as presented here is but one approach to work with memories, and is extremely productive in bringing up themes and issues for further analysis. As such it can be highly recommended as a pilot project, before an extensive empirical research project is embarked upon. I have myself used it that way, to enlighten a research project on sexual harassment and in another project on the sociality of tiredness. But Memory Work can of course also be the main project, demonstrated not least by Haug's work on female sexualisation (Haug, 1987) but also by Crawford and her colleagues on emotion and gender (Crawford et al., 1992). Each theme and approach has its own challenges and merits regarding knowledge claims. Yet there are of course also some challenges that are shared, affecting knowledge claims that not only call for our attention but also for the exploration of approaches, such as Memory Work.

As Freeman (1993) has pointed out, we live our lives in episodes. The overall plot of the life history that is made up of all these episodes is something we cannot know until afterwards. Remembering is therefore not only a recounting of the past, but also a reinterpretation. It is an interpretive act that aims to expand our understanding of the 'I'. Through memory, a new relation between the past and the present is created, one that can give structure to past and present experiences. Memories from the past are therefore not memories of facts, but memories of how we imagine and construct facts.

Further, what we remember is dependent on language and on culture. Now that we are adults, language plays such a decisive part in the formation of an experience that we find it hard to remember anything from our pre-verbal childhood. Language thus both enlightens and darkens an experience. Culture, on the other hand, is decisive to what is considered important and accordingly what we remember. That is why what is remembered will vary with culture and historical period. People from different cultures who share the 'same' experience may well remember it quite differently. The same is true for different groups within a culture. Oppressed groups, for example, often do not want to or even cannot remember. This has been interpreted (Taylor, 1993) as an expression of resistance towards the submission or oppression pervading their experiences and their memories of these. In order to survive and regain dignity they learn to forget. And if, and when, they do remember, the unbearable makes the memories incoherent and fragmentary. This unwillingness to remember and the way one remembers if forced to, is highlighted in the literature on sexual assault, for example.

To remember, finally, especially in writing, is not only to gain something – for better or for worse. It is also to lose something. Once the memories are written down, it is hard to remember anything but what has been written. Likewise, what we tend to recall of visual impressions of childhood is very much determined by the photos in the family album. In a way, the text or picture locks or fixes the memory, and thereby perhaps also future experiences – registered, reflected and remembered in the light of what we have of memories of our past.

These brief comments on some aspects of the memory process constitute, I believe, an argument for developing methods to unfold memories other than those that culture compels us to tell and also to live by. Memory Work is such an approach to be used and developed in research and teaching so as to fit the occasion, subjects and theme.

I have here tried to illustrate how it can be used and what kind of knowledge can be gained. Hopefully these illustrations can inspire further use and development of the approach. There is so much left to discover and so many ways to develop the approach so as to suit the occasion. A dream situation for us all; student and teacher, researcher and research subject.

---

### Box 4.2: Further reading

Crawford, J., Kippax, S., Onyx, J., Gault, U. and Benton, P. (1992) *Emotion and Gender: Constructing Meaning from Memory*, London: Sage.

Haug, F. (ed.) (1987) *Female Sexualization: A Collective Work of Memory*, London: Verso.

Kaufman, J., Ewing, M. S., Montgomery, D. and Hyle, A. (2003) *From Girls in their Elements to Women in Science: Rethinking Socialization through Memory-Work*, New York: Peter Lang.

Kaufman, J., Ewing, M. S., Montgomery, D. and Hyle, A. (eds) (2008) *Dissecting the Mundane: International Perspectives on Memory-Work*, Lanham, MD: University Press of America, Inc.

Widerberg, K. (1998) 'Teaching gender through writing "experience stories"' *Women's International Forum*, 21 (2): 193–198.

Widerberg, K. (2010) 'In the homes of others: exploring new sites and methods when investigating the doings of gender, class and ethnicity', *Sociology*, 44 (6): 1181–1196.

# References

Crawford, J., Kippax, S., Onyx, J., Gault, U. and Benton, P. (1992) *Emotion and Gender: Constructing Meaning from Memory*, London: Sage.

Davies, B. (2000) *(In)scribing Body/Landscape Relations*, Walnut Creek, CA: Alta Mira Press.

Davies, B. (2008) 'Practicing collective biography' in A. Hyle, M. S. Ewing, D. Montgomery and J. Kaufman (eds) *Dissecting the Mundane: International Perspectives on Memory-Work*, Lanham, MD: University Press of America, Inc.

Deutsch, F. (2007) 'Undoing gender', *Gender & Society*, 21 (1): 106–127.

Freeman, M. (1993) *Rewriting the Self: History, Memory, Narrative*, London: Routledge.

Haug, F. (ed.) (1987) *Female Sexualization: A Collective Work of Memory*, London: Verso.

Kaufman, J., Ewing, M. S., Montgomery, D. and Hyle, A. (eds) (2003) *From Girls in their Element to Women in Science: Rethinking Socialization through Memory-Work*, New York: Peter Lang.

Kaufman, J., Ewing, M. S., Montgomery, D. and Hyle, A. (eds) (2008) *Dissecting the Mundane: International Perspectives on Memory-Work*, Lanham, MD: University Press of America, Inc.

Smart, C. (2011) 'Families, secrets and memories', *Sociology*, 45 (4): 539–553.

Taylor, C. A. (1993) 'Positioning subjects and objects: agency, narration, relationality', *Hypatia*, 8 (1): 55–80.

West, C. and Zimmerman, D. (1987) 'Doing gender', *Gender & Society*, 1 (2): 125–151.

Widerberg, K. (1998) 'Teaching gender through writing experience stories', *Women's International Forum*, 21 (2): 193–198.

Widerberg, K. (1999) Alternative methods – alternative understandings: exploring the social and multiple "I" through memory-work', *Sosiologisk tidskrift*, 2: 147–159.

Widerberg, K. (2008) 'For the sake of knowledge: exploring memory-work in research and teaching', in A. Hyle, M. S. Ewing, D. Montgomery and J. Kaufman (eds) *Dissecting the Mundane: International Perspectives On Memory-Work*, Lanham, MD: University Press of America, Inc., 113–133.

Widerberg, K. (2010) 'In the homes of others: exploring new sites and methods when investigating the doings of gender, class and ethnicity', *Sociology*, 44 (6): 1181–1196.

Widerberg, K. (2011) 'Memory work: exploring family life and expanding the scope of family research', *Journal of Comparative Family Studies*, 42 (3): 329–337.

Widerberg, K. et al. (2001) *Doing Body/Texts: An Explorative Approach*, Oslo: Department of Sociology and Human Geography, University of Oslo.

# 5

# Material relationships: object interviews as a means of studying everyday life

Helen Holmes

## Introduction

Since the material turn in the social sciences, researchers have been exploring new ways to engage with the objects and materials of everyday life. Such methods aim to overcome subject–object binaries, placing the very substance of materials at the core of their inquiry (Gregson and Crewe, 1998). This chapter takes one such approach – object interviews – to explore how objects and materials structure our everyday lives and relationships. This method involves not only unearthing the significance of objects to their owners, but also and importantly investigating the biography of the object itself. Drawing on the work of Humphries and Smith (2014) such an approach reveals an object's materiality, biography and practice; interconnecting the object and the subject in novel and illuminating ways. This approach explores how an object's material qualities – its fibres, textures, patterns and forms (Miller, 2005) – influence the relationship we have with it; and its importance within our mundane, everyday lives.

Objects form part of networks with other objects. They have past and future lives, they enable and afford certain practices and activities, and they often play a central role in the relationships we have with others. Rather than thinking of objects as inert containers of our memories, stories and selves, this approach takes account of the importance of the object and its story. In other words, it explores its trajectory as well as its owners. Importantly, this approach is not just about extraordinary or 'special' objects but can be applied to ordinary items, things we use every day and probably pay little attention to; such as the mug we drink our coffee from each morning, our desk at work or the shoes on our feet. As I discuss, often it is this focus on the material minutiae of everyday life which can be so revealing. These unremarkable objects are often the overlooked crucial components of our daily lives. As I illustrate with empirical examples, object interviews are a means of understanding and making sense of everyday life, and the social, political and economic factors which structure it.

This chapter begins by appraising the importance of objects in everyday life and their significance within social science following the material turn. It draws on existing literature on materiality and the role of objects in everyday life. I briefly discuss the variety of material methods available for those interested in studying material culture, before focusing specifically on object interviews and varying ways in which these have been approached. The chapter then offers some guidance as to why the method may be used, before moving on to provide a proforma for approaching object interviews which remain object–subject neutral and are focused upon three key categories: materiality, practice and biography. Using empirical examples from my work on thrift (see Holmes, 2018, 2019a, 2019b), I offer advice on each of these categories. Finally, I offer some practical advice for anyone thinking of using object interviews as a research method.

## Background

The 1990s heralded a 'rematerialisation' of social and cultural studies, and a renewed focus on objects and materials (Jackson, 2004: 172; see also Hall and Holmes in this collection). Such work drew on anthropological theories of material culture to critique the then preoccupation with the 'spectacular' within social science. In particular, scholars called for recognition of the 'substance' as opposed to the 'symbolism' of material goods (Gregson and Crewe, 1998: 40). Much of this critique was levelled at cultural studies and, specifically, work on consumption which prioritised the cultural role of commodities as markers of identity. In other words, 'you are what you buy' and what you eat, wear and do makes a statement about who you are (Featherstone, 1991; Goss, 1993). Instead academics called for recognition of objects as more than cultural symbols, and that attention should be paid to the very materiality of things (Miller, 2005). Taking account of the substance of objects, their sensory and material properties – how they look, feel, what they do – gave rise to a whole new field of social science devoted to material culture and the study of materiality.

This material turn brought about a sea change in consumption studies – no longer were the cornucopia of shopping malls and conspicuous forms of consumption the focus (Slater, 1997), but instead ordinary forms of consumption were explored (Gronow and Warde, 2001). From second-hand stores and car boot sales (Gregson and Crewe, 2003; Gregson et al., 2013); to food shopping and purchasing everyday items (Miller, 1997, 2002); to household thrift and networks of neighbourly reciprocity (Holmes, 2018, 2019b) – the mundane became interesting. This work prioritises material culture, illuminating the significance of everyday, ordinary objects and their material qualities. Indeed, it forms part of the more recent move within the social sciences towards exploring the everyday and the mundane. Work such as that of Coole and Frost (2010) calls for recognition of what they term 'new materialism', and the need to take account of the relational and everyday sense of materiality. Through this new genre of materiality studies, the focus is on rethinking the subjectivity of materials, 'to give materiality its due while recognising its plural dimensions' (Coole and Frost, 2010: 27). This focus is important methodologically.

To date, methods for engaging with objects and materials to illuminate their sensory and material qualities have been relatively limited. Those which are available tend to prioritise either the subject – the person/persons the object is owned by or relates to – or the object in its own right. Very few attempt to combine the two to overcome this object–subject dichotomy. This is important to ensure that the material qualities and agencies of objects are not rendered invisible at the expense of a focus on the subject or participant. For instance, one of the most well-known methods for exploring materiality is follow-the-thing, an approach which essentially tracks an object from raw material through to disposal (also see Hall et al., this collection). This method has been used to chart the trajectory of papaya and its supply chain from Jamaica all the way to North London (Cook et al., 2004); and the movement of second-hand clothing from the West to less developed countries (Norris, 2005; Tranberg-Hansen, 2005). However, by focusing purely upon an object's trajectory this approach tends to render the subject(s) silent. The focus of these accounts is all about the journey of the object and the places and spaces it encounters. Such narratives do not delve into the influence the object has on the people with whom it comes into contact, or its socio-material significance in their lives.

At the other end of the spectrum are methods such as cultural probes (Gaver et al., 2004) and objects as containers for stories (Digby, 2006) which focus on the role of objects in people's lives. With these approaches the object is the means through which the subject is able to tell their stories. For example Susan Digby's (2006) work explores how souvenirs become part of identity construction and home making. Similarly, Rachel Hurdley (2006) on her study on mantlepieces studies the narratives people construct around objects on display and the connections made between identity and memory (see also Horton and Kraftl, 2012; Roberts, 2012). In these approaches objects act as receptacles for memories and stories, the object acting as the reminder of the memories, narratives the people associated with them. As Harre (2002: 25) notes, 'an object is transformed from a piece of stuff, definable independently of any storyline, into a social object by its embodiment into a narrative'. In such accounts the agency of the object and its biography are underplayed as the subject is always prioritised. Thus the object is rendered silent to the advantage of the subject.

We therefore reach something of an impasse – on the one hand our available material methods silence the subject, and on the other they silence the object. Neither set of approaches seemingly tries to equally prioritise both object and subject. While scholars of new materialism call for a removal of Cartesian dualisms, this dichotomy is a concern for those wishing to research materiality (Coole and Frost, 2010). How does one research objects and materials while paying attention to both the objects of interest and the people that come into contact with them?

One approach is Actor Network Theory (ANT) (Latour, 2005). This approach posits that everything in the social and natural world exists through networks of relationships. Through a flat ontological structure, humans and non-humans are perceived through varying networks. While there is not space to delve into ANT in any depth here, this approach is valuable because of its recognition of the equal importance of both objects and subjects, human and non-humans. However, it is not without critique. For Humphries and Smith (2014), this lies in ANT's recognition that 'actants' (humans and non-humans, alongside ideas, processes and really anything about the world) only exist through the relationships which they are part of, not in and of themselves; thus they can only be described and accessed through these networks. Humphries and Smith believe this extreme view misses any emerging actors or networks, and does not take account of change or resistance. As they note, if we are going to 'question the treatment of objects as mere instruments for social and functional performance' (2014: 479), then we must also 'query the treatment of objects as independent entities which reveal an autonomous reality'. As a corrective to accounts which focus on either the object or the subject, and to ANT's focus on networks, Humphries and Smith put forward their own approach. Through their work exploring encounters with a 914 Xerox copier, they collect object-centred narratives which give objects a 'louder voice' (2014: 479) and take account of their 'enmeshed relationships' with subjects (2014: 482). To do this they propose focusing on three key areas when thinking about objects. These are *object materiality*, *object practice* and *object biography*.

Object materiality requires the interviewer to take a 'common-sense view of objects' (Humphries and Smith, 2014: 483). In other words, to pay attention to an object's physical properties and sensorial material qualities. Object practice requires one to take account of the activities that enmesh objects and people, and how narratives of objects are illuminated through use. Object biography relates to 'the multiple and past lives' objects have and how these are often entangled with people over time (2014: 488). These three overlapping categories are central to the method of object interviewing I use and describe below. Building upon Humphries and Smith's approach, the method of object interviewing discussed here involves trying to place equal emphasis on both the object and the subject, alongside thinking reflexively about the role of the researcher in encountering the object and the subject. Furthermore, I try to appreciate the messiness of materiality – that objects, just like subjects, are not static but can and do change.

## Why choose object interviews?

Before I go on to outline how I use object interviews, it seems worthwhile paying some attention as to why you might use them. First, and while seemingly obvious, it is worth noting that this form of object interviews, focused on giving equal emphasis to both object and subject, only really works if you are interested in researching materiality. Nonetheless, object interviewing more generally can be used for a variety of subjects (see below). As discussed above, that might be researching materiality as a way of understanding the subject better, or it might be about understanding an object and its role, or both, as I attempt to do. An important distinction to make is between having a research focus on materiality, as opposed to using materials as a means to engage in a particular topic. The former we would refer to as object focused and would include all of the material methods we have discussed so far, while the latter is more about using materials as a method of inquiry. For example, this may involve using plasticine, lego or drawing to get people to engage with a subject unrelated to the materials with which they are working. Of course, there can be crossover, but the main point is that object interviews are not a method which can simply be shoe-horned into any research design; there has to be an interest in the significance of the material – whether that be to reveal a narrative of someone's life (subject focused) or to illuminate an object's biography (object focused) or both.

Secondly, your reasons for choosing object interviews might relate to the sorts of data you can expect them to generate. For Sheridan and Chamberlain (2011), who focus on objects as containers for stories, objects create depth and enhancement to otherwise only audio narratives. They note how objects can often validate an interviewee's lived experience while also 'thickening' their account. Similarly, the use of objects may force the emergence of new memories or recollections which may have been forgotten, buried or hidden. For Sophie Woodward (2016), object interviews evoke sensory experiences. Her work on denim jeans reveals how object interviews were able to add a sensory depth to the life history interviews she was initially conducting. Being able to see, touch and hold the material objects brought the materiality of the jeans to life – not just for the interviewees whose accounts were embellished by holding the jeans as they talked about them, but also for the researcher, Sophie, who felt connected to the jeans and the stories told about them. Therefore object interviews often produce very embodied, sensory accounts. Sometimes these may be accompanied by photographs or other visual depictions (drawings, video), even the objects themselves, as I discuss below, and these too generate particular sorts of data requiring specific analysis (see also Pink, 2013). If you are planning to undertake object interviews these aspects need consideration.

## A proforma for conducting object interviews

I now outline how I approach object interviews, building upon Humphries and Smith's (2014) three-pronged approach of materiality, practice and biography. Notably my focus is not on the object within each of these, but on *both* object and subject to overcome the aforementioned dichotomy, and includes the researcher thinking reflexively about their role. I deal with each thematic category in turn, providing a list of questions to consider, alongside empirical examples of how I have used this method. It must be noted, however, that these categories are not distinct, and as the following describes often all three merge together. Thus the questions are meant as a guide to the sorts of things you could ask during an object interview.

### Theme 1: materiality

- Explore the materiality of the object with both the participant and researcher.
- What are its physical properties?
  – Colour, texture, size, feel, smell, taste?
  What is it made of?
  – Are there signs of wear and tear?
  – What are they? Describe them.
  – Has it been repaired or altered?
- How does the participant handle the object during the interview? How do you the researcher handle it? Is this important?
- Are there any material features of the object which are prominent? Either visibly or stressed by the participant?

'Materiality' seems an obvious thing to consider if you are interested in objects. Yet often, particularly in an interview situation, it is easy to overlook the very minutiae in which we are interested. It is therefore worth spending time to consider the object in question, making notes about its physical and sensorial qualities, perhaps even sketching or maybe photographing the item. This was especially important during my research on thrift. This three-year research project explored everyday contemporary forms of thrift through the lens of materiality, practice and time. I was particularly interested in the ways in which people were thrifty in the home, and the sorts of objects and materials these thrifty practices incorporated (see Holmes,

2018, 2019a, 2019b). Part of this involved interviewing householders about everyday items they deemed as 'special'. They could be special because of something the objects did, or because of the significance they held – or often, as discussed, a bit of both. Often this line of inquiry would lead interviewees to bring out items which had been handed down or inherited from kin (see Holmes, 2018a). Such items ranged from kitchen equipment, to tools, to items of furniture, as Figures 5.1 and 5.2 illustrate.

Two things became very poignant within these interviews. First, and not surprisingly, many of these items were old – therefore they had very visible signs of wear and tear. Some had even been repurposed and turned into something else. For example, one participant, Heather, had turned the bottom part of her grandmother's wardrobe into a seat for which she had fashioned a cushion. Trying to account for these signs of wear and tear and sometimes object transformation in my data was difficult, but entirely necessary to capture the materiality of these items and their significance. Taking pictures helped this process and subsequently my data analysis – as it meant I could

**5.1  An inherited, well-used casserole dish**

**5.2** Heather's seat fashioned from her grandmother's wardrobe

access at least a visual representation of the object's materiality whenever I needed to, reminding me of its physical qualities. These pictures also worked to support my arguments in any writing (with consent from object owners).

Secondly, my own reaction to the objects I was presented with became an unexpected element of the research process. Given the age of these items, and the sentimental significance they held for many interviewees, I found myself often reluctant to touch or handle them for fear of damaging them or dropping them. One particularly noteworthy example was participant Edna, who at ninety-five was my oldest participant. Edna had a china tea set, a collection which had been her pride and joy as a young married woman in the 1950s. As she remarked, 'years back, if you had a china tea set you were everybody'. I was completely terrified by the tea set, yet Edna insisted I held it! This nerve-wracking moment stuck in my mind, and cemented the significance of not just the sentimentality attached to these items, but also the sheer potency of their existence and power within the research setting. I would therefore always recommend being reflexive about how an object makes you as a researcher feel as well as your interviewee's feelings. Are you repulsed by it, not bothered by it, eager to hold it? This links to Rebecca Collins's account of auto-ethnography during life drawing classes (this collection) and the need to remain continually reflexive to one's reactions during the research process. Answering these questions can be just as informative about the materiality of an object as understanding what an object means to its current owner.

## Theme 2: practice

- What is the practice of the object? Does it have one?
  - This could be practical or symbolic significance.
  - If so – how is it significant?
  - Is the practice of the object missing? Maybe it has several uses? Or is used in an alternative way than it was designed for?
- How is the object stored? Why is it stored where it is?
- Are there any connections or collections apparent?
  - With other practices? Objects? People?
  - Think about networks, collections, assemblages, relationships.

As per Humphries and Smith's argument (2014), the second thing to consider when researching objects is 'practice'. What does the object do? Or, as Humphries and Smith (2014: 486) describe, 'how are people and objects mingled together?' This may seem like an obvious question – for example a coffee cup is used for drinking coffee out of, a table for sitting at, and so forth. However, the set of questions I have developed above are about thinking broadly about the variety of practices that objects are a part of but also recognising their relationality.

So, first, a coffee cup may be used for drinking coffee out of, but then it may also be used to store pens, decant cereal or hold flowers. The point is that often objects are not used as intended and that is of interest to scholars of materiality. This could be intentional upcycling – one of my participants used an old, unused CD rack as storage for children's shoes – or it may just be something that has happened to an object over time. Nonetheless the use of an object, whether as per its intended design or not, is relevant. Why is it used in this way?

What does that illustrate about the object and the owner? Maybe it is not used at all? This leads to another important question – how is the object stored? Many objects are simply held on display, such as Edna's tea set above, never to be used again, gathering dust. Others are relegated to attics or the back of cupboards and never see the light of day, as examined in the work of Sophie Woodward (this collection) and her work on 'Dormant Things' or Horton and Kraftl on their work on cupboards (2012). These decisions about storage are vital to understanding the materiality of the object and its biography.

Secondly, and relatedly, does the object have symbolic significance? Maybe the coffee cup is used to hold pens because it has a sentimental significance and the owner wants to make sure it is not subjected to the usual wear and tear of the dishwasher/hot drinks or risk of being broken. Maybe it was given to them by someone special, or signifies something in their life. Importantly, symbolic items are not just the spectacular or extraordinary but can and do include mundane, everyday objects like the coffee cup. Many of my participants held on to everyday items because they held some symbolic significance. One participant, Alex, had an old spade which was his father's (see Figure 5.3). There was nothing spectacular about the spade, but for Alex every time he used it, it reminded him of his father (see also Holmes, 2019a). Other participants kept children's clothes or teddies – dormant reminders of different times in their life. Often these symbolic attachments are crucial to understanding why the object is used or kept in such a way.

Thirdly, it is important to think about the object and its networks and relationships. This set of questions borrows from ANT and the idea that everything exists as part of a network or assemblage. There is not the space here to discuss Actor Network Theory in any depth (see: Latour, 2005 for more information), nor is the method I use and describe here a strictly ANT approach. It is the idea of thinking about how an object is connected to other objects, practices and people which I think is most useful. So, to return to the coffee cup example, it might (depending on what it is used for) be connected to the kettle, other cups, milk, coffee, maybe tea, teaspoons, the dishwasher. It may be enmeshed in a range of practices, from making coffee, being drunk from, being in the dishwasher, sitting in a cupboard. And, it may connect to other people – perhaps someone else uses the cup or someone washes it up. Maybe it is part of a collection of cups and, if so, why and what is its role? (See also Woodward, this collection, which

**5.3 Participant's spade inherited from his father**

discusses the value of collections as a means of studying the everyday.) Thus understanding how the object connects to other objects, people and practices is valuable to exploring its material significance.

## Theme 3: biography

- How is the object part of the biography of the participant?
  - For example, object used to describe life events, discuss a relationship.
- What about the biography of the object?
  - For example, who made the object, previous owners, previous lives, relationships with other objects?
- How are the two intertwined?
- Is one more prominent than the other?

The final aspect to consider when object interviewing is 'biography'. Unlike Humphries and Smith (2014: 488), who advocate a focus on the biography of objects to reveal 'the lives they have shared with their human users', I argue that we must focus equally upon an object and the owner's biography. While the whole point of object interviewing is to reveal the hidden and invisible lives of objects, focusing only on its biography in an interview situation not only overlooks the importance of the owner, but is also quite difficult; particularly if the owner has limited knowledge of the object's origins, trajectory or previous owners. Therefore I would advocate first asking the owner or keeper of the object about how it came into their possession. This then may tie into 'practice', as they may explain its significance in their life. Aligning with subject-centred approaches, this may produce a narrative whereby the object is used as a means to access the subject's life events, memories and relationships. In other words the object becomes a container for the subject's story (Digby, 2006). However, this approach brings forth the opportunity of also questioning the object's biography. Once we know how the object fits into the owner's biography it is a more natural segue into exploring what the owner knows about the object's biography.

So, we may ask questions such as where does the object come from, where was it made, who owned it before? Often this may link to practice and sentimental significance, as the object may be handed down or inherited from a family member. There may also be material clues on the object which can help with some of these questions, such as labels, or markings revealing country of origin, original raw materials or perhaps when the object was made. All of these markers along with information from the owner/keeper help us to piece together some resemblance of the object's biography. Unfortunately these will often be piecemeal unless we are deploying a follow-the-thing approach, but they may be enough for us to understand the object's material significance.

## Practical advice

### Interweaving the object interview into a broader interview

I have already noted how all three categories – materiality, practice, biography – interweave with one another, and that you will probably find that it is not as straightforward as asking about each category in turn, as they blur together. However, it is also important to note that often object interviews are interwoven into broader and more traditional semi-structured interview formats. I have never performed a standalone object interview; it has always been part of a wider interview. This point is important for several reasons. First, being part of a more traditional interview method often helps put the interviewee at ease. Many interviewees may feel a bit uncomfortable at first, being asked about objects in their homes or other familiar spaces. There have been many occasions where my requests to view the contents of someone's cupboards have been met with alarm, despite prior information being given in the participant information sheet about the type of interview and focus of research this will involve. Asking questions which require just 'talk' to begin with can gain the interviewee's trust and help them to relax before you start asking about objects.

Secondly, ensuring your object interview is part of a wider and more traditional interview approach is a way of enhancing its rigour as a form of data. While novel methods are alluring, they are also often experimental and this can raise questions about their robustness. Great thought needs to be given about their relevance to the research and their application. Combining object interviews with standard interviews (or with life history methods, as per Woodward, 2016) is one way of limiting this risk. The object interviews form part of something bigger, rather than being the entire focus.

Thirdly, this combined approach helps with analysis. The object data forms part of the bigger data set and can be analysed in the same way, rather than as standalone. For me this has always meant taking a thematic approach, and using the object data and photographs of objects as a means of interpreting the overall interview, and vice versa. With the great things that analysis software can do now, this comprehensive approach is becoming easier and easier. Although I am still a fan of manual coding with crayons!

## Remaining object–subject neutral

I have already addressed this throughout the chapter, but this is just to warn any would-be object interviewers that trying to remain object–subject neutral is challenging. It can be very hard to steer your interviewee (and yourself as researcher) from only seeing the object as container for stories. This is because we are conditioned to think of objects as inert, as powerless and as 'our' stuff to do with what we will. Therefore it is easy to only think about objects as playing roles in our biographies, rather than us in theirs. Always try to remain open to the power and agency of the object. It cannot speak for itself, but you can try to give it a voice and to reveal its agency.

## Do not ignore the mundane!

I am hoping that if you have chosen to read a text such as *Mundane Methods*, you are already well aware of this, but often with studies of objects there is a temptation to explore the spectacular and the extraordinary at the expense of the everyday. As this chapter has hopefully illustrated, even the most banal of objects – spoons, pans, spades, coat hangers – can be of huge sociological significance and are worthy of our study.

## Taking pictures

A word of warning that if you are taking pictures of objects to help with your analysis, do get consent from the owner/interviewee (you made need it from both if they are two different people). Even if pictures are of inert, everyday things with nobody visibly present in them, objects, even mundane ones, can be identifiable. It is worth noting on your consent form that with permission you will take pictures and that these may be used in publications and other research outputs in the future. If participants do not want photographs taking you could always sketch objects. Sue Heath and Lynne Chapman's chapter on sketching in this collection gives some guidance on doing this.

## Conclusion

Object interviews can be a crucial method for anyone interested in materiality and material culture. The approach outlined above offers

---

### Box 5.1: Training, tools and equipment

Equipment used included:

- a Dictaphone;
- a digital camera or camera phone for object photos;
- paper and pen – for any notes or sketches (if photographs are not permitted).

a guide to object interviewing which tries to remain object–subject neutral, privileging neither one nor the other. Through a focus on materiality, practice and biography, developed from the work of Humphries and Smith (2014), the proforma offers a means of illuminating the material significance and potency of objects as well as their role as containers for people's memories and stories. It requires the interviewer to be sensitive to the sensory and embodied nature of objects and also to be reflexive about their own position within the interview and their interaction with both the interviewee and the object. This method can be interwoven with standard interviews and can also involve the collection of other data such as photographs and videos to support and enhance the material-based data. It also requires little equipment other than a Dictaphone and a camera if you want to take pictures.

Object interviews offer a way for researchers to engage with materiality; exploring how objects and materials are part of everyday life without seeing them as merely containers for our stories. This method is part of a broader set of methods around ways to engage with materials (see Woodward, this collection), recognising the importance of their agency and how it is interwoven with our own.

---

### Box 5.2: Further reading

The work of Humphries and Smith (2014) is a great place to start to explore object interviewing:

Humphries, C. and Smith, A. (2014) 'Talking objects: towards a post-social research framework for exploring object narratives', *Organization*, 21 (4): 477–491.

As is Sophie Woodward's book:

Woodward, S. (2019) *Material Methods: Researching and Thinking with Things*, London: Sage.

The empirical account of object interviews on which this chapter is written may also help:

Holmes, H. 'Material affinities: doing family through the practices of passing on', *Sociology*, 53 (1): 174–191.

## Bibliography

Cook, I. et al. (2004) 'Follow the thing: papaya', *Antipode*, 36 (4): 642–664.

Coole, D. and Frost, S. (2010) 'Introducing the new materialisms', in D. Coole and S. Frost (eds) *New Materialisms, Ontology, Agency and Politics*, London: Duke University Press.

Digby, S. (2006) 'The casket of magic: home and identity from salvaged objects', *Home Cultures*, 3 (2): 169–190.

Featherstone, M. (1991) *Consumer Culture and Postmodernism*, London: Sage.

Gaver, W., Boucher, A., Pennington, S. and Walker, B. (2004) 'Cultural probes and the value of uncertainty', *Interactions – Funology*, 11 (5): 53–56.

Goss, J. (1993) 'The magic of the mall: an analysis of form, function and meaning in the contemporary retail built environment', *Annals of the Association of American Geographers*, 83 (1): 18–47.

Gregson, N. and Crewe, L. (1998) 'Tales of the unexpected: exploring car boot sales as marginal spaces of contemporary consumption', *Transactions of the Institute of British Geographers*, 23: 39–53.

Gregson, N. and Crewe, L. (2003) *Second-hand Cultures*, Oxford: Berg.

Gregson, N., Crang, M., Laws, J., Fleetwood, T. and Holmes, H. (2013) 'Moving up the waste hierarchy: car boot sales, reuse exchange and the challenges of consumer culture to waste prevention', *Resources, Conservation and Recycling*, 77: 97–107.

Gronow, J. and Warde, A. (eds) (2001) *Ordinary Consumption*, London: Routledge.

Harre, R. (2002) 'Material objects in social worlds', *Theory, Culture and Society*, 19 (5/6): 23–33.

Holmes, H. (2018) 'New spaces, ordinary practices: circulating and sharing in diverse economies of provisioning', *Geoforum*, 88: 138–147.

Holmes, H. (2019a) 'Material affinities: doing family through the practices of passing on', *Sociology*, 53 (1): 174–191.

Holmes, H. (2019b) 'Unpicking contemporary thrift: getting on and getting by in everyday life', *Sociological Review*, 67 (1): 126–142.

Horton, J. and Kraftl, P. (2012) 'Clearing out a cupboard: memory, materiality and transitions', in O. Jones and J. Garde-Hansen (eds) *Geography and Memory: Explorations in Identity, Place and Becoming*, London: Palgrave Macmillan, 25–44.

Humphries, C. and Smith, A. (2014) 'Talking objects: towards a post-social research framework for exploring object narratives', *Organization*, 21 (4): 477–494.

Hurdley, R. (2006) 'Dismantling mantelpieces: narrating identities and materialising culture in the home', *Sociology*, 40: 717–733.

Jackson, P. (2004) 'Local consumption in a globalizing world', *Transactions of the Institute of British Geographers*, 29: 165–178.

Latour, B. (2005) *Reassembling the Social: An Introduction to Actor Network Theory*, Oxford: Oxford University Press.

Miller, D. (1997) 'Coca-cola: a black sweet drink from Trinidad', in D. Miller (ed.) *Material Cultures*, London: UCL Press, 1–19.

Miller, D. (2002) 'Making love in supermarkets', in B. Highmore (ed.) *The Everyday Life Reader*, London: Routledge, 339–345.

Miller, D. (2005) 'Introduction', in S. Kuchler and D. Miller (eds) *Clothing as Material Culture*, Oxford: Berg, 169–188.

Norris, L. (2005) 'Cloth that lies: the secrets of recycling in India', in S. Kuchler and D. Miller (eds) *Clothing as Material Culture*, Oxford: Berg, 83–105.

Pink, S. (2013) *Doing Visual Ethnography* (3rd edn), London: Sage.

Roberts, E. (2012) 'Family photographs: memories, narratives, place', in O. Jones and J. Garde-Hansen (eds) *Geography and Memory: Explorations in Identity, Place and Becoming*, London: Palgrave Macmillan, 91–108.

Sheridan, J. and Chamberlain, K. (2011) 'The power of things', *Qualitative Research in Psychology*, 8 (4): 315–332.

Slater, D. R. (1997) *Consumer Culture and Modernity*, Cambridge: Polity Press.

Tranberg-Hansen, S. (2005) 'From thrift to fashion: materiality and aesthetics in dress practices in Zambia', in D. Miller and S. Kuchler (eds) *Clothing as Material Culture*, Oxford: Berg, 107–120.

Woodward, S. (2016) 'Object interviews, material imaginings and "unsettling" methods: interdisciplinary approaches to understanding materials and material culture', *Qualitative Research*, 16 (4): 359–374.

Woodward, S. (2019) *Material Methods: Researching and Thinking with Things*, London: Sage.

# 6

# Food for thought? Material methods for exploring food and cooking

Sarah Marie Hall, Laura Pottinger, Megan Blake,
Susanna Mills, Christian Reynolds and
Wendy Wrieden

## Food: the stuff of the everyday

Food is, quite literally, the stuff of the everyday. It punctuates daily rhythms, constitutes social relationships, and shapes economic and political systems. Whether by looking at its origins, cultural relations, environmental and health impacts, or economic implications, social researchers have long been fascinated with food. As a material substance, food brings people together, whether at dinner tables or at certain times of the year, as well as being a point of shared memories, experiences and practices (see Bell and Valentine, 1997; Warde, 2016). At the same time, food is also the result of a series of mundane and wonderful transformations of various materials, through cultural practices and techniques (see Wilbur and Gibbs, 2018).

Preparing, cooking and devouring food is a process, and one which involves a series of embodied skills and visceral repertoires, as well as material engagements (also see Goodman, 2016; Hayes-Conroy and Hayes-Conroy, 2010, 2013; Roe, 2006; Wilbur and Gibbs, 2018). With this chapter we focus on food and cooking practices, particularly preparation and making. We explore methods that allow for the investigation of different facets of food as a social object. Advancing well-worn methodological approaches to food stuffs, such as the biography of things or 'follow the thing' (see Cook et al., 2004), we look at methodological means of tracing the transformation of food; from ingredient, to par-cooked, to creation, to eating. With methods of talking, doing, documenting and observing, in the guise of cook-alongs and food-for-thought discussions, the material transformations of food are seen anew. Our focus here is, then, on where material methods meet embodied practices, exploring mundane manual and tactile tasks of making food, as well as using the body as an instrument through which to smell, taste, eat and digest (also see Longhurst, Ho and Johnston, 2008; Roe, 2006; Wilbur and Gibbs, 2018).

To do this, we open with a discussion of foodie methods, detailing some of the many ways in which the mundane materialities of food have previously been researched across the social sciences. After this, we move on to describe our research project – 'The personal and political potential of cookery classes in low-income communities in Manchester' (2017–2018, funded by the N8 Agri Food Network) – which employed cook-alongs and food-for-thought methods. This includes a discussion of reflections on the fieldwork process and our broad findings, before positing some pieces of advice for other researchers considering similar methodological approaches. We offer suggestions throughout for replicating our approach, or alternatively for applying these and similar methods to other forms of 'following'. Either way, we hope readers leave feeling full of new ideas!

## Following food: popular methodological recipes

The most obvious starting point for a brief genealogy of food-as-material methods is the notion of material or product biographies. This idea stems from an approach heavily influenced by Marxist theories of exchange value; that as raw materials are transformed into commodities – for example tea leaves into tea bags, or blackberries into jam – the monetary value of the material increases. This process of accruing value in a material object, food or otherwise, as it moves through a series of production and consumption practices has been of intense interest to social scientists, particularly for how it intersects with ideas about workers' rights and labour conditions, waste and resource use, and the cultural place of consumer goods in everyday life. Here, the commodity is depicted as having a 'lifespan' or a 'life history' (Appadurai, 1986; Cook et al., 2004; Cook, Crang and Thorpe, 2004), stretching from the processes of production onwards.

This progression of food as material, from raw product to disposal (as the product 'life'), has been described using different metaphors, such as 'biographies', 'social lives' and even 'geographies' of products (Bridge and Smith, 2003; Cook, Crang and Thorpe, 2004; Kopytoff, 1986). Indeed, readers might be more familiar with the 'follow the thing' approach, including Cook et al.'s (2004) piece following the papaya fruit from extraction to consumption (though other objects have also been 'followed', see for example Pfaff, 2010). These many interchangeable metaphors refer to the socio-economic relations that commodities encounter and, in turn, produce. Increasingly, too, these product life-cycles take account of the environmental consequences of production, consumption and disposal (including recycling for reproduction). This work has been influential in moving accounts away from heavily economic analysis (particularly in the 'production' phase of a commodity) towards questions about the politics of food access, waste and surplus where economic and cultural values are difficult to pick apart. As will be discussed later in the chapter, the politics of accessing, making and creating everyday goods like food can also work to reframe understanding of materials in everyday life. "

Nonetheless, it is argued that an advantage of a commodity-centred approach, when tracing the materialities of food, is that the links between production, distribution and consumption become visible for inspection (Jackson, 1999). Acknowledging the various stages through which products progress, the life history of materials, may therefore reveal a number of crucial connections between the commodity as an object, and a range of social practices and relationships. Likewise, Castree (2004) argues that commodities are transgressive, and that it is important to consider the socio-spatial universe of places, peoples, identities and beliefs when researching the commodity-form. In this chapter we too are interested in these transgressive politics of food and other materials, and how they can be researched in practice.

Where the writings discussed above have placed their focus on the cultural and monetary value of the object (the food item or items), biographical and life-cycle approaches have since spawned a range of empirical developments that involve following the thing(s) using different techniques; talking, observing, feeling. Within this body of work, 'focus is directed not [just] to the producers or consumers of food' but also towards 'the bodies of humans and nonhumans' (Roe, 2006: 104). It is widely acknowledged that sociable, participatory methods, of doing research together and alongside others, is one approach by which to observe moments of material transformations *as they occur*. For instance, Hayes-Conroy's (2010) visceral fieldwork approach investigating Slow Food involved participant-designed encounters around food. Ethnographic interviews and participant observation were carried out while 'doing' food alongside participants in various ways, from tasting food products to cooking, handling plants in gardens and so on. This brings to light how food-based material methods have lots of possibilities, for they might involve food at different stages – as it is growing, harvested, processed, prepared, eaten and so on (see Pottinger, 2017; Wilbur and Gibbs, 2018). Roe (2006: 105), for example, using video methods, develops an approach of what she calls 'things becoming food' as 'a tool to trace the materiality of foodstuff through the practice of eating'. There are lots of possibilities here for going beyond food followings to explore other material forms to follow.

On the matter of food, some scholars have used the method of cooking as a form of inquiry (Brady, 2011), exploring how 'food acquires its meaning through the place it is assembled and eaten' (Law, 2001: 275). Turner (2011), writing on the embodied dimensions of community gardening as an example of 'doing food' methods (Hayes-Conroy, 2010), suggests that 'intimate', 'micro-level' bodily engagements in garden places hold significant potential for long-lasting and deep commitments to sustainable environmental practices. Pitt (2015) also identifies 'planty methods', drawing on ethnographic research in community gardens, showing how techniques of 'walking, talking, doing and picturing' can encourage research participants, both human and non-human, to share their expertise. Longhurst, Ho and Johnston's (2008) vignettes reflecting a shared lunch with new migrants from different countries similarly involved observational and participatory methods that account for the spatial–temporal dimensions of eating alongside others, with the researchers later digesting their thoughts on the experience as a group. And, of particular relevance to the discussions in this chapter, Wilbur and Gibbs's recent paper on bodily engagements with the more-than-human explores 'embodied methods for researching the processes involved in producing and consuming food' (2018: 2).

Again focused on the embodied and corporeality of food, eating and making, Hayes-Conroy and Hayes-Conroy (2010, 2013) draw on the work of Probyn (2000) and Longhurst, Johnston and Ho's (2009: 334) understanding of the visceral as pertaining to 'sensations, moods and ways of being that emerge from our sensory engagement with ... material and discursive environments'. As Goodman (2016: 259) indicates, an emphasis on the visceral connotes recourse to our 'gut' feelings about food. Mol (2008: 30) also asks about the relationalities between bodies and food: 'does my apple only start to have subjectivity once it has become part of me, after I have digested it[?]' This work has been formulated predominantly (though not exclusively) with reference to specific food and social movements, and questions how 'we can begin to recognize and utilize the body as an instrument of progressive political projects' (Hayes-Conroy and Hayes-Conroy, 2010: 1277). However, in contrast to strategies aimed at changing behaviours by providing information, the relational understanding of the body here 'complicates the notion of individual choice or behaviour' (Hayes-Conroy and Hayes-Conroy, 2010: 1278). Instead what is stressed are 'embodied forms of learning where people are doing, walking, chatting, moving, tasting, sensing with each other and with nonhuman others, and potentially registering the world in more articulate and more sensitive ways' (Cameron, Manhood and Pomfrett, 2011: 505). As Holmes (2019: 117–118) explains, the body is 'not just a site where consumption is displayed and identities represented, but also a material means through which everyday personal life is produced, experienced and negotiated'.

A key element that emerges here is that a focus on the material substance of food necessitates an appreciation of *transformation*, since the materiality of food is a moveable feast. This marks food out from other following approaches. A material substance might not yet be food – it may not be edible – but its socio-economic engagements are nevertheless a part of food practices. Similarly, a food item might have been digested or even perishing, rotting perhaps, but this still tells us something interesting about, say, cultural practices of eating, the corporeal relationship we have with food, or about taste and everyday rhythms. The body itself is likewise 'in constant flux', with changing corporealities and meanings (Holmes, 2019: 122). This, then, makes the study of food materialities really quite fascinating, open to multiple possibilities and directions.

## Cook-alongs and food-for-thought discussions: our methodological ingredients

Our project on community cooking was grounded in an understanding that being taught cookery skills can empower individuals to be imaginative, resourceful and healthy in their food creations. However, we were aware that only a limited body of research had to date explored the overlapping material, social and relational benefits of cooking food together. Using the case of community cooking classes, the project sought to unpack the potential and possible impacts of social cooking for individuals from low-income backgrounds. Partnered with Cracking Good Food (a social enterprise based in Manchester, UK), we set to work as an interdisciplinary team of researchers from three UK institutions and across a diverse range of subject areas – from human geography, public health and nutrition – to investigate everyday relationships with food and cooking. Exploring foodstuffs, stories and sociality, the project shifted the focus from common stigmatising discourses of (un)healthiness, (in)convenience and (mis)education, towards exploring long-term personal and political capacities of community cooking and collaboration.

Experimenting with methods of ethnographic cook-alongs and food-for-thought discussions, we sought to develop rich social methods to ascertain the potential of cookery classes, for participants, their families and wider communities. Working with Cracking Good Food, we used ethnographic, observational and interviews methods with participants of two parallel sets of cooking classes based in two of Manchester's most deprived areas – Fallowfield and Old Moat. We wanted to follow the food as it transformed from ingredients and raw products, was chopped and cooked, and then as it became a meal to be eaten. The cooking classes were a great place to develop these exploratory methods, since they involved attendees cooking meals from scratch and then eating their creations together at the end. We opted to use methods that enrol observations through the body as a vessel for research, as well as opportunities to talk and reflect on food in the making, eating and digesting (also see Cameron, Manhood and Pomfrett, 2011; Hayes-Conroy, 2010; Longhurst, Ho and Johnston, 2008; Pitt, 2015). More specifically, we carried out:

- three ethnographic cook-alongs during community-cooking classes in each of the two communities, with six lessons in total and 4–8 people per class;

- food-for-thought discussions at the end of community-cooking classes while participants ate the meals they had made;
- post-class follow-up interviews, with ten participants.

To recruit participants we utilised the networks of Cracking Good Food, and of the venues for the cooking classes (one a primary school, the other a Sure Start children's centre). The fact that the classes were being provided for free was also a draw, and in addition we arranged for a crèche at one of the venues so that parents with childcare responsibilities could attend. Furthermore, we also used free taster food to draw people in (such as a recruitment day in a school playground during pick-up times), which seemed to work in generating interest. One participant told us in a post-class interview that

> when they did everything outside … you know, your attention was drawn, 'oh, what is this, let me go and see' … The way they did it, it was like they wanted us to do more, 'come on, you can do it differently, you can …'. So it was really attractive. It was a nice approach. (Interview, June 2018)

In this way, the fact that food is the stuff of the everyday, as well as a conduit for political and personal discussions, means it can also work as an incentive in the recruitment stages of foodie-based research.

## Cook-alongs

Our empirical methods for the cook-alongs were heavily focused on visual and sensory methods. Like Roe (2006) and Holmes (this collection), we were acutely aware of the tensions in using talk alone to research practice, and so chose instead to rely more on what was unspoken. At least one member of our project team – Laura Pottinger – was present at each class to lead the data collection. Laura took part in the classes like the other members of the group, following instructions from the class instructor. Where possible, she also made handwritten notes in a field diary (both during the class and afterwards) on how the food was made, presented, shared, devoured or wasted during the class. Photographs were also taken on a mobile smartphone at key moments during the class, working both as a memory device for the researcher and as a way to capture the mundane material transformations of food from ingredients into a meal – although, as

**6.1   Photographs documenting food transformations**

we explain later in the chapter, this was only really possible when there was more than one researcher attending the class.

In one of the classes we observed, the group were tasked with making savoury pancakes. Members of the class expressed that they usually made sweet pancakes, with sugar and lemon, or banana and chocolate spread, and would not think to make savoury ones for themselves and their families. As the photographs displayed together in Figure 6.1 illustrate, materials as well as opinions were transformed during the class; from clean chopping boards and unwrapped aprons, to messy bowls of whisked eggs and flour, and from wet cold mixture to hot fried solids, to finally being eaten by researcher(s) and participants as a group.

At the same time, the space of the room and the bodies within it were transformed during the class (also see Wilbur and Gibbs, 2018). As participants gained in confidence they would walk around the room, making the space feel somewhat cramped yet more intimate, drifting away from their set cooking 'station' (marked with different coloured chopping boards) to look at what their classmates were creating and the types of skills they were displaying. Some even picked up new tips from the instructor and from other participants. Examples included the use of different tools, like using scissors instead of a knife to chop spring onions, and norms of food preparation and hygiene, like whether to wash mushrooms before eating.

In addition, one of the aims of Cracking Good Food, aside from giving people the confidence and skills to cook, is about showing how the latest flashy gadgets for food preparation are not always necessary, and so they also educate in making do; a fork can be a whisk, a glass tumbler can be a rolling pin. While our focus here is on food transformations, we nevertheless also saw other material transformations occurring within the classes. We posit that these small, quietly indiscriminate practices would likely not have been identified or remembered by participants as having any significance had a researcher not been co-present to document such moments (also see Pottinger, 2017). The class then became a space for interaction and mutual support, an intervention even (also see Holmes, 2018).

Being a participant researcher present in the class was really important in methodological terms, as well as conceptually. We observed healthy eating and cooking messages being conveyed subtly throughout the classes, in a non-patronising way. This was interesting for how our research sought to bring together ideas about the personal politics of food, wherein communications can quite readily be translated as stigmatising and judgemental (also see Hall, 2016). Fieldnotes were full of examples, such as the following:

> As the meatballs go into a pan and begin to fry in olive oil, the course leader tells a story about her grandmother, who had a bad fall at eighty-seven, but didn't break any bones, which she attributed to her diet with lots of olive oil and fish. Rather than framing the classes (or the research) in terms of healthy eating, little nuggets of info – 'gram flour is full of iron', or 'plenty of protein in borlotti beans' – are relayed to the group conversationally, as and when the occasion arises. And information about the healthiness of different ingredients is delivered in the same way as advice about thrift or flavour – 'If you know which trees are bay leaf, you can just pick some when you walk past, that's what I do!'; 'parmesan rind is full of umami flavour – don't throw it away!'. (Pottinger, Fieldnotes, April 2018)

By researching food-as-material transformations in these group settings, we could observe as new habits were being formed and old habits were corrected.

Nonetheless, our observations also highlighted the possibility for misinformation about food and ingredients to spread in these classes; again, this is not something that would likely have been identified in pre- or post-class discussions alone, or through the use of photo-graphs. The process of not just being co-present but also cooking *with* participants was methodologically significant, being part of shared conversations about food while also making the meals in the class. Analysis of our fieldnotes brought this to light; for instance:

> As we're preparing to make the pancakes, the course leader tells us we won't be using eggs – this will be a vegan recipe. Prompted by this, one participant who has been quite vocal throughout the class so far, tells the group that corn flour is not vegan, because it contains bone meal. Her brother told her this after refusing to eat a meal she had prepared containing the ingredient. Her claim is met with some surprise from the group – 'Really?', 'I've never heard that before …' – but the state-ment is not challenged directly. (Pottinger, Fieldnotes, March 2018)

Observing this moment of spreading misinformation was really inter-esting, and gave us an insight into the potentially sticky and personal nature of people's relationships with food, to the point that incorrect information is not corrected for fear of (we assumed) upset or embar-rassment (also see Longhurst, Ho and Johnston, 2008). This approach therefore complements and develops follow-the-thing methods (i.e. Cook et al., 2004; Cook, Crang and Thorpe, 2004) by encouraging participant and researcher engagement and co-present interaction with materials as they transform.

## Food-for-thought discussions

As well as handling and creating food alongside participants, the sharing of the meal at the end of the class provided an obvious space to also share in experiences of the class and food and cooking in general. We referred to these as 'food-for-thought discussions', finding that participants related more to this type of (context appropriate) language than if they were asked to take part in a 'focus group'. Using the shared experience of making and eating a meal as the main prompt, as well as the food itself, an informal conversation followed each class (recorded using a Dictaphone, with participants' consent), covering questions such as:

- How did you find taking part in this class?
- Were there any tricky bits?
- Are you pleased with your cooking creation? How does it taste?

- Have you made anything like this before?
- Can you see yourself cooking this again?
- Did you feel like you learned anything new at this cooking lesson?

As we expected, these post-class transcripts were filled with discussions about the flavours and textures of the food being eaten, often with silences or full mouths as people ate. Eating the meal together also raised memories for participants of foods they might have previously eaten or made that were similar, or different. Sometimes participants reflected on the future possibilities of the foods they were eating, too. As one female class member explained, 'my daughter, if she joins in ... she might think, "oh, I could do that, I might like to eat it". Because at the moment, she doesn't want to eat anything green!' (post-class discussion, May 2018). Using the embodied experiences of both cooking and eating was therefore a methodological tool for teasing out mundane practices and relationships with food (Longhurst, Ho and Johnston, 2008; Pottinger, 2017; Wilbur and Gibbs, 2018), adding to a rich body of literature that uses embodied participant observation techniques to study everyday life. But it was also part of the process of food transformation, following the food from ingredients, to the shared meal created, then being eaten and digested (also see Cook et al., 2004; Hayes-Conroy, 2010; Roe, 2006).

Added to this, and in part because of our interest in both the material and political transformative potential of the cooking classes, we undertook a small number of follow-up interviews with class attendees. These interviews were intended to continue our 'followings' approach, as well as a means of potentially tracking the impact of the classes on the communities and for participants. The interviews were carried out up to two months after participants had attended the last of the three classes, and involved asking questions such as:

- What was your overall experience of the cooking classes?
- Have you continued with your new cooking skills?
- Did you make any of the meals again? Who for? Did you change/innovate? Why (might be taste, preference, cost, availability, seasonality)?
- Did your family/friends like the food you cooked?
- Have the classes changed your experiences of eating and cooking? If so, in what ways?
- Would you recommend the classes to other people?

The interviews were successful in so much as they provided an opportunity to record changes in eating and cooking practices over time as a result of the classes, as mundane instances of everyday food transformations. Participants described changes in their everyday cooking habits, creative practices and even taste buds, for example:

> Most of my cooking dishes are not changed, but I add some different herbs, the garlic, and some vegetables. So it has changed a little bit for me, yeah. [My family] noticed the garlic, they enjoyed it. (Interview, April 2018)
>
> It's changed a little bit ... some of the ingredients, and added something new to our Chinese recipes. (Interview, June 2018)

Moreover, we decided it was best that these interviews were conducted by Laura, who attended the classes alongside our participants. This meant that the interviews were an extension of the in-class conversations, discussing the class as a shared experience, and Laura could also jog participants' memories about the food creations they had made and eaten together.

With a focus on material transformations, embodied practice and shared reflections, there is much potential for these methods to be used in other forms of making, crafting or art practice, where a material item is created and developed in the process (see Slater, this collection, and Holmes, this collection). We also think there is scope to apply these methods to collective gardening and growing projects, to look at food through the different stages of growth and production. Furthermore, our approach could also be applied and adapted to other different types of class-based activities or encounters in which skills and techniques are shared, taught or learnt, like pottery making, woodwork, glassblowing or crocheting. Furthermore, they might be used by colleagues whose work is focused more on evaluation, impact and assessment of the relative success (or otherwise) of class-based skill transfer projects. In this regard, in what follows we offer some advice for other researchers considering using these and similar methodologies who hope to replicate or develop our approach.

## Using similar methods? A dollop of advice

We found there to be multiple benefits of using methodological techniques for simultaneous talking and doing with participants in the

## Box 6.1: Training, tools and equipment

Equipment used included:

- a Dictaphone;
- a digital camera or camera phone for in-class photos;
- a field diary and pen.

  Please bear in mind that arranging a cooking class, as we have done, requires an amount of forward planning and practical arrangements, including:

- appropriate spaces for the food/making activity; for example, here we needed a kitchen, hobs, running water and space for lots of 'work stations';
- consideration of hygiene and food safety standards in the preparation of food; Cracking Good Food staff already held hygiene certificates relevant for our research;
- we arranged a crèche for participants attending the daytime classes so that access to childcare was not an obstacle to their participation.

cooking classes as a means to explore food transformations. Key advantages are that being a participant observer and part of the class enables more natural conversations. In being more informal and less structured, these conversations are also less intimidating. We found the 'doing with' technique a way of accessing everyday practices that may be less easy to talk about in a formal, structured interview, for example. It would be fair to say that our method involved innovating with a combination of traditional ethnographic techniques of participant observation, group discussions and interviewing. The tools and equipment outlined in Box 6.1 are therefore typical of those used within ethnographic projects.

While these methods are relatively low cost and require few resources, they tend to be time and energy consuming. Furthermore, a key challenge we found during the class-based fieldwork was keeping our focus on the food when there was so much going on within the room. Practical considerations include background noise (like blenders or cutlery clattering, or the class instructor giving out orders) which would make it difficult to only audio record the sessions. Taking handwritten fieldnotes during the class was also tricky because hands were often already full with keeping up with instructions, as well as covered in food (see Wilkinson, this collection, for discussion of alternative forms of note taking). We imagine this would be similar in crafting classes and such like. The same applies to taking photographs, which was much easier when there was more than one member of the team present. However, there is a trade-off. We found that when more than one researcher attended the class, the space felt strangely unbalanced, as though there were too many of the project team present. As the saying goes, too many cooks spoil the broth! Additionally, we found talking and eating during the post-class discussions to be a little tricky, although we enjoyed the intimate atmosphere that was conjured by eating with participants.

It is also worth noting that by our very presence as researchers we might have altered the spaces, practices and material interactions within the cooking class; albeit this is a well-worn critique of ethnographic methods. It can also be argued that there are ethical advantages to this approach, too, since our co-presence through embodied participant observation and variously visible researcher tools (such as field notebooks and a Dictaphone) means participants have multiple material cues available to remind them that they are involved in a research project.

There are also distinct ethical considerations in the use of photographs and retaining participants' anonymity, although since our research focus was on food, we chose to take photographs that did not feature people's faces. Others considering conducting similar research will also need to be aware that the positionality of the researcher can shape the outcomes of a project, particularly in participant observation and participatory research when compared with other research methods. Indeed, we would argue that a more informal 'doing with' approach to some extent breaks down the barriers that traditional interview methods tend to reinforce (also see Blake, 2007). These issues are not of course confined to research on food.

If we were to use this method again we would want to employ video methods in order to capture the full range of practices, discussions and silences within the classes (see Pink, 2013; Roe, 2006). This might require having multiple cameras set up around the room where the class is held, or finding ways to film from above with a panoptican perspective (see Lyon, this collection); although of course this comes with ethical issues around the possibilities for anonymising the data. This method could also offer opportunities for participants to lead classes – sharing their own skills and recipes – rather than being led and directed by someone else. This would also be applicable when researching other types of 'making' spaces, such as embroidery, metal soldering or flower arranging classes, as well as for research on other forms of classes like exercise, dance or singing classes; though again this is not without further ethical considerations.

At times we also wondered whether the layout of the classroom space was affecting the types of interactions taking place. For example, in the school venue there was a worktop on which hobs were arranged, which worked well for demonstrating but could also act as a barrier between cooking and preparation areas, as well as obscuring the view of the researcher in being able to observe transformations within the class. One option could be to have different work stations for different types of activity – heating, chopping, mixing and so on – making it easier for people to move around and for the practices to be documented. Again, this is something to consider for researching within other making spaces, too. Also on a practical note, we think that having more time to eat and discuss the food cooked would have been advantageous, as at times the shared meal and post-class discussion could feel rushed. Giving adequate time to taste, smell and touch, and to take time over food presentation, would help to capture more data on sensory interactions with food. Furthermore, food is often a conduit to talk about other social and economic circumstances, so the ethics of group discussions should also be considered.

## Finishing up

With this chapter we have explored how following food from ingredients to a shared meal, in the context of cooking classes, can be one way of exploring material transformations. Placing our methodological focus on cook-alongs and food-for-thought discussions, we posit that material-focused methods can also open up opportunities for thinking about the transformation of practices and habits, as well as the body as a space for research. Drawing on a rich and varied tradition of foodie methods, our approach considers participants' relationships with food as more than consumers. Using a food–centric approach that can be applied to other everyday materials, we look at how people can be actively involved in the transformation of food. Rather than documenting the decisions made about buying or choosing food, or

---

### Box 6.2: Further reading

Here are some articles we mention in our chapter, which we think make a really great starting point for others thinking of using similar approaches to researching food or making activities:

Brady, J. (2011) 'Cooking as inquiry: a method to stir up prevailing ways of knowing food, body, and identity', *International Journal of Qualitative Methods*, 10 (4): 321–334.

Hayes-Conroy, J. and Hayes-Conroy, A. (2010) 'Visceral geographies: mattering, relating, and defying', *Geography Compass*, 4 (9): 1273–1283.

Longhurst, R., Ho, E. and Johnston, L. (2008) 'Using "the body" as an "instrument of research": kimch'i and pavlova', *Area*, 40 (2): 208–217.

And here is the website address of our partner, Cracking Good Food, which might give you some ideas for how to work with foodie charities and organisations in your area: www.crackinggoodfood.org/.

---

thinking about the different points in a production network that brings food to consumers, these material methods can help work through the ways in which participants as consumers and producers actively appropriate, modify and are creative with food.

We have shown that being co-present in the context of these transformative moments is important for being able to take note of unassuming, perhaps trivial expressions and practices that people would not typically think to talk about or highlight themselves if asked about food-related practices. In addition, being more than just co-present but also a participant observer opened up possibilities for shared experiences when spoken reflections on cooking were sought; as they might for sewing, gardening or woodwork if those were the transformative practices being studied. As both a methodological and conceptual finding, we ultimately concluded that the cooking class is a space of subtle social significance: a space for connecting and bringing people together through, around and about food, a space of personal and political transformation.

## References

Appadurai, A. (1986) *The Social Life of Things: Commodities in Cultural Perspective*, Cambridge: Cambridge University Press.

Bell, D. and Valentine, G. (1997) *Consuming Geographies: We Are What We Eat*, London: Routledge.

Blake, M. (2007) 'Formality and friendship: research ethics review and participatory action research', *ACME: An International E-Journal for Critical Geographies*, 6 (3): 411–421.

Brady, J. (2011) 'Cooking as inquiry: a method to stir up prevailing ways of knowing food, body, and identity', *International Journal of Qualitative Methods*, 10 (4): 321–334.

Bridge, G. and Smith, A. (2003) 'Intimate encounters: culture–economy–commodity', *Environment and Planning D: Society and Space*, 21 (3): 257–268.

Cameron, J., Manhood, C. and Pomfrett, J. (2011) 'Bodily learning for a (climate) changing world: registering differences through performative and collective research', *Local Environment*, 16 (6): 493–508.

Castree, N. (2004) 'The geographical lives of commodities: problems of analysis and critique', *Social & Cultural Geography*, 5 (1): 21–35.

Cook, I. et al. (2004) 'Follow the thing: papaya', *Antipode*, 36 (4): 642–664.

Cook, I., Crang, P. and Thorpe, M. (2004) 'Tropics of consumption: "getting with the fetish" of "exotic" fruit?', in A. Hughes and S. Reimer (eds) *Geographies of Commodity Chains*, London: Routledge, 173–192.

Goodman, M. K. (2016) 'Food geographies I: relational foodscapes and the busyness of being more-than-food', *Progress in Human Geography*, 40 (2): 257–266.

Hall, S. M. (2016) 'Family relations in times of austerity: reflections from the UK', in S. Punch, R. Vanderbeck, and T. Skelton (eds) *Geographies of Children and Young People: Families, Intergenerationality and Peer Group Relations*, Berlin: Springer, 51–68.

Hayes-Conroy, A. (2010) 'Feeling slow food: visceral fieldwork and empathetic research relations in the alternative food movement', *Geoforum*, 41 (5): 734–742.

Hayes-Conroy, J. and Hayes-Conroy, A. (2010) 'Visceral geographies: mattering, relating, and defying', *Geography Compass*, 4 (9): 1273–1283.

Hayes-Conroy, J. and Hayes-Conroy, A. (2013) 'Veggies and visceralities: a political ecology of food and feeling', *Emotion, Space and Society*, 6: 81–90.

Holmes, H. (2018) 'New spaces, ordinary practices: circulating and sharing within diverse economies of provisioning', *Geoforum*, 88: 134–147.

Holmes, H. (2019) 'The body in personal life', in V. May and P. Nordqvist (eds) *The Sociology of Personal Life* (2nd edn), London: Global Press, 117–129.

Jackson, P. (1999) 'Commodity cultures: the traffic in things', *Transactions of the Institute of British Geographers*, 24 (1): 95–108.

Kopytoff, I. (1986) 'The cultural biography of things: commoditization as process', in A. Appadurai (ed.) *The Social Life of Things: Commodities in Cultural Perspective*, Cambridge: Cambridge University Press, 64–94.

Law, L. (2001) 'Home cooking: Filipino women and geographies of the senses in Hong Kong', *Cultural Geographies*, 8 (3): 264–283.

Longhurst, R., Ho, E. and Johnston, L. (2008) 'Using "the body" as an "instrument of research": kimch'i and pavlova', *Area*, 40 (2): 208–217.

Longhurst, R., Johnston, L. and Ho, E. (2009) 'A visceral approach: cooking "at home" with migrant women in Hamilton, New Zealand', *Transactions of the Institute of British Geographers*, 34 (3): 333–345.

Mol, A. (2008) 'I eat an apple: on theorizing subjectivities', *Subjectivity*, 22: 28–37.

Pfaff, J. (2010) 'A mobile phone: mobility, materiality and everyday Swahili trading practices', *Cultural Geographies*, 17 (3): 341–357.

Pink, S. (2013) *Doing Visual Ethnography* (3rd edn), London: Sage.

Pitt, H. (2015) 'On showing and being shown plants – a guide to methods for more-than-human geography', *Area*, 47 (1): 48–55.

Pottinger, L. (2017) 'Planting the seeds of a quiet activism', *Area*, 49 (2): 215–222.

Probyn, E. (2000) *Carnal Appetites: FoodSexIdentities*, London: Routledge.

Roe, E. (2006) 'Things becoming food and the embodied, material practices of an organic food consumer', *Sociologia Ruralis*, 46 (2): 104–121.

Turner, B. (2011) 'Embodied connections: sustainability, food systems and community gardens', *Local Environment*, 16 (6): 509–522.

Warde, A. (2016) *The Practice of Eating*, Cambridge: Polity.

Wilbur, A. and Gibbs, L. (2018) '"Try it, it's like chocolate": embodied methods reveal food politics', *Social & Cultural Geography*, https://doi.org/10.1080/14649365.2018.1489976.

# Part II

## Senses and emotions

# 7

# The art of the ordinary: observational sketching as method

Sue Heath and Lynne Chapman

## Introduction

In recent years there has been a modest resurgence of interest within academia in the methodological affordance of observational sketching. Within the social sciences, this is a method historically associated with anthropological fieldwork (Soukup, 2014), and much of the growing interest comes from this quarter (see, for example, Ingold, 2011; Kuschnir, 2011; Azavedo and Ramos, 2016; Causey, 2017). However, sociologists and others have also been drawn to the method (e.g. Hurdley et al., 2017), and this chapter reports on a collaborative experiment in sketching involving observational artist Lynne Chapman and a group of researchers – mostly, but not all, sociologists – from the Morgan Centre for Research into Everyday Lives at the University of Manchester. Elsewhere we have provided a detailed account of the residency and some of the methodological lessons we learnt from the collaboration, in particular highlighting the usefulness of sketching as an alternative way of seeing and as a tool for thinking (Heath and Chapman, 2018). Here we explore observational sketching as a particularly useful method for engaging with taken-for-granted aspects of everyday life: aspects which may sometimes appear to researchers as somehow *too* mundane, *too* ordinary, to merit our attention, yet which, when looked at in new ways, can often speak volumes about the nature of the social world around us.

An openness to the remarkable nature of ordinary things also happens to underpin the philosophy of the 'Urban Sketchers' movement, a global network of observational sketchers to which Lynne is affiliated. Urban Sketchers pledge in their manifesto to 'show the world, one drawing at a time', and in so doing often shed light on places, things and people that can be overlooked even by many artists, perhaps because they are not considered to be sufficiently pleasing to the eye. This openness to the quotidian also chimes with the novelist and essayist Georges Perec's celebration of 'the infra-ordinary', an idea which we both encountered for the first time early in the development of the residency, and which resonated for both of us, as sociologist and artist respectively. We explore these influences further below, and then outline some of the approaches we adopted for sketching 'ordinary things'. We include a simple exercise designed to encourage reluctant sketchers to overcome their anxieties about putting pencil to paper, and which can also be used in research contexts. We conclude with some reflections on the value of observational sketching for increasing our openness to the resonance of ordinary things.

## Urban sketching, the infra-ordinary and the art of everyday life

The Urban Sketchers movement was founded by Spanish journalist and illustrator Gabriel Campanario in 2007, when he established an online forum for sharing on-location drawing (for more on the origins of Urban Sketchers, see www.urbansketchers.org/p/our-mission.html). Now consisting of a large global network of observational sketchers, the Urban Sketchers movement has a manifesto which reads as follows:

1. We draw on location, indoors or out, capturing what we see from direct observation.
2. Our drawings tell the story of our surroundings, the places we live and where we travel.
3. Our drawings are a record of time and place.
4. We are truthful to the scenes we witness.
5. We use any kind of media and cherish our individual styles.
6. We support each other and draw together.
7. We share our drawings online.

We show the world, one drawing at a time. (Ibid.)

In seeking an authentic representation of the world as it is rather than how we might like it to be, there are many parallels between the approach of the Urban Sketchers movement and that of many qualitative researchers. Anthropologist Karina Kuschnir has, for example, argued that

Many authors from both the art world and the field of anthropology have persuaded me that a bridge can be built between fieldwork and observational sketching. On the art side, the books by Salavisa (2008), Gregory (2003) and Campanario (2012) were crucial in terms of defining a pathway for contemporary urban drawing. As I wrote in 2011, the drawings of these urban sketchers are not simply drawings: they are 'informed-shaped' by a particular 'worldview.' In many respects, a worldview similar to the anthropological one: the emphasis on drawing 'on location,' the use of direct observation, the search for a narrative, the providing of a context and the moral basis (to be truthful). (Kuschnir, 2016: 106)

An awareness of these kinds of parallels informed the collaboration between Lynne and the Morgan Centre from the outset of the residency. It was through going on 'sketchcrawls' with the Yorkshire Urban Sketchers group – led by Lynne – that Sue first got to know Lynne. Sketchcrawls involve groups of sketchers getting together *en masse* to draw on location and then share their work, a process that invariably leads to fascinating discussions of perspective and interpretation. In this respect, Sue was immediately struck by the parallels between urban sketching and social research. Having an observational artist in and around the Morgan Centre for the duration of an academic year would of course have been inspirational and fun in its own right, but Sue was convinced that there was a great deal that a group of qualitative researchers could learn from Lynne about alternative modes of perception and how that might affect their work.

Once the residency was underway, we were particularly drawn to urban sketching's embrace of the mundane and the unremarkable. In elaborating upon the movement's manifesto commitment to 'show the world, one drawing at a time', for example, founder Gabriel Campanario writes the following:

The urban sketcher's quest to draw the world is not limited to city landmarks or historic locations. Any scene, no matter how mundane, is worth drawing. A sketch has the ability to elevate the least picturesque location into something worth looking at and reflecting upon. (Campanario, 2012: 23)

The metaphor of elevation is an interesting one, highlighting how the simple act of making a drawing of an otherwise everyday object, activity or place has a transformational effect. It is as if by so doing the object is placed within a frame, making it the legitimate centre of attention rather than something that usually only exists in the shadows of peripheral vision. Foregrounding everyday objects in this way goes against what we usually expect to see; as Danny Miller has written, '[things] work by being invisible and unremarked upon, a state they usually achieve by being familiar and taken for granted'. This he refers to as 'the humility of things', noting that 'the surprising conclusion is that objects are important, not because they are evident and physically constrain or enable, but often precisely because we do not "see" them' (Miller, 2010: 50). So, for example, when we first discussed the potential focus of the residency and Lynne asked Sue what we as academics did all day, Sue expressed the view that the average academic's day was not really very exciting from a visual perspective. How wrong she was proved to be! Through Lynne's eyes the everyday ordinariness of academia became instead an exotic world of colour and intrigue, and our everyday worlds were reflected back at us in exciting new ways.

Shortly before the residency officially started, we both encountered for the first time the work of Georges Perec, the French essayist and novelist. Perec was often preoccupied with exercises in listing and categorising. For example, in one essay (Perec, 1999b) he writes of his desire to list all the places he had ever slept, sub-divided by categories such as 'my bedrooms', 'makeshift beds', 'friends' bedrooms' and 'unusual conditions'. This is typical of the playfulness and quirkiness that characterises much of his writing. In another short essay, originally written in 1973, entitled 'Approaches to what?', Perec muses on the prevalence in the media of the scandalous, the abnormal and the extreme – 'the big event' – at the expense of the ordinary. He asks,

> How should we take account of, question, describe what happens every day and recurs every day: the banal, the quotidian, the obvious, the common, the ordinary, *the infra-ordinary*, the background noise, the habitual? ... How are we to speak of these 'common things', how to

track them down rather, flush them out, wrest them from the dross in which they remain mired, how to give them a meaning, a tongue, to let them, finally, speak of what is, of what we are? ... What we need is to question bricks, concrete, glass, our table manners, our utensils, our tools, the way we spend our time, our rhythms. *To question that which has ceased forever to astonish us.* (Perec, 1999a: 210, emphasis added)

One of Perec's solutions to this dilemma of 'not seeing' was to try systematically to catalogue the world around him, exhaustively to describe *everything* he could see while trying not to prioritise certain things over others. Lynne's work can, in many respects, be seen as a visual equivalent of Perec's suggested strategy, inasmuch as her drawings give as much importance to a forgotten corner of the office or the recycling bins as they do to architectural grandeur or beautiful objects. By coincidence, Perec's ideas were also evoked by Les Back (also see Back's foreword in this collection) in a plenary address which he gave towards the end of the residency at a Morgan Centre event on creative approaches to qualitative research, which included a workshop on observational sketching. Speaking of Perec's 'extraordinary attentiveness to things', he argued that Perec

manages to enchant the mundane through noticing detail and its significance ... it makes us think ... about attentiveness as a vocation – a matter of training our senses and then sifting imaginatively what we find for significance, like panning for gold on the surface of life. (Back, 2016: 2, 3)

We could of course have attempted to do something like this, like Perec, in the written form with which most of us were much more comfortable. Yet, as we found out over the course of the residency, producing a visual image provided us with an alternative register of attentiveness that encouraged us to see in new ways (also see Collins, this collection), which we now go on to outline.

## The art of everyday life

Throughout the 2015/2016 academic year, Lynne Chapman spent two days a week based in the Morgan Centre for Research into Everyday Lives as an Artist in Residence funded by the Leverhulme Trust. Lynne sought to capture a year in the life of the Morgan Centre and to refine her sketching skills in new contexts, while members of the

Morgan Centre sought to learn some drawing techniques and to explore whether and how the Centre might be able to use sketching in its own research. Lynne sketched virtually every aspect of our academic lives – meetings, tutorials, conferences, fieldwork, lectures, office time, meetings with students, work spaces, campus life generally, even a short spell of industrial action – and by the end of the year had managed to fill forty-four two-metre-long concertina-style sketchbooks with her vibrant artwork. Lynne was adept at training her artist's eye on aspects of academic life that might on the face of it be thought of as routine and mundane, yet which she rendered distinctive through her colourful drawings and her ability to enhance an image through the use of text. So, for example, departmental business meetings were brought to life in ways unimaginable to those who are familiar with enduring them; the gender politics of the shared staff–student kitchen were laid bare for all to see; and the contents of desk drawers, office shelving and open plan desks were transformed into exotic cabinets of curiosity. Figure 7.1 provides an example of Lynne's ability to shed light on the overlooked aspects of everyday

**7.1 An example of one of Lynne's sketches: an overlooked corner of the office**

life, reproduced here in black and white but in the original bursting with colour.

But what about those of us who were not trained artists? How did we rise to the challenge of capturing ordinary things? First, and rather critically, Lynne needed to find a way of instilling in us some confidence in our abilities, as most of us had not drawn or painted for very many years, except perhaps with younger family members, and we were all rather nervous at exposing our lack of experience to each other. Lynne led us through a series of drawing workshops which gradually built up our confidence and our repertoire of drawing techniques, and by the end of the residency most of us had become reasonably comfortable users not just of pencils and pens, but also of watercolour and other media. The exercise we include at the end of the chapter is in fact one that Lynne led us through in one of our workshops and which she also used in public workshops at the end of the residency, as we outline below. In addition to completing a number of homework tasks linked to the workshops, we each kept a personal sketchbook throughout the year, which we used as a visual diary of both work and non-work activities, and Lynne also led us on several sketchcrawls. Individual members also joined Lynne from time to time as she sketched out and about on campus throughout the year.

Another group challenge which Lynne set for us was to maintain a set of collaborative 'chain sketchbooks' which were circulated between us across the year. These consisted of a series of concertina-style sketchbooks which were passed between us rather like an old-fashioned chain letter, each of us adding our own sketch before passing it on to the next person. Each sketchbook was devoted to a specific theme and in most cases was linked to an existing research interest in the Morgan Centre. There was, then, a sketchbook devoted to 'weather' (linked to Jennifer Mason's 'Living the Weather' research project), another devoted to 'dormant things' (linked to Sophie Woodward's research project of the same name – also see Woodward, this collection), and others related to the themes of 'home' (a research interest of several of us), 'today', 'the office' and 'food'. Figure 7.2 shows Susanne Martikke displaying the chain sketchbook on the theme of weather, to give readers a sense of what these sketchbooks looked like. Over the course of the year most of us added at least one image to each of these sketchbooks, often with added text, and they were exhibited alongside Lynne's sketchbooks at an end-of-residency exhibition at a

**7.2** The chain sketchbook on the theme of weather

Manchester art gallery. These images, and their often humorous and sometimes poignant comments, almost invariably captured an ordinary, usually unnoticed or unremarked upon aspect of everyday life, whether an object, an event or a place of some kind.

Take, for example, the sketchbook devoted to the theme of 'dormant things', which was linked to Sophie Woodward's research exploring 'the accumulation of things in domestic spaces'. Sophie's research is concerned with shedding light on the items that most people tend to accumulate in their homes over time, sometimes deliberately stored and concealed, but often placed somewhere for later consideration and then forgotten about. As Sophie writes on her project website, 'like archaeological layers, these accumulations tell us about the histories of a house, the people who live and have lived there, and their wider relationships and lives' (http://projects.socialsciences.manchester.ac.uk/dormant-things/). This theme provided us all with a wonderful opportunity to engage in the 'concentrated seeing' of objects which had become almost invisible to us in our own homes. We not only sought to capture images of some of these things but also tried to convey in accompanying text something of their broader significance to us and quite why it was that we had kept these objects despite no

**7.3   A sketch from the 'dormant things' book**

longer using them. Figure 7.3, for example, is part of a larger sketch by Hazel Burke of her 'dormant sewing kit', which includes a needlecase with 'a glamorous tassle' (text just out of view) that had belonged to her gran, and a second needlecase which she thinks was made by her mother ('did my mum make this?'). Also, in the top right hand corner, is a thimble drawn by Hazel's son, with (just out of view) the words 'guest sketch, by a five year old who wants a piece of the action'. This image is both fun and poignant, connecting four generations over the page.

Building on this technique of drawing everyday objects, Lynne and members of the Morgan Centre ran two public sketching workshops in collaboration with Manchester Museum as part of the 2016 ESRC (Economic and Social Research Council) Festival of Social Science. The first workshop was on the theme of belonging and the second on the theme of thrift, relating to research interests of Vanessa May and Helen Holmes respectively. Members of the public were invited to bring along personal objects which they associated with the theme of their chosen workshop and, following a brief sociological introduction to the theme from Vanessa and Helen, they were then invited to sketch either their own objects or objects linked to these themes from the Museum collections and to then add text. In order to make this not too daunting a task, Lynne taught some simple drawing techniques which we include as an exercise in the next section. The exercise was followed by a discussion between participants of their choice of object and the ways in which they had chosen to illustrate and describe them. Participants found the drawing method taught by Lynne to be relatively straightforward and not too challenging, and they appeared to enjoy looking closely at their chosen object, often seeing it in a new light as part of the process. This was then reflected in the conversations that followed about their drawing and the object itself. Although we did not design these workshops as formal research encounters, we came away convinced that this method would work well as an elicitation technique in a group context.

## Passing it on

Once we had developed some confidence, most of us developed a love of sketching and continued to draw after the residency came to an end. Sketching is certainly not for everybody, but our experience suggests that keeping a personal sketchbook can be a novel and thought-provoking way of connecting with our research interests. Keeping a chain sketchbook as part of a research project could also be an innovative and engaging way for members of a research team to reflect on key themes. As themes emerge in fieldwork, team members could, for example, attempt to address the same theme visually and then pass the sketchbook on to the next member for further elaboration and reflection, which could be fed into broader processes of reflection and analysis. This is certainly a practice that Sue hopes to incorporate into future research projects. Alternatively, a chain sketchbook could be passed around between research participants in the context of research where participants are known to each other, asking them to reflect visually on the research topic in question as an additional form of data generation.

We also think that there is potential for using sketchcrawls in research contexts. As part of Jennifer Mason's 'Living the Weather' project, for example, Lynne led a public sketchcrawl in Hebden Bridge, the small West Yorkshire town which formed the focus of Jennifer's research. Over twenty-five members of the public responded to an open invitation to join Lynne in the centre of Hebden Bridge one rainy October morning. Over several hours, dozens of sketches were produced. The event ended over hot drinks and discussion in a local café, with strangers talking to each other and to Jennifer about living with the weather in the Calder Valley and the significance of their drawings in relation to this theme (see Figure 7.4). Our experience of this and other sketchcrawls that some of us were involved in suggested that this method could work particularly well in research

**7.4** Hebden Bridge sketchcrawl

contexts where place, space and location are central themes. One could, for example, ask participants to sketch in relation to a particular theme, such as spaces and places where they feel at home and those where they feel less comfortable. Or they could be asked to sketch the things that they can hear or smell, by way of tapping into different sensory dimensions of space. Again, these are all ideas that we hope to try out in future.

The issue of perceived level of ability is an important one, though. As already indicated, inexperienced sketches can, at least initially, find the method daunting. Sketching together can also be a double-edged sword; there is certainly safety in numbers when sketching in public, but it can also be quite exposing to then share one's work with sketchers of differing abilities. Lynne has extensive experience of leading workshops with novice sketchers and we include here the details of the exercise that she used with us and with participants in the museum workshops which we referred to above.

## A simple exercise in observational sketching

When we are at school, we generally learn to judge our drawing abilities by the degree to which our outcomes match the reality of the subject in front of us; the more photographically accurate our results are, the better. This straight-jacket of realism is one of the main reasons that people give up on art as they become adult: as a benchmark for success, it is doomed to failure. One key shift in thinking which can liberate a novice sketcher is the understanding that a sketch does not have to look like the real thing. A successful sketch can work on its own terms, so long as it is visually interesting and communicative. Once created, the sketch need never be compared to the original subject again; it becomes a new and unique creation.

There are various techniques which can be employed to lift a sketch out of the need to ape photography. We used three of these techniques during the museum workshop.

1.  *Colour collage.* A splash of colour makes a massive difference to the drama of a drawing, but colour can be a minefield and so is usually avoided by the novice. We asked sketchers to choose from a selection of coloured papers. The colour could approximately match the actual colour of the object they had selected to sketch

but, crucially, it did not need to. They were asked to tear a shape which, again, need have no bearing on their subject, and then stick it down on to their paper, *before* beginning to draw. The eventual line-drawing's mismatch with the coloured shape added an excitement to the sketch, complementing the drawing.

2.  *Contour line-drawing.* A hesitant, spidery drawing is rarely appealing. During the workshop, we used a contour-drawing exercise to demonstrate the power of a more confident line. Sketchers were asked to draw using a continuous line, describing the shape of their object without taking their pencil from the paper. The best results are achieved if the sketcher looks at the object, rather than at their paper, and draws without stopping. To incentivise speed and movement, sketchers were asked to do this in just one minute. The results included inevitable inaccuracies, but the line-drawings were nevertheless enticing and powerful.

3.  *Text as design.* Sketchers were asked to consider why they had selected their particular object. What was the object's relevance to the theme, or its resonance with the individual? Sketchers were asked to describe this in a sentence or two but, rather than 'labelling' the object in their sketch, they were asked to wrap the text around the drawing, to think of the words as an intrinsic and decorative element of the composition, rather than just added information. Coloured pencils were provided, and sketchers were encouraged to think about the colour of their text and whether there were any words of significance which could be 'highlighted' in a complementary colour.

The sketch reproduced in Figure 7.5 is a good example of the sorts of images that can be produced using these techniques. In the original, the image is drawn over a torn piece of light blue paper.

## Conclusion

The research tools of sociologists do not typically consist of sketchbooks, pencils and paints deployed for the purposes of observational sketching. Yet, our collaboration highlighted how the respective crafts of qualitative researcher and artist can intersect really well in the act of sketching. As sociologists, we are used to selecting, interpreting, telling stories and capturing atmospheres. What observational

**7.5** 'A bottle of holy water left by the previous owners and that I am too superstitious to discard ... ' by Susanne Martikke

sketching does is to provide a new and intriguing register in which to do this. Sketching is also a slow method (see Law, 2004). It stops us in our tracks and forces us to concentrate. It creates a new space for creative thought amidst a world where we are so often rushing around from one task to the next. It is a revelatory process and it has undoubtedly changed our view of ourselves and of our craft. It has also allowed us to develop a new appreciation of the ordinary things around us by forcing us to look in new and more intense ways (Heath and Chapman, 2018) and to engage with them over extended moments of time: to learn to see, one drawing at a time.

---

**Box 7.1:** Training, tools and equipment

The tools and equipment needed for the sketching exercise are easily accessible:

- coloured paper;
- glue;
- coloured pens or pencils.

Our broader toolkit included:

- watercolour paints;
- paintbrushes of various size;
- sketchbook.

---

**Box 7.2:** Further reading and useful resources

Canadian anthropologist Andrew Causey's *Drawn to See: Drawing as an Ethnographic Method* (Toronto: University of Toronto Press, 2017) is an excellent hands-on guide for novice researcher-sketchers. Brazilian anthropologist Karina Kuschnir has written a comprehensive account of the potential benefits of sketching in academic contexts and how she uses the method with her own students: 'Ethnographic drawing: eleven benefits of using a sketchbook for fieldwork', *Visual Ethnography*, 5 (1): 103–134. Cartoonist Linda Barry is also an Assistant Professor of Interdisciplinary Creativity ('AKA Professor Long Title') at the University of Wisconsin-Madison. She has written a wonderfully fun primer for anyone wanting to gain the confidence to draw anything and everything around them: *Syllabus: Notes from an Accidental Professor* (Montreal: Drawn and Quarterly, 2014). Finally, Lynne Chapman's own blog, *An Artist's Life for Me!*, is a fantastically inspiring resource for thinking about the use of observational sketching as a potential research method (https://lynnechapman.blogspot.com/). Since finishing her residency with the Morgan Centre, Lynne has gone on to undertake several other academic projects, including sketching sheep shearers in the Australian outback, and these are all covered in her blog.

## Acknowledgements

Lynne Chapman's residency was funded by the Leverhulme Trust [2104-AIR-008] as part of their Artist-in-Residency funding programme. We are extremely grateful to the Trust for funding this initiative.

# References

Azavedo, A. and Ramos, M. J. (2016) 'Drawing close – on visual engage-ments in fieldwork, drawing workshops and the anthropological imagina-tion', *Visual Ethnography*, 5 (1): 135–160.

Back, L. (2016) 'A qualitative research renaissance: ten years of the Morgan Centre', plenary address at the Morgan Centre 'Summer Spectacular' event on 6 July 2016, Friends Meeting House, Manchester, www.socialsciences.manchester.ac.uk/morgan-centre/connect/past-conferences/ (accessed 2 October 2019).

Campanario, G. (2012) *The Art of Urban Sketching: Drawing on Location around the World*, Beverly: Quarry Books.

Causey, A. (2017) *Drawn to See: Drawing as an Ethnographic Method*, Toronto: University of Toronto Press.

Gregory, D. (2003) *Everyday Matters: A Memoir*, New York: Hyperion.

Heath, S. and Chapman, L. (2018) 'Observational sketching as method', *International Journal of Social Research Methodology*, 21 (6): 713–728.

Hurdley, R., Biddulph, M., Backhaus, V., Hipwood, T. and Hossain, R. (2017) 'Drawing as radical multimodality: salvaging Patrick Geddes's material methodology', *American Anthropologist*, https://anthrosource.onlinelibrary.wiley.com/doi/abs/10.1111/aman.12963 (accessed 2 October 2019).

Ingold, T. (2011) *Being Alive: Essays on Movement, Knowledge and Description*, London: Routledge.

Kuschnir, K. (2011) 'Drawing the city: a proposal for an ethnographic study in Rio de Janeiro', *Vibrant: Virtual Brazilian Anthropology*, 8 (2): 609–642.

Kuschnir, K. (2016) 'Ethnographic drawing: eleven benefits of using a sketchbook for fieldwork', *Visual Ethnography*, 5 (1): 103–134.

Law, J. (2004) *After Method: Mess in Social Science Research*, London: Rout-ledge.

Miller, D. (2010) *Stuff*, Cambridge: Polity Press.

Perec, G. (1999a) 'Approaches to what?', in G. Perec, *Species of Spaces and Other Pieces*, Harmondsworth: Penguin, 20–25.

Perec, G. (1999b) 'The bedroom', in G. Perec, *Species of Spaces and Other Pieces*, Harmondsworth: Penguin, 205–207.

Salavisa, E. (ed.) (2008) *Diários de Viagem: Desenhos do Quotidiano – 35 Autores Contemporâneos*, Lisbon: Quimera.

Soukup, M. (2014) 'Photography and drawing in anthropology', *Slovak Eth-nography*, 62 (4): 534–546.

# 8

# Sensing rhythm

Dawn Lyon

## Introduction

Percussionist Evelyn Glennie knows a thing or two about rhythm. Profoundly deaf since the age of twelve, she uses her body to feel rhythm. Playing barefoot she can hear vibration and feel sound in her legs and other parts of her body. She has explicitly cultivated this capacity for detecting rhythms, heightening her body's sensitivity and recognition of different kinds of resonance. Sight, too, is central to how she 'hears'; sounds arise within her to correspond to what she sees (Glennie, 2015). I am listening to a recording of one of her performances (on YouTube) as I'm writing this. The rhythm inspires me. It is as if it gets hold of me. My body responds and I am moving as I type in a sort of exaggerated nod towards the screen. It even seems to help my concentration.

Some weekday mornings, I am woken up by the sound of a car engine. My neighbour has a different rhythm from the rest of the street, often setting off before it is light. I am not sure whether it is the noise of the van's ignition that wakes me or the persistent drone of the engine that disturbs my sleep. But it is not something I can tune into. My body registers the sound as intrusive and literally cannot incorporate it. There is no differentiation in the noise that allows this. It is pure repetition. And without difference there can be no rhythm.

As I am describing these experiences, I am making sense of them through the concepts and ideas proposed by Henri Lefebvre, the

French philosopher, sociologist, urban scholar and literary critic who devised 'rhythmanalysis'. *Éléments de rythmanalyse: introduction à la connaissance des rythmes* was published in French in 1992, one year after Lefebvre's death and in English in 2004 as *Rhythmanalysis: Space, Time and Everyday Life*. This short book is widely considered as the fourth and final volume of Lefebvre's hitherto three-volume *Critique of Everyday Life* (Lefebvre, 2014) and has attracted considerable interest in the twenty-first century. It adds a temporal dimension to Lefebvre's long-standing analyses of space and attempts to think time and space together.

As the instances I described above suggest, rhythmanalysis is helpful as a means of sensing and making sense of rhythm in the everyday across different sites and scales. In this chapter, I discuss some of the challenges and possibilities of using rhythmanalysis as a mundane method in social research. While rhythm is pervasive in everyday life, its intangibility makes it difficult to research and requires some inventive and experimental practices. I present the different strategies and methods I used to explore rhythm as a tool of analysis in the everyday unfolding of London's Billingsgate fish market and discuss the opportunities and challenges of sensing rhythm in these ways.

The chapter is organised as follows. The next section discusses Lefebvre's thinking for doing rhythmanalysis and considers rhythmanalysis as a fundamentally embodied and sensory research practice. Following on from this, I discuss my own research from three starting points: learning to feel rhythm; attending to rhythm; and the use of audio-visual techniques to record rhythm and reveal what our senses cannot directly perceive. In my critical reflections on these approaches, I highlight their limitations, in particular the restricted spatial and temporal frames of these forms of empirical research. However, I also argue that they can help researchers to identify the different co-existing rhythms of everyday life in sensitive and creative ways. Overall, this approach sheds light on how we inhabit time and space and sense rhythm, in this instance in the setting of a fish market.

## Lefebvre's *Rhythmanalysis*: the body as a metronomic device

Lefebvre intended rhythmanalysis as an object and tool of analysis to show how change occurs through the imprinting of new rhythms on an era (Lefebvre, 2004: 14). He was concerned with what he described as capitalism's 'colonisation' of different spheres of life. The resulting fragmentation and alienation dominated what he called 'la vie quotidienne', or everyday life (and wrote about at length – see Lefebvre, 2014). Capitalism's invasiveness into routine practices resulted in more abstract and linear forms of space and time structuring everyday experience. He contrasted the *linear time* (or rhythms) of technology, industry, the city and consumption with the *cyclical rhythms* of nature which are apparent in the seasons and the practices of rural life. These tensions resonate today in the celebration or critique of the acceleration of everyday life, which reinforces linear time, on the one hand, and calls for alternative 'slow' ways of living, which make space for the cyclical, on the other. For Lefebvre, capitalism was not seamless and the everyday was also the site of revolutionary possibility that would put an end to alienation. So rhythmanalysis challenges any reductive opposition between speed and slowness (mobility and inertia). It offers a more intricate spatio-temporal grasp of lived experience as a means through which to explore and critique social life (Lyon, 2018).

Rhythmanalysis has been described as both conceptual and corporeal since on the one hand it offers a critique of spatio-temporal relations in capitalist society and, on the other, it suggests a research practice. However, the challenge of doing rhythmanalysis remains. Readers have argued that rhythmanalysis is more of an 'orientation' (Highmore, 2002: 175) or 'a speculative invitation to think rhythmically' (McCormack, 2013: 42) than a method. Rhythmanalysis might be thought of as a 'strategy of inquiry', making use of a range of documentary, ethnographic and audio-visual methods as well as quantitative analysis. Indeed, although it is most often associated with a qualitative tradition, DeLyser and Sui (2013) argue that it cannot be captured within a qualitative–quantitative divide. Rhythmanalysis has been taken up and developed across the social sciences, notably within geography. It has been used in particular to study mobility, place, work and nature, as well as consumption and leisure practices, education and identity (also see Wilkinson, this collection).

For Lefebvre rhythmanalysis was principally an embodied phenomenological research practice and this is how it has been most widely used since. Indeed, one way of thinking about doing rhythmanalysis is as a form of ethnography that is especially attuned to time and space and explicitly uses the body as an instrument in the research process (Longhurst, Ho and Johnston, 2008). The rhythmanalyst 'listens – and first to his [*sic*] body; he learns rhythm from it, in order consequently to appreciate external rhythms', Lefebvre writes. The rhythmanalyst takes her own rhythms as a reference such that the body serves as a 'metronome' in relation to broader patterns and interactions. 'The rhythmanalyst calls on all his senses,', Lefebvre continues. 'He thinks with his body, not in the abstract, but in lived temporality.' Indeed, 'to grasp a rhythm, it is necessary to have been grasped by it; one must let oneself go, give oneself over, abandon oneself to its duration' (Lefebvre, 2004: 19–21, 27). How, though, does this happen in practice?

## Learning to feel rhythm: disruption and *dressage*

Walking into the market hall at Billingsgate feels like really arriving somewhere. The space is already buzzing with movement and noise. The brightness of the lights and the chill of the ice are strangely enlivening despite the early hour. As I approached the side entrance from the car park on each visit, my pace would quicken and I found myself eager to enter this world. A brief pause would make for a good start. Standing at the north eastern corner of the market hall, I would look around and gather a sense of what was going on, looking out for familiar patterns as well as anything out of the ordinary, sensing the mood of the day and the direction I would take.

When the idea of doing a visual ethnography of Billingsgate first emerged (a couple of years earlier), I went there to try to trace the circulation of fish from the wholesale market to the retail space in South East London I was researching at the time (with Les Back – see Lyon and Back, 2012). With the ethnographer's combination of audacity and uncertainty, I told fish merchants and salespeople about my imagined project on the work involved in bringing fish 'from sea to table', testing the water for viability, access and whether I had the nerve to put myself into this space. 'Well, if you really want to understand, you should come and work for me one day!' My encounter with the long-established fish merchant, Roger Barton, a well-known figure in the market at the time, threw me in at the deep end. One cold winter night, I worked on his stand and experienced first hand the unfolding of the market from a 2am start to a late morning finish.

Researching the fish trade meant that I had to 'calibrate' my body to the market's rhythms from the outset (Sharma, 2014). Ben Snyder (2016) documents something similar in his ethnography of truck drivers where he mirrored the drivers' sleeping and waking patterns to feel for himself, albeit briefly, the demands of their work. Billingsgate is predominantly a wholesale market (although open to the public) selling fish and seafood (fresh, frozen and smoked) serving the hotel and catering industry, fishmongers and other consumers. It is located on the Isle of Dogs in east London next to where Canary Wharf now stands and is dominated numerically and culturally by older, white, working-class men. The site comprises a covered hall for the display of fish (it is a 'samples' market) with adjacent buildings for cold storage, a shellfish boiling room and an ice-making plant. It opens for trade at 4am but buyers browse before then. The market floor closes at around 8am but there is work to be done after that still – sorting stock, cleaning, finalising orders in the office and preparing for the following day or week. If I felt excited to be driving to Billingsgate in the relative quiet of the night, I have rarely felt as tired as after that one shift on the market floor. Indeed, that such working patterns take their toll on the bodies and relationships of workers is well documented.

I mostly started to sense the rhythms of everyday market work through being out of synch and out of place. I couldn't lift boxes, fish or differentiate between the sizes of prawns quickly enough; I was slow to add up bills or get out of the way as the porters approached with their trolleys and cries to 'mind your legs!' This disjuncture was instructive though, revealing the fluid rhythms that underpinned the embodied skill and knowledge of the fish merchants, salespeople and regular buyers who knew the space. Lefebvre, together with his last wife and collaborator, Catherine Régulier, point out how we largely become aware of our rhythms 'when we suffer from some irregularity' or disorderliness (2004: 77): disruption reveals rhythm and offers a 'heuristic device' for doing research into rhythm (Edensor, 2000: 135–137).

Some scholars have explicitly sought to go against dominant rhythms in order to detect them. For instance, Caitlin Bowdler and her colleague undertook rhythmanalysis using dance. They performed on a footbridge in Manchester as people awkwardly attempted to pass them, provoking both laughter and hesitation. Dancing bodies

'defamiliarise' a sense of place and in so doing offer an enticing practice for the sensory grasp of the city (Edensor and Bowdler, 2015; see
Wilkinson, this collection). They bring to the fore the rhythmanalyst's awareness of different rhythmic relations: discordance between
rhythms, or being 'out of step' (which is what Lefebvre (2004) calls
*arrhythmia*); eurhythmia when rhythms combine smoothly; and the
ways in which rhythms shift across these registers.

It was only once I started my Billingsgate ethnography in a sustained way that I learnt how to inhabit the space. For a period of
several months in 2012, I went to the market as an observer two or
three times a week. My routine involved a 2, 3 or 4am start and a
series of repeated encounters with the people who became my key
interlocutors, or 'informants' as I spent time on the market floor and
in the on-site cafés (see Lyon, 2016). I literally absorbed the rhythms
of market life, knowing when to move and 'bend' to its activity – an
instance of what Lefebvre calls *dressage*. This refers to the entrainment
and constitution of the body through rhythm and the production of
rhythm through corporeal gestures (Lefebvre, 2004: 39–40). Doing
rhythmanalysis also involves making use of this process explicitly. For
instance, I sought to match my stride to the porters I shadowed on
their way to take orders from a chill store to a waiting van, registering
rhythm at a kinaesthetic level in relation to my usual pattern and pace.
In addition, this focus on a singular rhythm was helpful to disentangle
elements of the 'polyrhythmic assemblage' of Billingsgate (Chen,
2017). Indeed, through this level of embodied attention, I came to
appreciate how the porters' movements contributed to the polyrhythmic production of the market space; in other words, how different
rhythms combine to produce the synchronisation and spatio-temporal
entanglements of the market.

## Attending to rhythm: listening and looking

If moving about the market was central to sensing rhythm in this
project, I certainly did not give up on the idea of articulating rhythm
or its effects in talk. My time at the market included lots of informal
exchanges with fish merchants, salespeople, inspectors, porters, customers and other workers (e.g. in the café spaces). Once I had established some ongoing conversations, I approached people to undertake
more formal interviews about working at Billingsgate which usually

took place on site after the market was formally closed for the morning.[1] Two sets of rhythmic relations emerged most prominently in these exchanges. First, people reported feeling in tune and in synch with one another and with the life of the market as it repeatedly took its everyday familiar shape in time and space. The other side of the coin, however, was the experience of arrhythmia, of being out of synch with the outside world. In particular, people discussed the implications this had for familial and personal relationships and there were many tales of discord and divorce as well as instances of accommodation and compromise. One of the younger fish merchants on the market, Ryan, explained how he stays up in the afternoon (unlike some of his colleagues) and that he and his wife 'go out and have lunch or something like that' after work. However, he goes to bed at 7pm which means 'we don't go out in the evenings, I don't anyway. Which makes it a bit difficult at times.'

Secondly, these discussions revealed how traders' work is characterised by several different temporalities, themselves marked by distinct rhythms or combinations of rhythm. Traders actively think about matching buyers and sellers when they make decisions about what products to offer; they plan in terms of seasons and holidays, and manage the vagaries of the weather and regulation and their implications for supply. At the level of the everyday, when they negotiate a sale, this often happens in the context of an ongoing relationship between buyer and seller. So while the rhythms of the day's exchanges are in the foreground, other rhythms make themselves felt that relate to past deals and of course the availability of the fish itself. Roger, for instance, explains that he starts making calls at around four o'clock in the morning, letting his best customers know what he's got, offering them 'first refusal' on the day's offers. At the same time, he updates them on orders from the previous day and together they make provisional decisions for the next. He is keenly aware of the broader rhythms within which he operates: 'I'm on call twenty-four hours a day – and I'm dependent on the weather', he says. He plays with this knowledge, plotting ahead and anticipating who will buy what, and constituting future preferences in how he makes a sale.

Jim Dillon, a salesman with considerable knowledge of fish, emphasises speed when he first starts explaining how trade operates, stating: 'If it is still good enough for sale you've just got to get the fish into the system.' However, the rhythm of the exchange might be slowed or even paused. He continues: 'If the fish is very good to begin with … if someone was to come up and offer silly money, I, for this fish, you don't have to accept it … because it's got another three, four, five days life in it.' The rhythms of decay – slowed by care and ice – are central to these evaluations. Roger also reports holding stock back as he gambles on tomorrow's sales in relation to his judgements about demand and supply. No one gets it right all the time. 'Everybody at times gets a little stung with a certain amount of fish', he states, but 'the first loss is the best loss.' Or as Brian Roper, another long-established and well-respected salesman, puts it: 'These aren't antiques, you know. We can't, we can't just store them, [*laughter*] you know. Take, bring them out later, somehow.'

In addition to listening to accounts of people who worked in the market, attending to the soundscape of the space was a vital part of sensing rhythm in this project (see also Rose, this collection). Walking into the market hall, there is a crescendo of sound marked by different 'layers' (Makagon and Neumann, 2008): the close ring of a telephone, someone shouting nearby, background chatter, or the pervasive squeak of the polystyrene boxes being moved around. While the chaos of noise alone 'has no rhythm' according to Lefebvre, 'the attentive ear begins to separate out, to distinguish the sources, to bring them back together to perceive interactions' (2004: 27). He instructs the rhythmanalyst to 'listen to the world, and above all to what are disdainfully called noises, which are said without meaning, and to *murmurs* [rumeurs], full of meaning – and finally he will listen to silences' (2004: 19). He continues: rhythmanalysts should learn 'to listen to a house, a street, a city, as one listens to a symphony or an opera'. And he recognises the benefits of sound recording: 'Putting an interview or background noises on disc or cassette enables us to reflect on rhythms, which no longer vanish whenever they appear' (2004: 69). At the present time, sonic methods seem to be gaining ground as a sensory approach, in part as an important counter to the dominance of the visual in accounts of urban experience (e.g. Hall, Lashua and Coffey, 2008; Revill, 2013).

I also sought to document the space of the market using photography. Indeed, when I first set out to do this project, I anticipated that I would construct collages or sequences of images of the market to capture the rhythms and sensory mood of the space. An example can be seen in Figure 8.1, which shows the material context of market work well. Roger is surrounded by fish and seafood and he makes notes or calculations at his stand. On the far left of the images, boxes of differently sized prawns stand tall as they await customers and a set of scales wide enough for the largest fish on display is ready for the next sale. However, photographs and collages turned out not to be as effective as I had hoped as a means of sensing rhythm. Fish are sold whole or pre-filleted at Billingsgate, so there is not the work of gutting, cleaning or skinning fish that can be observed in a retail setting (Lyon and Back, 2012). There is nevertheless important work of the display of fish, as each stand presents 'samples' which require sorting, organising and maintaining in a liminal state. The fish is iced, checked for temperature and 'aestheticized and *staged* in the sphere of exchange' (Bohme, 2003: 72). While I could see this process happening in real time, my images did not capture the sensory richness of the scene. I persisted for a while but became stuck in how I was looking with the camera. My photographs quickly replicated one another and after two or three weeks I stopped taking them altogether.

**8.1** A photo collage of Roger Barton's stand, Billingsgate Fish Market, London

## Extending the senses: audio-visual methods for researching rhythm

I spent most of my time at Billingsgate wandering around letting myself get caught up in or 'grasped by' the rhythms of the place. I absorbed and enjoyed the atmosphere and left stimulated and satisfied by the spectacle. I talked to people, listened to the space, took photographs and still I had a sense that there was more to the market than I could take in with the tools I was using. Walking around the market hall, I noticed that I kept looking over my shoulder – a kind of bodily expression of the uncertain sense of where exactly the market was happening. Immersion turned out to be an obstacle to the perception of the ebb and flow of the market (Lefebvre, 2004: 28; Lyon, 2016). How, then, could I deal with this sensory excess and 'catch' this polyrhythmic complexity?

Rhythmanalysis requires 'critical distance' as well as immersion (Elden, 2004: 113): 'In order to grasp and analyse rhythms, it is necessary to get outside them, but not completely', Lefebvre writes (2004: 17). When trying to grasp the rhythm of the street, he recommended the 'marvellous invention' of a balcony, and failing that a window, from where the flow of sounds and movements can be disentangled. At Billingsgate, I repeatedly found myself climbing the stairs and looking down on the market hall from the first-floor gallery in an effort to contain and clarify the sensory overload of being there. And here, the possibility of making a film based on time-lapse photography to 'capture' the rhythm of the market began to take shape.

Lefebvre was sceptical of the capacity of the visual to apprehend rhythm, stating: 'no camera, no image or series of images can show these rhythms' (2004: 36) – and he was right in relation to my 'failed' photographs. However, his call to tune into the environment is something which can be enhanced by the audio-visual technologies available today (Latham and McCormack, 2009; Wunderlich, 2008, 2013). With film-maker/collaborator, Kevin Reynolds, I used time-lapse photography to record one night in the life of the market from set-up to close – from one o'clock in the morning until midday. Following Paul Simpson, time-lapse photography provides an opportunity to record 'the qualitative unfolding of events as they happen' in linear clock-time and reveal 'how various rhythms and routines interrelate and interfere' (2012: 431, 440). From the gallery location, we took one photograph

**8.2** A still from *Billingsgate Fish Market*

every ten seconds. In addition, each hour I did some 'soundwalking' on the market floor (Hall, Lashua and Coffey, 2008), walking around casually and making audio recordings on a hand-held digital device (see Rose, this collection, for more work on soundwalks). The resultant film or audio-visual montage is a combination of a selection of these sounds with the sequence of images speeded up so one hour is presented in thirty seconds. This was a 'creative-analytic process' in which we sought to evoke Billingsgate with an 'affective force' that goes beyond representation (Garrett and Hawkins, 2015: 145–146). Figure 8.2 shows the market at 4am, poised for the official start of trade, after which time fish can legally leave the site. The samples of fish can be seen on display and several sales are already taking place.

The construction of the montage is explicitly artificial – and effective for revealing rhythm and exposing the polyrhythmic complexity of the market. By losing the richness of the detail, we sidestep the sensory overload that live presence and video entail, and begin to distinguish some threads. As from Lefebvre's window, 'the flows separate out, rhythms respond to one another' (Lefebvre, 2004: 28). Most of the frame of the film is taken up with the market floor, reaching up to the level of the clock suspended from the ceiling at the centre of the market hall, which explicitly marks linear time for the viewer. It highlights the sequential process of the market from preparation through to the sale, then closure and cleaning up as different groups of workers occupy the space in turn, from sellers and buyers to inspectors and cleaners. But these sequences happen alongside the cyclical unfolding of the life of the market with its multiple, changing rhythms across the night. Recursive loops, 'repetition, rupture and resumption' (Lefebvre, 2004: 78) mean there is an 'always emergent interaction' of the linear and cyclical (Simpson, 2008: 823). It is a contained world when trade is at its peak in its eurythmic flow, but once the inside lights are switched off and daylight is seen reflected in the wet floor, the viewer recognises the rhythms of the market as being at odds with the city space around it – an instance of arrhythmia.

## Researching rhythm: tips and pitfalls

In this chapter I have discussed several means of sensing rhythm: directly with the body as an instrument of research (see also Hall et al., this collection), with a focus on listening and looking, and using audio-visual methods to perceive rhythms that exceed the capacity of the senses. None of this was clear to me at the outset of the research. I had some lines prepared to tell people about the scope of the project when I began work at the market but I only came to know what I was doing there and how I was doing it through experiment and discovery. Uneasiness, frustration and hunches were all important guides. What I now write as the methodology for this project emerged through an unfolding process of trying out different tactics for doing rhythmanalysis (e.g. disruption) and seeing what might lie the other side of some of the project's failures (e.g. still images). Each element of the research – successful or not – directly or indirectly took me to the next and was effective for different things. The interviews really helped me understand the temporal complexities of the fish traders' work which I could not perceive through my own observations. However, it was in the film that their collective working rhythms became apparent and meaningful and offered a form in which I could better explore the relationships between rhythm, atmosphere and mobility, and the interconnections of different types of work in the market space.

That said, the audio-visual montage as a mode of doing rhythmanalysis also has its limitations. Most obviously, the spatial frame of the film is restricted to the market hall and the temporal frame is also narrow, focusing on the market through the night. While this is effective for showing the unfolding of the life of the market as it takes place, it ignores other processes and rhythms that underpin the movement of fish through Billingsgate. In particular, the viewer cannot observe the anticipation of rhythms that are beyond the present that make the market happen the next day, and the one after – orders placed and deals done in processes that extend well beyond its temporal and spatial reach. It is therefore important to recognise that any one rhythmanalytical research strategy may be insufficient to grasp the full workings of rhythm or that rhythmanalysis may be one strand of a research design that uses different tools to address different aspects of a study.

With the experience of having done this project now behind me, if I were starting again I would focus more on sound, both as a source for registering rhythm in itself and for transforming other data into an audible form. Here I might take inspiration from the work of Michaela Palmer and Owain Jones (2014), who have made use of rhythmanalysis to explore the tides and other non-human patterns in nature that are not directly available to human senses. They convert data from environmental processes such as the movement of water, silt and other elements in estuaries and around the coast to produce fascinating 'sonifications' in which they translate these inaccessible rhythms into different arrangements of sound. Instead of directly recording sounds at Billingsgate, it might have been possible to generate an alternative soundscape or sonification based on the visual representation of the market as seen in the film. I also wonder how Evelyn Glennie might 'play the space' at Billingsgate, either by interpreting the film directly or through responding to vibration if she were to be present live at the market (and I did try to make this happen!). She did something similar following a visit to the Mini car factory in Oxford, 'hammering out a metallic improvisation inspired by the rhythms of the production line' (www.bbc.co.uk/programmes/b0bgfqx7).

## Conclusions

When I am doing ethnographic research I often feel the sheer unintelligibility of what is going on around me. I have a sense of slipping in and out of understanding which escapes my grasp as something else catches my attention. Indeed, the sensory excess of being in the field is often confusing as well as stimulating. In this chapter, I have reflected on my own experience of trying to use rhythmanalysis as a research practice in the study of a fish market. I have traced the specific means of sensing rhythm I deployed in my research at Billingsgate. In this, I relied on the body and the senses, in particular practices of looking and listening, as well as seeking to extend the senses using audio-visual technologies. These mundane methods were not settled in advance of being in the field. Rather, they came to be formalised through a process of trying different things out. Once they were clear to me, however, they offered some focus for doing rhythmanalysis. Having drawn attention to the challenges and limitations of working in these ways, I would suggest that in the end they were effective for identifying and analysing the different co-existing rhythms of the everyday life of the market. And these – or similar – techniques might be used by others to further develop and promote spatially, temporally and sensually attuned practices of research for the study of everyday life.

---

### Box 8.1: Training, tools and equipment

As this chapter has discussed, rhythmanalysis can be undertaken in a variety of ways. For general observation, the tools and equipment needed are attentive eyes and ears, notepads and audio-visual recording devices. I collaborated with a film-maker for the creation of the audio-visual montage of the market which included access to professional cameras and editing software. However, it would certainly be possible to make a similar film with more modest kit.

---

### Box 8.2: Further reading and additional resources

- Progressive Geographies: https://progressivegeographies.com/resources/lefebvre-resources/.
- Rhuthmos: https://rhuthmos.eu/.
- Lyon, D. (2018) *What is Rhythmanalysis?*, London: Bloomsbury Academic.

## Note

1 With the exception of Roger Barton (see above), who already has a public profile, the names of traders mentioned in this chapter are pseudonyms.

## References

Bohme, G. (2003) 'Contribution to the critique of the aesthetic economy', *Thesis Eleven*, No. 73: 71–82.

Chen, Y. (2017) *Practising Rhythmanalysis: Theories and Methodologies*, London and New York: Roman and Littlefield.

DeLyser, D. and Sui, S. (2013) 'Crossing the qualitative–quantitative divide II', *Progress in Human Geography*, 37 (2): 293–305.

Edensor, T. (2000) 'Moving through the city', in D. Bell and A. Haddour (eds) *City Visions*, Harlow: Pearson Education Limited, 121–140.

Edensor, T. and Bowdler, C. (2015) 'Site-specific dance: revealing and contesting the ludic qualities, everyday rhythms, and embodied habits of place', *Environment and Planning A*, 47: 709–726.

Elden, S. (2004) *Understanding Henri Lefebvre: Theory and the Possible*, London and New York: Continuum.

Garrett, B. L. and Hawkins, H. (2015) 'Creative video ethnographies: video methodologies of urban exploration', in C. Bates (ed.) *Video Methods: Social Science Research in Motion*, Abingdon: Routledge, 142–164.

Glennie, E. (2015) 'Hearing essay', www.evelyn.co.uk/hearing-essay/ (accessed 10 October 2018).

Hall, T., Lashua, B. and Coffey, A. (2008) 'Sound and the everyday in qualitative research', *Qualitative Inquiry*, 14 (6): 1019–1040.

Highmore, B. (2002) 'Street life in London: towards a rhythmanalysis of London in the late nineteenth century', *New Formations*, 47: 171–193.

Latham, A. and McCormack, D. (2009) 'Thinking with images in non-representational cities: vignettes from Berlin', *Area*, 41 (3): 252–262.

Lefebvre, H. (2004 [1992]) *Rhythmanalysis: Space, Time and Everyday Life*, London: Continuum International Publishing Group Ltd.

Lefebvre, H. (2014 [1947,1961,1981]) *Critique of Everyday Life: The One-Volume Edition*, London and New York: Verso.

Lefebvre, H. and Régulier, C. (2004 [1985]) 'The rhythmanalytical project', in H. Lefebvre, *Rhythmanalysis*, London: Continuum International Publishing Group Ltd.

Longhurst, R., Ho, E. and Johnston, L. (2008) 'Using "the body" as an "instrument of research": kimch'i and pavlova', *Area*, 40 (2): 208–217.

Lyon, D. (2016) 'Doing audio-visual montage to explore time and space: The everyday rhythms of Billingsgate Fish Market', *Sociological Research*

*Online*, 21 (3): 12, www.socresonline.org.uk/21/3/12.html (accessed 10 October 2018).

Lyon, D. (2018) *What is Rhythmanalysis?*, London: Bloomsbury Academic.

Lyon, D. and Back, L. (2012) 'Fish and fishmongers in a global city: socio-economy, craft, and social relations on a London market', *Sociological Research Online*, 17 (2): 23, www.socresonline.org.uk/17/2/23.html (accessed 10 October 2018).

Makagon, D. and Neumann, M. (2008) *Recording Culture: Audio Documentary and the Ethnographic Experience*, London: Sage.

McCormack, D. (2013) *Refrains for Moving Bodies*, Durham and London: Duke University Press.

Palmer, M. and Jones, O. (2014) 'On breathing and geography: explorations of data sonifications of timespace processes with illustrating examples for a tidally dynamic landscape (Severn Estuary, UK)', *Environment and Planning A*, 46: 222–240.

Revill, G. (2013) 'Points of departure: listening to rhythm in the sonorous spaces of the railway station', *Sociological Review*, 61 (S1): 51–68, Special Issue: 'Urban rhythms, mobilities, space and interaction in the contemporary city'.

Sharma, S. (2014) *In the Meantime: Temporality and Cultural Politics*, Durham and London: Duke University Press.

Simpson, P. (2008) 'Chronic everyday life: rhythmanalysing street performance', *Social & Cultural Geography*, 9 (7): 807–829.

Simpson, P. (2012) 'Apprehending everyday rhythms: rhythmanalysis, time-lapse photography, and the space–time of everyday street performance', *Cultural Geographies*, 19 (4): 423–445.

Snyder, B. (2016) *The Disrupted Workplace: Time and the Moral Order of Flexible Capitalism*, Oxford: Oxford University Press.

Wunderlich, F. M. (2008) 'Walking and rhythmicity: sensing urban space', *Journal of Urban Design*, 13 (1): 31–44.

Wunderlich, F. M. (2013) 'Place-temporality and urban place-rhythms in urban analysis and design: an aesthetic akin to music', *Journal of Urban Design*, 18 (3): 383–408.

# 9

# Everyday ethnographies and the art of eavesdropping: capturing ordinary human–animal encounters

Becky Tipper

## An ethnography of everyday encounters with creatures

Ethnographic research offers a way of attending closely to people's ordinary, lived experience – practising the 'art of listening' that Les Back (2007) argues should drive the sociological endeavour. Here, I discuss the use of a neighbourhood ethnography which explored one aspect of everyday British life: people's encounters with animals.[1]

Creatures of all kinds are enmeshed in ordinary human lives: people eat them, own them, live alongside them. We might take their presence for granted, but once we orient to them, they raise compelling questions: how do people draw the line between 'animal' and 'human'? What ethical responsibilities do humans feel they owe to other animals? What symbolic meanings do animals carry? Can our connections with other species meaningfully be understood as friendship, kinship or love?

Although European and North American anthropologists have long recognised the significance of animals in 'Other' cultures, social science has been slower to acknowledge that animals also matter in human lives closer to home. In recent years, however, qualitative research has explored sites of human–animal encounter in Western societies, such as slaughterhouses, farms and research laboratories. This research is insightful, but these are still often intense and rarefied situations rather than commonplace experiences. Relationships with household pets, of course, are more widespread, and there is a rapidly growing body of research into these intimate and complex relationships. But I wanted to look beyond this focus on pets and their owners to other everyday ways that people encounter animals – encounters which are less marked, more ordinary and often mundane.

In British cities and towns, even people without pets (or any particular interest in animals) regularly encounter a multitude of creatures in the course of their everyday lives: garden wildlife (including birds, mammals and amphibians), domestic 'pests', urban wildlife in public spaces and parks, free-roaming cats, and dogs being walked. My research took as its focus a suburban neighbourhood to explore how people made sense of these ordinary, often-overlooked encounters with creatures, and to ask how far everyday sociability might be seen as a 'more-than-human' affair (Tipper, 2012).

But, like many of the creatures which skitter, flutter and scurry through our ordinary lives, the everyday *itself* is elusive and hard to capture; seemingly unremarkable and taken-for-granted. It is difficult to articulate what is considered mundane. Of course, the 'everyday' is not interchangeable with 'mundaneity': everyday life encompasses remarkable, astonishing and singular moments, whereas the mundane is the routine, unexamined part of quotidian life that seems hardly worth considering. But, by using a locality-based ethnographic approach, I hoped to explore the encounters with other species – both remarkable and mundane – that occurred in the everyday lives of people in this particular neighbourhood.[2]

## Locating the everyday in ethnographic research: immersion, reflexivity and attentiveness

Ethnographic research is well suited to a study of the everyday. Although widely employed by social scientists, its origins, of course, are in the anthropological study of the ordinary worlds of (usually unfamiliar) cultures. The interpretivist approach that often informs ethnographic research is 'not an experimental science in search of law but an interpretive one in search of meaning' (Geertz, 1993: 5) – meanings discovered through detailed attention to ordinary practices and local understandings of mundane life. And it was this sort of everyday 'meaning' I wanted to capture in my own research.

It is worth noting that ethnographers have often taken for granted that humans are the only beings who make meanings, in contrast to inanimate objects and the non-human world (e.g. Hammersley and Atkinson, 2007: 97). For ethnographers of human–animal relations, this simple distinction is, of course, blurred. Some researchers even seek to include the actions and perceptions of animals alongside those of humans, arguing that it is not only humans who participate in social interactions (see Jerolmack, 2009 for a discussion). However, even if an ethnographer's concern is explicitly with how humans make sense of their interspecies relations (as was the case in my research), people's own understandings may well focus on animals as thinking and meaning-making individuals, with their own creaturely perspectives on the world.

In a sense, ethnography involves simply 'gathering whatever data are available to throw light on the emerging focus of enquiry' (Hammersley and Atkinson, 2007: 3), although in practice ethnography usually draws on a combination of participant observation (semistructured or informal) interviews and analysis of documentary data. In participant observation, the researcher immerses themselves in the everyday world they are studying, in the hopes of gaining a rich understanding of people's lives. This intense living-with, working-with and talking-with has been described as 'deep hanging out' (Wogan, cited in Crang and Cook, 2007: 37). The aim is to create a 'thick description' which brings to life the world of the study (Geertz, 1993). In fieldnotes, an ethnographer creates a rich record of experiences, encounters and people's own words, categories and understandings. Ethnographic research incorporates the ethnographer in complex ways – it is, after all, through their interpersonal relations, understandings, reflections and writings that an ethnography comes into being (e.g. Coffey, 1999). As such, fieldnotes (and the final written text) can also incorporate a great deal about the researcher's own perspectives, actions and reflections. Although auto-ethnographers focus entirely on analysis of their personal experience (see Collins, this collection), many ethnographers (myself included) seek to strike a more delicate balance between introspection and an account which risks becoming 'more about the ethnographer than the people being studied' (Davies, 2008: 17); an account which, although reflexive, is 'not about narcissism or self-absorption but common likenesses, and by extension, contrasts' (Back, 2007: 159).

Ethnographic methods seem to offer an ideal way to explore every-day life, although it is worth pausing to ask what exactly we mean by 'everyday life'. There are many definitions of the 'everyday', but Rita Felski (1999) offers a practical, lucid basis for thinking about precisely how and where it might be found. Felski argues that the everyday emerges through everyday temporality (routine and repetition), modality (ordinary habits) and the experience of spatiality (in both public and domestic spaces).

Participant observation, then, can immerse the ethnographer in Felski's everyday 'habits' and 'routines', but it is also a means to appreciate the role of movements through everyday space (Davies, 2011; Ross et al., 2009) – and, as Ingold and Vergunst observe, 'the ways along which we walk are those along which we live' (2016: 1). In addition, since so much of the 'everyday' occurs not-in-public, an ethnographic attention to life, talk and routines in the domestic realm is also important – accessed perhaps through home-based interviews (Hockey, 2002), or even inviting people to give tours of domestic spaces (Pink, 2004).

An ethnographic attention to the everyday also includes an analysis of how it unfolds and is represented in documentary sources – for instance, in organisational policies, archives, news media or the internet. Images produced by researchers, or by participants, or which exist already in the social world of the study, can also add a layer to a 'thick description' of everyday life. Back suggests that photographs can 'communicate what is outside language' (2007: 17–18) and allow us to listen more closely to the multiple, embodied aspects of everyday experience. And, when presenting ethnographic data, photographs might bring the reader into a visceral, intense appreciation of what cannot easily be expressed in words.

Although ethnographic methods are ideal for exploring what is lived, felt, observed and experienced, this is not to suggest that simply *asking* people about their everyday lives is impossible. It is, however, potentially problematic – as Crang and Cook observe, 'a great deal of what researchers might like to know about other people's lives is unlikely to be noticed by them or easily put into words' (2007: 77). In particular, the mundane might resist direct scrutiny: in Daniel Miller's research on ordinary shopping, participants often tried to deflect him towards other people who relished spending to excess; they assumed that everyday shopping was entirely unremarkable and that 'shopping' would be better understood by exploring extreme practices (1998: 69). Nevertheless, qualitative, semi-structured interviews (often in participants' homes) allow for an attention to aspects of everyday life that unfold domestically, and provide insights into how people account for and represent their own lives (Hammersley and Atkinson, 2007: 97). Interviews can be seen as an integral part of ethnographic approach; Hockey and Forsey suggest that interviews are as complex and rich as participant observation when conducted with an 'ethnographic imaginary' (2012: 83) which finds participant meanings in the subtle contours of what is said, unsaid, and experienced by both interviewee and interviewer.

However, potential problems of eliciting talk about the everyday are compounded when the research focus is also ordinary for the researcher: explanations about ordinary life might be readily offered to an 'outsider', but when the researcher shares the everyday life of the participants, it will probably be assumed they already understand what everyone in the study takes for granted. And it can require careful attention and close analysis for a researcher to see their own familiar world as 'anthropologically strange' (Hammersley and Atkinson, 2007: 9).

Nevertheless, ethnographic research 'at home' also has the potential to radically reframe academic discourses. Crang and Cook argue that 'ethnographers, rather than focussing on poor and powerless Others,' might instead 'study our "own" cultures, cease taking them as some universal benchmark and problematise their values' (2007: 28). Researching what (even to the researcher) seems 'already understood' might allow us to see the world in entirely new ways. While my own research drew much inspiration from the neighbourhood ethnographies conducted by North American urban sociologists (often focusing on poor, marginalised communities – Mitch Duneier's *Sidewalk* (2000) is a relatively recent example), I located my own ethnographic research much closer to home: in the neighbourhood where I already lived.

Research 'at home' does not have to be entirely auto-ethnographic (although it might be), but it often involves a particularly intricate meshing of 'personal' and 'research' identities (see Collins, this collection). Often, an ethnographer's personal relationships can play a key role; Cudworth (2011) engaged in participant observation with dog walkers accompanied by her own dogs, and Stewart's (2007) neighbourhood-based study incorporated her own walks in the area with her young child. Bringing these personal relationships 'into the field' can grant access to some aspects of ordinary social life (Levey, 2009), and might offer an opportunity for a deepened reflexivity and a richer understanding of everyday life.

Ultimately, ethnography offers a means to practise the sociological 'art of listening' that Back calls for. For Back, such listening is 'not simply a matter of transcription or just emptying people of their expertise and wisdom … It involves artfulness precisely because it isn't self-evident, but a form of openness to others that needs to be crafted, a listening for the background and half-muted' (2007: 8). The established techniques that comprise ethnography can be customised and fine-tuned in a way that is alert to the subtleties of everyday life: immersion in ordinary experience, oriented to the multiple ways in which it is seen, said, unsaid, done and felt. It can generate an understanding of what everyday life *means* to the people whose everyday life it is.

## Ethnography in practice: capturing creaturely encounters

My study was situated in the neighbourhood in which I already lived – a suburb of a mid-sized northern English city, intersected by a river, with a park and duckpond, and a mix of terraced and semi-detached houses with back gardens where the largely white-British, middle-class and working-class residents lived. Of course, to claim this is 'ordinary' is not to claim universality. However, it was ordinary to me, and I would suggest that many other British people would find at least some aspects of the neighbourhood's everyday life to be familiar and unremarkable. This 'un-remarkability' is important: there was no reason to suppose that animal–human relations in this neighbourhood would be marked, significant or problematic. Nor was it uncharted and 'exotic' like the foci of many neighbourhood ethnographies – it seemed readily understood. Choosing a neighbourhood that there was, ostensibly, 'no reason to choose' (Miller, 2008: 5), would, I hoped, offer a site where I could explore the ordinary business of encountering creatures.

My residence, of course, allowed me to immerse myself in the everyday life of the locality – the spaces, habits and routines that Felski (1999) describes. My own domestic relationships and my movements through local space even became a key part of the research – in particular, walking my dog, and dropping and collecting my young son from nursery implicated me in the 'multiple interlacing routes' (Ross et al., 2009) of everyday social life in the area.

Some aspects of neighbourhood life lent themselves perfectly to an ethnographic analysis. For instance, one notable example of interspecies entanglements was the ongoing debate about Canada geese in the local park. For many residents, the geese – who damaged the grass, behaved aggressively and deposited large volumes of excrement – were a destructive presence. The city council had made several efforts to address the problem, even proposing a cull (a suggestion welcomed by some residents but vehemently opposed by others), and the issue was frequently the topic of articles and letters in the local newspaper. This debate offered a wealth of documentary data and evocative photographs, as well as interview accounts (from both city officials and local residents). And my participant observation alongside people in the park (as they attempted to feed ducks only for the bread to be snatched instead by geese, or as they walked near the pond and shooed away belligerent geese) offered another strand of ethnographic insight.

In another instance, when a well-known local cat was run over by a car, many local people left flowers and tributes at a bench where they had often met him. This impromptu memorial even featured in both local and national newspapers. My ethnographic analysis drew in media coverage, discussions with local people including the cat's owners, and – since I had personally crossed paths with this cat as I walked through the neighbourhood – my own reflections on my fleeting connection with him. Visual data also offered some surprising insights; as I discuss elsewhere (Tipper, 2016), the sight of an elaborate roadside memorial for a dead cat had a striking impact, leading people to express not only sadness but sometimes also amusement or mild outrage that an animal's death should be marked and mourned in this way – highlighting how complex and contested everyday engagements with animals can be (see Figure 9.1).

The memorial for the local cat and the goose controversy unfolded in the flow of ordinary and everyday life, although at the same time both issues were quite noteworthy and remarkable – inspiring animated discussion and debate amongst local people. But other, subtler, aspects of the everyday can be harder to research. Participant observation in public spaces allowed me to attend to a range of less remarkable everyday encounters. In addition to my everyday dog walking, I spent time in spaces such as the riverside path and local streets, alert to human–animal interactions, and alongside other people as we participated in ordinary practices such as feeding ducks in the park.

Even small encounters could be significant. For example, as my son and I walked to and from his nursery each day, we passed a small

**9.1  Floral tributes in memory of a neighbourhood cat**

industrial estate, where a desultory German Shepherd guard dog lived in a seemingly unoccupied yard. My son habitually greeted it with a cry of 'Doggy!', as did other young children (who seemed to find its presence remarkable). On more than one occasion, however, I witnessed older children taunting it. Although the dog appeared well fed, I never saw its owners, and it troubled me slightly to see it lying there listlessly and alone each time we passed. One day, I encountered a woman in her sixties or seventies passing scraps of food through the chain-link fence and murmuring comforting words to the dog. We began to talk, and she said that she came to see it often. Before this, she told me, there had been another dog who she had also visited – 'then someone told me she'd died. Maybe poisoned, they said.' She seemed, even now, deeply upset about the death of the previous dog – 'And I just kept thinking I could have *done* something. I should have been there for her.' The woman told me how thinking of the dog 'out here on her own in all weathers' haunted her. 'On the cold nights', she said, tearfully now because it was almost too much for her to bear, 'I think about her before I go to sleep. I'm in my warm bed and I can't stop thinking that she's out here in the cold all alone.' Her sudden and intense outpouring startled me – an amplified version of the passing concern I myself had felt. And I was enfolded into a complex web of interactions and meanings about this particular dog – one of the everyday meetings between the species in this particular neighbourhood.

Alongside observations of animal encounters in public spaces, I recruited people to participate in at-home interviews about the creatures in their homes and gardens. I delivered informational leaflets to homes in one particular street, and subsequently knocked on their doors to invite them to participate (see also Davies, 2011; Miller, 2008). Altogether, I interviewed thirty people; only three people directly declined to take part, although when no one answered the door, I returned only once and did not pursue recruitment any further.

Like the participants in Miller's (1998) shopping study, many interviewees initially remarked that if I was interested in animals, I really ought to speak to someone they knew who was, for example, passionate about pets or phobically terrified of spiders (people with remarkable perspectives on human–animal relations). But despite this, all participants talked readily for between one and three hours about a wide range of creatures – garden wildlife of all sorts (most notably birds), infestations of house-mice, entanglements with insects, memorable encounters with unusual creatures (such as a bat in the house or a heron in the garden), their own household pets (although only nine currently owned pets), their acquaintance with neighbourhood cats, their experiences walking dogs or encountering dog walkers, and their opinion about local animal-related issues such as the geese in the park. Interviews were tape recorded and later transcribed.

I also invited interviewees to give me a 'tour' of their gardens (see also Pink, 2004, who also asked research participants to give a 'tour' of their domestic space). In these tours, people showed me where they engaged in ordinary practices such as feeding birds; recalled encounters with visiting wildlife including foxes and hedgehogs; spoke of their efforts to attract pollinators; or lamented their battles with slugs and snails. For instance, one woman, Sandy, and I spent a substantial portion of a three-hour interview in her garden, searching her small pond for baby frogs. When at last she found one nestled under a leaf, Sandy was delighted. Addressing the frog tenderly – 'Oh, you little *darling!*' – she picked it up to show me. 'Now you know why I'm absolutely *enraptured* by them!' she said. 'They're like little jewels, they are *adorable* aren't they? So small and so delicate.' And Sandy and I

**9.2** Encountering tiny frogs in a garden tour

took turns holding the creature for some time, both of us marvelling aloud at its tininess (see Figure 9.2) In other cases, living room windows allowed a full view of the back garden, and interviewees frequently drew my attention to visiting birds, so that we could watch them together, often joining to express delight at their behaviour (for further discussion on in-situ interview methods see Stoodley, this collection).

It was striking that much of what people wished to say about their relations with animals was not easily expressed in words. And, as illustrated in Sandy's interview, it was often the case that I joined with participants in long periods of silent (or largely wordless) contemplation or laughter. As people recalled experiences of delight, enchantment and wonderment in their engagements with animals, their talk was peppered with sighs, gasps or softened voices (murmuring as if the moment being recounted were itself as fragile as a tiny creature). Talk of distressing experiences was characterised by cracking voices, silence or even tears, underlining how those experiences also pushed at the limits of language. Such moments illustrate how the 'realm of embodied social life that operates outside of talk' (Back, 2007: 95) is part of everyday experience, but perhaps especially so in relations with animals, who are themselves non-verbal. I found it essential to annotate interview transcripts (that might otherwise show only silence or laughter) with detailed descriptions of wordless interactions, and notes about these non-verbal expressions (see also Crang and Cook, 2007: 82ff.; Hockey and Forsey, 2012).

There were other ways, though, in which listening out for something 'more' than the ostensible talk of the interview was useful. In several cases, people interrupted the interviews in order to tell other household members something interesting that they had remembered – that they'd recently seen a frog or unusual bird in the garden (in one case, for instance, a starling with only one leg). Conceptualising such comments as 'data' rather than 'interruptions' means they can also offer an important glimpse of the mundane (see also Hockey and Forsey, 2012; Mason and Tipper, 2014). Increasingly, it became clear that these comments *mattered* – everyday social life is punctuated with fleeting moments where people orient to creatures and remark with passing wonderment at their presence. They are a small way in which animals are woven into the texture of everyday domestic life.

It was also interesting that interviewees often spoke at length about encounters with animals which had been profoundly moving, yet wrapped up such stories with a dismissive joke. One woman, Belinda, gave a detailed recollection of caring for orphaned baby blackbirds in her garden was followed by a quip that such concern was ridiculous and made her 'sound like a silly old lady'. Similarly, Sandy tenderly recalled how she had carefully kept a chrysalis until it hatched into a moth and then had released the creature one night, before laughing and commenting that it was 'probably eaten by a bat' immediately afterwards. It was tempting to see the detailed stories as the 'real' account, and the subsequent joke as an aside, even an irrelevancy, but I came to see that such jokes were a crucial part of the way people spoke about their engagements – employing irony and humour as they explored what it meant to care about animal lives, implicitly asking how seriously it is possible to think about such care.

As can be the case in interviews, talk often strayed from the purported topic (e.g. Crang and Cook, 2007: 71). For example, one woman, Frances, was a widow in her eighties. She spoke readily about the pleasure she took in feeding garden birds (and her angst about

squirrels who pilfered the birdseed). But much of the interview concerned the recent loss of her husband. Frances wept as she recalled his
death and told me how lonely she often felt – isolated in her home
with very little social engagement. Seeing the interviews less as a
means for 'extracting' data from participants, and more as a human
encounter characterised by the interviewer's 'welcoming disposition,
which leads one to make the respondent's problems one's own … a
sort of *intellectual love*' (Bourdieu, cited in Back, 2007: 94–95), I did
not try to redirect Frances (or two other widowed interviewees who
similarly spoke at length about their bereavement). Nevertheless, I
could often draw links between these apparent digressions and my
research interests; it became unsettlingly clear that in the absence of
human relationships, everyday sociability with garden wildlife often
took on an increased significance and meaning.

But it was not only in interviews that an attention to these 'overheard' elements mattered. As I have suggested above, my participant
observation yielded useful data from almost incidental observations
– my chance encounters with the cat who subsequently died; and my
engagements with geese, which occurred as I simply spent time in
the park alongside other people who happened to be in the same place
at the same time.

In fact, much of my participant observation had a similar sidelong
character – an attention to things noticed in passing. For example,
I wrote (and analysed) a lengthy fieldnote after I happened upon a
mother duck and string of ducklings using a zebra crossing to traverse
a road – the incident attracted the attention of many passers-by, laughing and commenting to one other. It illuminated the everyday delight
and hilarity of ordinary human–animal encounters, and how a shared
attention to creatures sometimes mediated social interaction between
strangers. Such moments were crucial for understanding mundane
encounters with animals, but could not have been sensibly explored in
other ways; they were quintessentially fleeting – it would have seemed
bizarre, even unnerving, had I approached these people to interrogate
them in more detail about their reactions, or asked to tape record them.

## Cultivating an art of eavesdropping

My interest in the tangential and incidental – in both observations
and interviews – certainly resonates with Les Back's (2007: 8) call for
an attention to 'the background and half-muted'. However, through

the course of my research, I came to feel that not only was I practising an art of listening but, equally, cultivating an 'art of eavesdropping' – an alertness to things overheard or observed in passing.

Eavesdropping is, admittedly, a controversial metaphor for social research (too close, perhaps, to the characterisation of researchers as deceptive spies, for example Spicker, 2011). Eavesdropping, at its worst, is unethical and dangerous – the eavesdropper snoops, hearing things not intended for their ears that have the potential to damage and upset both the listener and others. Although my own everyday eavesdropping was not (I hope) as risky as this, I think it offers a productive (and perhaps provocative) metaphor for research. As Van Maanen (2011) notes, metaphors can be an excellent way of expressing what exactly an ethnographer *does*. Framing mundane ethnography as a kind of eavesdropping is, I suggest, a useful way of articulating how everyday ethnography can (and perhaps *should*) be somewhat happenstance, surprising and even occasionally uncomfortable.

Ethnographers traditionally value the rich, slow understanding that accrues from extended time in the field, and qualitative interview questions often seek in-depth, detailed accounts of the interviewee's experiences. However, an art of eavesdropping emphasises a distinctive kind of ethnographic temporality. It foregrounds those experiences and expressions which are necessarily momentary and fleeting, which can only ever be glimpsed (see also Tipper, 2013). The philosopher Friedrich Nietzsche wrote evocatively on this point:

> [D]oes a matter necessarily remain ununderstood and unfathomed merely because it has been touched only in flight, glanced at, in a flash? Is it absolutely imperative that one settles down on it? That one has brooded over it as over an egg? ... At least there are truths that are singularly shy and ticklish and cannot be caught except suddenly – that must be surprised or left alone. (Nietzsche, cited in Pearson and Large, 2006: 382)

As I have explored here, in some cases brief or suggestive responses are all that can be said about certain experiences (which must be, as Nietzsche says, 'surprised or left alone'). Some encounters cannot be *better* accessed through in-depth and focused discussion, and must be instead 'touched only in flight, glanced at, in a flash'. Framing mundane research as a kind of eavesdropping foregrounds such 'shy and ticklish' truths – those aspects of social life that are inherently fleeting. It acknowledges that the edges, the outskirts and the tangential are, in fact, often *central* to understanding everyday life.

## Doing everyday ethnographies: perils and possibilities

As I have suggested, my methodological approach evolved through the course of the research as I developed an understanding of my research questions and a sense of where useful data might be found. The method that I ended up with – a neighbourhood ethnography embedded in both public and domestic space, employing and custom-ising a range of established methods – allowed me to develop a deep appreciation of people's ordinary interspecies encounters.

However, not all aspects of the research were entirely 'successful'. For instance, although the garden tours enabled rich discussions, in some cases they were less productive. I interviewed one man, Pat, who savoured the moment in his day when he would return home from work and sit in his back garden with a cup of tea, feeding and watching the birds. When I asked him more about this, Pat simply made me a cup of tea and sent me into his garden for ten minutes to watch the birds myself (while he returned indoors to watch a televised golf tournament). Although I could rationalise this as an opportunity to gain embodied experience of Pat's everyday habits and routines, sitting alone outside – while my 'interviewee' watched TV – certainly made me question my efficacy as an 'interviewer'! When we resumed the interview, however, Pat was articulate about his concern and interest in birds – a reminder that abandoning traditional qualitative interviews in favour of more creative formats is not always necessary or desirable.

Ethnographic research is often an intensive exercise. The kind of insights I sought – through reflective immersion and close attention to people's accounts – generated vast amounts of data and required sustained emotional and intellectual effort. This was intensified by my (developing) interest in the fleeting and incidental – I annotated interview transcripts with non-verbal, interactional details (including comments made before and after the interview), and even momentary public encounters could result in pages of in-depth fieldnotes. Manag-ing and analysing such data is time consuming. And doing justice to it in a finished report is challenging: 'thick' descriptions that 'bring to life the people we work with and listen to' (Back, 2007: 17) require detailed, crafted writing that contextualises and evokes those people's lives and words.

This intensity also had an emotional dimension (as qualitative research often does, for example Hockey, 2002). Even now, years later, some moments still haunt me: the encounter with the woman and the guard dog; the overwhelming grief of Frances (and two other widowed interviewees) whose accounts of everyday encounters with animals were interwoven with still-raw grief at the loss of their spouses. As I discussed, sometimes these confidences informed my understanding of the questions I had set out to answer, but this still remains problematic – did lonely interviewees who opened up to my 'welcoming disposition' really imagine that I would utilise everything they said to me? Like the other forms of 'eavesdropping' that I have discussed, it raises the question of how researchers can use such incidental data. The woman feeding the guard dog, for instance, had no idea that I would write about our encounter. And, although seemingly innocuous, the kind of sidelong observations in public space that informed my understandings could equally be seen as research on people not aware they were being researched.

Paul Spicker (2011) distinguishes between covert research (where a researcher does not identify themselves) and actively *deceptive* research. Undisclosed research in public places is covert, but not as ethically problematic as research which intentionally misleads or deceives. And, since the public sphere is already publicly accessible, it could be argued that researching it raises no particular ethical questions. All the same, even public interactions can be blurry – although my passing encounter with the woman feeding the guard dog occurred in public, her emotional confession brought us into much more personal and intimate relationship.

Ultimately, attending to what is overheard (either in public or in interviews) is necessarily complex. I did embrace this data, but I also sought to minimise any harm to participants, and to take seriously the responsibility to write about people's lives and words carefully and respectfully. Although an art of eavesdropping might open our eyes and ears to whole dimensions of the everyday, it also embroils the researcher in complex, unfinished ethical relations that need to be scrutinised anew with each fresh interaction.

Mindful of these corollaries, this kind of ethnographic research has potential to explore many other aspects of everyday life. Centrally, I have suggested that a neighbourhood ethnography can capture phenomena *not necessarily thought of as neighbourhood-specific*. By focusing on the quotidian life of a locality which seems unremarkable, we might begin to access what is 'everyday' about a phenomenon.

## Box 9.1: Training, tools and equipment

- Ethnographic research does not require extensive equipment. Beyond a notebook and pen, a camera may be useful (photographs can be used to supplement the final text and to trigger memories of incidental and sensory details).
- While it is standard practice to record qualitative interviews, ethnographers do not necessarily record participant observations (although Duneier (2000: 339) argues that recording *all* interactions gives a valuable verbatim record and, I'd suggest, may even capture subtleties that an ethnographer does not notice in the moment). In either case, careful transcription is crucial – rather than outsourcing this job, a researcher may benefit from transcribing recordings themselves, annotating them with subtle details such as non-verbal aspects of interactions, as well as comments or jokes made before and after the recording.
- If observations are not recorded, perfecting the practice of ethnographic note taking is important. Emerson, Fretz and Shaw (1998) offer a comprehensive overview of the skills and process of taking initial 'jottings' (of basic phrases or events), expanding them into fuller accounts with rich details and reflections, and fusing these fieldnotes with 'analytic memos', as the researcher develops and refines their emerging theories.

The ordinary meaning of encounters with other non-human elements of a neighbourhood (such as the built environment, plants, weather or changing seasons) might also be understood by exploring how these are layered through the routines, habits and spaces of everyday neighbourhood life; in talk and encounters in homes and gardens; in discussions in local media; in the ways they are addressed by the local council; as part of everyday movement through the locality; and even in passing engagement and conversations with strangers on these topics. Even the experience of more abstract concepts – from happiness to conflict – could be explored as they are experienced in these everyday modes and spaces. More generally, an 'art of eavesdropping' might provide a conceptual tool that could inform research on the everyday experience of many issues (including classic sociological areas of concern such as gender, class, race or political identity) by focusing not only on what is said, but also on what is found *only* in jokes, asides, fragments of casual talk, fleeting comments and other oblique and unintentional data.

## Conclusion

I have argued that a locality-based ethnography that draws in the researcher's own ordinary life, and where there is no reason to expect the issue will be especially remarkable, is a good way to explore a research question. Following a question through the day-to-day life of people in a particular neighbourhood offers one way to think about its everyday manifestation.

This kind of everyday ethnography relies largely on well-established methods and tools, although they may be customised to develop an attention to ordinary things. This attention to the ordinary might involve rethinking exactly what constitutes data, and where we might find it. And, I have suggested, 'eavesdropping' offers an apt and useful (albeit slippery) metaphor for conceptualising the sort of attention that listens out for the mundane. Finding the everyday is, in part, about locating what is often overlooked, and perhaps can *only* be overheard.

Ethnography that is intimately 'at home' and reflexive is a potentially demanding task for a researcher, but the mundane experience of such everyday research might bring remarkable moments of dazzling insight where a familiar world takes on entirely new dimensions.

---

### Box 9.2: Further reading

Crang and Cook's *Doing Ethnographies* (London: Sage, 2007) is an excellent guide to all aspects of ethnographic research. Emerson, Fretz and Shaw's *Writing Ethnographic Fieldnotes* (Chicago: University of Chicago Pressaw, 1998) offers detailed, practical information about how to produce and work with fieldnotes.

Paul Spicker's 'Ethical covert research' (*Sociology*, 45 (1): 118–133, 2011) is a good starting point for thinking about the complexities of undisclosed ethnography.

Les Back's *Art of Listening* (Oxford: Berg, 2007) is an invaluable resource for social scientists conducting reflexive, attentive ethnographic research into everyday life.

## Notes

1 The term 'non-human animals' is preferred by some writers, since humans are, of course, also animals. Although mindful of this, I find 'animals' and 'creatures' less cumbersome, and use these terms interchangeably to refer to the range of non-human animals discussed in this study.

2 This research was undertaken for a PhD in sociology at the University of Manchester between 2006 and 2012, and was funded by an ESRC (Economic and Social Research Council) Quota Award (031–2006–00394).

## References

Back, L. (2007) *The Art of Listening*, Oxford: Berg.

Coffey, A. (1999) *The Ethnographic Self*, London: Sage.

Crang, M. and Cook, I. (2007) *Doing Ethnographies*, London: Sage.

Cudworth, E. (2011) *Social Lives with Other Animals: Tales of Sex, Death and Love*, Basingstoke: Palgrave Macmillan.

Davies, C. A. (2008) *Reflexive Ethnography: A Guide to Researching Selves and Others*, London: Routledge.

Davies, K. (2011) 'Knocking on doors: recruitment and enrichment in a qualitative interview based study', *International Journal of Social Research Methodology*, 14 (4): 289–300.

Duneier, M. (2000) *Sidewalk*, New York: Farrar, Strauss and Giroux.

Emerson, R., Fretz, R. and Shaw, L. (1998) *Writing Ethnographic Fieldnotes*, Chicago: University of Chicago Press.

Felski, R. (1999) 'The invention of everyday life', *New Formations*, 39: 13–31.

Geertz, C. (1993 [1973]) *The Interpretation of Cultures*, London: Fontana.

Hammersley, M. and Atkinson, P. (2007) *Ethnography: Principles in Practice*, Abingdon: Routledge.

Hockey, J. (2002) 'Interviews in ethnography? Disembodied social interaction in Britain', in N. Rapport (ed.) *British Subjects: An Anthropology of Britain*, Oxford: Berg, 209–222.

Hockey, J. and Forsey, M. (2012) 'Ethnography is not participant observation: reflections on the interview as participatory qualitative research', in J. Skinner (ed.) *The Interview: An Ethnographic Approach*, New York: Berg, 69–87.

Ingold, T. and Vergunst, J. L. (eds) (2016) *Ways of Walking: Ethnography and Practice on Foot*, London: Routledge.

Jerolmack, C. (2009) 'Humans, animals, and play: theorizing interaction when intersubjectivity is problematic', *Sociological Theory*, 27 (4): 371–389.

Levey, H. (2009) 'Which one is yours? Children and ethnography', *Qualitative Sociology*, 32 (3): 311–331.

Mason, J. and Tipper, B. (2014) 'Children as family members' in G. Melton, A. Ben-Arieh, J. Cashmore, G. Goodman and N. Worley (eds), *The SAGE Handbook of Child Research*, London: Sage, 153–168.

Miller, D. (1998) *A Theory of Shopping*, Cambridge: Polity Press.

Miller, D. (2008) *The Comfort of Things*, Cambridge: Polity Press.

Pearson, K. and Large, D. (eds) (2006) *The Nietzsche Reader*, Oxford: Blackwell.

Pink, S. (2004) *Home Truths: Gender, Domestic Objects and Everyday Life*, Oxford: Berg.

Ross, N., Renold, E., Holland, S. and Hillman, A. (2009) 'Moving stories: using mobile methods to explore the everyday lives of young people in public care', *Qualitative Research*, 9 (5): 605–623.

Spicker, P. (2011) 'Ethical covert research', *Sociology*, 45 (1): 118–133.

Stewart, K. (2007) *Ordinary Affects*, London: Duke University Press.

Tipper, B. (2012) *Creaturely Encounters: An Ethnographic Study of Human–Animal Relations in a British Suburban Neighbourhood*. Unpublished PhD thesis, University of Manchester.

Tipper, B. (2013) 'Moments of being and ordinary human–animal encounters', *Virginia Woolf Miscellany*, 84: 14–16.

Tipper, B. (2016) 'On cats and contradictions: mourning animal death in an English community', in M. DeMello (ed.) *Mourning Animals*, East Lansing, MI: Michigan State University Press, 91–100.

Van Maanen, J. (2011) *Tales of the Field: On Writing Ethnography* (2nd edn), Chicago and London: Chicago University Press.

# 10

# Smell walking and mapping

## Chris Perkins and Kate McLean

### Introducing the aroma

Smell offers a ubiquitous and powerful way to make sense of the world and strongly underpins social hierarchies, working as a key cue in social bonding. Smells also have a strong cultural resonance. They take on different meanings in different contexts, changing over time and across cultures. The perception of smells powerfully evokes memories of experiences and emotions associated with events. As such, smell is inevitably mundane, quotidian and central to life.

However, smell as a sense is largely taken for granted and as such is under-analysed. Artistic practice has privileged vision over smell (Drobnick, 2002). To date most research on smell has been scientific and technical, focusing on psychological aspects of the sensory modality, or the neuroscience of perception, or the utility of scent development and commodification. As such, olfactometers can be deployed to measure environmental odours and pollution monitoring can be carried out. But for most people smells can be difficult to research: they are discontinuous, intangible, ephemeral or episodic. They can be pleasant as well as a nuisance. Smells are ingested: volatile molecules are inhaled and processed by the limbic system in the brain, whereas a landscape that is seen can be framed as separate from our corporeal being and as such more subject to reason. So, perceptions of smell are emotional, subjective and more separate from cognition, which makes them challenging to deploy in our methodological toolkits. Just as modern society has become increasingly sanitised, with smell kept in its undervalued place, so has research tended to underplay the multiple social, cultural and *geographical* roles that smell can play. Sight allows fixed perceptions of the world to emerge, be mapped and shared but the more mutable, contingent and ambiguous qualities of smell present interesting challenges for researchers.

It is these challenges involving juxtapositions of vision and smell that form the focus of this chapter. The geographies wrapped up with smell relate to our everyday experiences and the mapping of these perceptions and their affects has great potential for revealing hitherto unseen social and cultural norms. The mundane can become extraordinary when designers translate what Porteous (1985) called the 'smellscape' into visual forms and share these with others. Mapping offers a method that is particularly appropriate for achieving this. Maps have historically usually fixed the ambiguous or ephemeral, tying down meanings and freezing time and allowing a shared worldview to emerge as a rational working tool. However, recent technological and epistemological change has encouraged a focus on more performative and narrative qualities of the form (Perkins, 2009). So, the time is appropriate for increased encounters and translations between smell and maps (for further discussion on encounters see Tipper, this collection).

This chapter examines some of the background and ways in which artists, designers and researchers have enacted these encounters and translated between sensory modalities. It explores the challenges of smell-mapping practice. It charts some of the practical fashions in which smell mapping might be enacted, focusing upon different temporalities associated with our smellscapes, and in particular on ways of carrying out a smell walk and mapping smell. It documents the potential of different technologies and mobilities for attending to smell, highlighting different kinds of smell walking (other sensory forms of walking interviews are discussed by Rose, this collection). The links between smell and other sensory geographies are explored. In so doing, this chapter argues for a multi-sensorial turn in mundane methods.

## The background to smelly mapping methods

In a ground-breaking review Porteous (1985) highlighted the marginalisation of senses other than vision and first developed the notion of the smellscape as a scaled, subjective assemblage of olfaction, people, contexts, histories and geographies; the olfactory equivalent of a landscape or soundscape. He flagged up the need for real-world investigation of smellscapes through what he termed 'smell walks', as against laboratory-based investigations. In the last decade of the twentieth century and the first two decades of the new millennium researchers have increasingly addressed the everyday aspects of smells in society and culture. Sensory studies has emerged in this period as an important cross-disciplinary field of interest to disciplines across the social sciences and humanities, with the journal *Senses and Society* available from 2006. Smelly research is much more on the agenda in 2019, with overview monographs in cultural history (Classen, Howes and Synnott, 1994); sociology (Low, 2008); social anthropology (Drobnick, 2006); and urban design (Henshaw, 2014) now situating smell in relation to their different concerns. Henshaw et al.'s (2017) collection drew authors from fields as diverse as museum curating, artistic practice, archaeology, history, landscape design, geography, psychology, literary studies, organisation studies, environmental management and education. Across these fields researchers are increasingly exploring the relations of smell to place.

However, this focus on smell has only rarely generated novel methods. Sarah Pink's (2015) overview of sensory methods charts a very wide variety of methodological innovations in everyday geographies. But her consideration of smell is very much in terms of its potential to elicit participation in conventional ethnographic methodologies. It is certainly true that most methodological work with smell focuses on environmental monitoring of odours or air quality, as part of strategies to manage nuisance, and are very much the domain of environmental consultancies and specialist technical equipment. Social scientific methods charted by Pink do incorporate smell into interviews, or focus groups, but do not directly attend to smell. By way of contrast to technical assessments, or smells' subsidiary role in other ethnographic approaches, this chapter focuses upon the creative deployment of mapping as a mobile method, building on Porteous's original suggestion and Henshaw's (2014) development of the concept, and drawing in particular on the work of one of the authors, sensory designer Kate McLean.

Mapping as a process begins with the planning of a strategy, incorporating thinking as well as doing. It reflects a research design relating to collecting information to be mapped and decisions about what and how to map. The mapping helps navigation, or is used to administer and control, or it focuses on distributions and relationships, or on a specific aspect of a place. It might map out a view of the past, imagine a future or chart something happening now. It might be an information source or serve as part of persuasive narrative. Maps can stand on their own right or be designed as part of a wider assemblage. They can serve as part of a neutral discourse or be strongly crafted to evoke particular emotional responses about a place as an artwork, a promotional device or as tools in a subversive protest. The poetics of a design come together with a political context. Mapping has historically been associated with facts, with best practice in cartographic enterprise and with the power of the nation state. But the aesthetics of mapping highlight interpretive and subjective qualities, and at the same time mapping also reflects and enrols people as a social practice. Mapping technology has profoundly impacted practice. Digital developments and the social network have removed past certainties and opened new opportunities for anyone wishing to map, arguably democratising the medium.

In the light of this complexity it makes sense to recognise that smell mapping becomes a performance that changes depending on the stage of mapping. On the one hand, it might involve the synthesising of smells – as in the work of Sissel Tolaas, who incorporates distilled essences of mundane smellscapes into exhibition spaces, such as in her 2012 work SmellScape KCK/KCMO (Lockard, 2013). On the other hand, there are published maps of smellscapes that seek to depict the olfactory environment by translating smell into visual equivalents. The history of publication of this kind of mapping has until recently focused upon the final stages of the process – the design of a map to depict a smellscape. Among design challenges that have to be addressed are how to classify smells, how to represent their intensity and how to deal with the transience of the smellscape. There is no published consensus on any of these issues but some of the practical issues relating to these design concerns are explored in more detail in the next section. Three methodological innovations have been significant in recent smell mapping.

The nature of data collection has changed in profound ways as a result of the capacity of social networking to crowdsource the collection of smells. Big data can be repurposed to map the smellscape.

Quercia et al. (2015) highlight this potential in their discussion of the scraping and subsequent mapping of geo-referenced picture tags from Flickr and Instagram and geo-referenced tweets from Twitter, and argue that this can allow an upscaling of data collection. The researchers derived a tenfold classification of smell tags, across two test data sets relating to the cities of Barcelona and London. Thus it became possible to map the base notes of smell for different cities: Barcelona was characterised by smells relating to food and nature, whereas London was represented predominantly by smells relating to traffic emissions and waste. The mid-level notes of the smellscape, with a finer spatial definition, can be displayed as heat maps in a mash-up against a map of the street segments to which the terms might apply. Borough Market in London is associated with high scores in posts relating to the twenty-four-hour city, with the smells of leisure and entertainment dominating. By way of contrast, high levels of posts relating to pollution cluster along significant roads across the capital.

Another data collection technology that is profoundly impacting smell collection is potentially driven by using mobile devices and customised apps to automate the smell-mapping production process. Apps such as Smell PGH allow posts about local perceptions of unpleasant smells. Prototypes of several different systems have already been designed to extend this idea to the wider range of smells, including the Smellscaper App from Kate McLean, which automates the smell-noting process described below.

Digital mapping also allows many different subsequent aspects of the mapping process to be automated. The fixed framing of the hard copy map is no longer a constraint. The angle of view onto a smell map can be altered, to convey different impressions of the data. McLean (2018) reports on changing the viewing angle in an animated smell map of Pamplona. A bird's-eye and top-down perspective (referred to as planimetric) allows the appearance of a smell to be charted. A view from above, at 45 degrees (known as an isometric perspective), allows dissemination of smells in the wind to be charted and maps changing durational perceptions of the smellscape. And a more immersive angle of view, moving through a smellscape in a horizontal fashion, charts the volatisation of smells as a person encounters an aroma that subsequently disappears. The technology enacting the display alters the impression. Models of smells diffusing can be simulated in exhibition displays. Digital animation can convey durational qualities of the smellscape. Display technology alters the interaction that might be possible. A map on a mobile device affords readers with many tasks that are beyond the fixed paper maps, such as panning, zooming and moving as the device itself moves through the smellscape, but even though the display may be egocentric, with the map moving as the reader moves, overview is limited by the screen size of the display.

So, the design choices around the mapping of smell are complex and dictated by contextual factors such as the environment, the temporality of the smellscape, the nature of mapping technologies, the desired impression for reading, and more pragmatic issues such as medium of dissemination and resources available to the designer or researcher.

## Smell walking and mapping in practice

This section explores some of the key practical issues that underpin mapping out smells, drawing on Kate McLean's artistic practice. Smell mapping entails many different activities: collecting smells, classifying them, representing them in mapped form and then displaying a map in different contexts. At each of these stages different configurations are possible and we highlight below the potential of smell walking as a data collection strategy; practices of map design; the multiple views of the smellscape that can be made; and the exhibition contexts in which smell maps have been displayed.

It has been argued that the smell walk is an essential initial step in the mapping of the smellscape which can serve as a useful real-world strategy for collecting sensory perceptions about a place (Porteous, 1985). It is now widely accepted that smell walking offers an active, researcher led, embodied methodology with the capacity to attend to more than vision and more than representation (for further embodied methods see Hall et al., Collins, and Tipper, this collection). Best practice in smell walking very much depends upon the kind of smell walk that is undertaken and McLean (2019) describes five different variations, according to the number of participants, the degree of expert participation and the use of different data collection technologies: she identifies the solo walk, the group walk, the buddy walk, the 'smellfie' and the app walk. Buddy walks enrol a local expert who knows the smellscape and is able to lead the researcher to the best locations. App walks deploy digital technology, instead of printed forms, to record smell notes. Smellfie walks are a kit that may be used by anyone to set up a smell walk instead of relying on a guided approach.

Between July 2011 and August 2018 133 different smell walks enrolling around 1,200 participants were led by one of the authors of this chapter as part of her ongoing doctoral research (McLean, 2019). The majority of these took place in urban contexts, where smell diversity might be expected to be greater because of the greater diversity of human activities, and in European or North American cities. Early walks were solo and during this process McLean developed best practice methods for different stages of the activity. In part they were a learning process for the researcher and changes in walking strategy reflected learning from failure. For example designing and using technology in app walks was initially very appealing, but this kind of walk was largely abandoned after 2017. This was mainly because using a mobile device to record smells distanced walkers from the world by demanding attention be given to the screen, and the app also discouraged discussion (for further walking-based methods see Rose, this collection).

Indeed discussion emerged as important in the process and the group walk has been the most common form of smell walking – ninety-five of the walks have deployed this format. Group walks allow the researcher to enrol many noses as sensors, and cover a much wider area, but also bring together sometimes-contested views of the smellscape. Practical advice about smell walking is described in the next section.

The design of mapping produced during this sensory work always uniquely reflects the particular smellscape. Practice usually takes many people's perceptions and translates these into maps – so the mapping is predominantly an artistic and phenomenological recounting of multiple sensory experiences, a creative re-mapping that speaks to aspects of a unique place experienced at a particular time.

The maps emerge from a wide variety of smells accumulated during smell walks. Smells are classified from perceptions during the smell walking. The Amsterdam map identifies 11 smells distilled from 650 smell perceptions. These classifications frequently evoke different notions of place, and do not always conform to expected stereotypes. Thus *SmellMap Amsterdam* does not record cannabis, which was only noticed in a few neighbourhoods, but instead more frequently records waffles, spicy food, floral scents, coffee and old books, set against the damp and all-pervading base notes of the canals (McLean, 2017). In other contexts a very different coded range of smells might be mapped.

In the Newport, Rhode Island map, for example, maritime smells dominate, whereas the 'scent mapping' of Singapore – so designated because of funding – reflects much more of an emphasis on food.

Many of these maps are designed in a consistent style, characterised by colour-coded points indicating where smells were perceived, alongside concentric circles denoting potential dispersal from these sources. Perceived smell intensity and wind strength and direction come together in the characteristic contoured patterns. The maps deploy pastel tones describing smells, which are set against restrained and frequently limited base information. The published maps do not capture the smellscape in a scientific way; instead they are akin to what landscape architect James Corner (1999) terms 'agentic mappings', emerging out of individual creative moments, but with the power to change perceptions of places. So, the published smell map becomes part of a narrative where the designer controls the final published output, while acknowledging the many noses that have come together in the process. These social or group perceptions of the smellscape are set against interpretation from the artist.

However, publication is only one of many aspects of mapping. Many of the maps are designed to facilitate the smelling process, such as route maps for a group smell walk. Or they exist as working diagrams, to be changed by the artist or researcher as the process crystallises. Some maps explicitly chart the dynamism of the smellscape, evoking aspects of the temporality of smell (McLean, Lammes and Perkins, 2018). They can indicate the duration of a smell, the tempo at which the smellscape changes, the sequence of encountering different smells and then losing them in the course of a walk, and the more rhythmic qualities of the smellscape. Mapping of Kyiv carried out by McLean in the winter of 2017 and emerging from group walks through the city, for example, highlights many different ways in which temporal qualities of the smellscape might be mapped out (McLean, 2019).

Published mapping is frequently displayed in exhibition spaces as part of a commissioned outcome. In some of these exhibitions maps serve as props to encourage participation from audiences. For example the Marais (Figure 10.1), Amsterdam and early Parisian maps (McLean, 2014) were exhibited alongside representative smells derived from natural and synthetic sources, and visitors to the exhibitions were encouraged to sniff the cases and at times to post their own reactions

**10.1**  Smellmap Le Marais (2018) exhibited at MAIF Social Club, rue de Turenne, Paris comprises two versions of the visual smell map on either side of a wall and sniffing bottles (hidden beneath a surface) containing essential oils and raw materials of the featured and mapped smells of bamboo, leather, painter's varnish, perfume, peach and wood

to the distillations against the visual representation of the smellscape, adding further layers to the complex exhibited assemblage.

Versions of the published mapping are also disseminated from the http://sensorymaps.com/ website. For the majority of the walks, however, mapping may not actually be created. So, the practicalities of smell walking and smell mapping very much depend on the priorities of researchers or practitioners deploying the method. We conclude this section by contrasting McLean's practice with research from different disciplines and contexts.

The strategy of smell walking and mapping can be deployed as part of many different inquiries in different kinds of spaces. The emotional correlates of smell strongly suggest that the technique has great potential in charting cultural geographies. It can be used by sociologists to map the spread of gentrification, for example by mapping out the distribution of beard oil and sourdough baking around markets in the east end of London (Rhys-Taylor, 2018). Historians can re-create past sensory geographies of cities, as evidenced for parts of Istanbul by Davis and Thys-Şenocak (2017). Smell can also be deployed as an active part of storytelling, to evoke emotional responses to place and unlock memories. But conversely it can also be used to chart the marketing of the city, highlighting ethnic districts which trade on the back of their smellscapes, as described, for example, by Henshaw (2014) in relation to Manchester's Chinatown. A more corporeal approach can document smell to explore the affect of the office as a place of work, as described by Riach and Warren (2015). Planners and landscape professionals can use smell walking as a means of investigating how a smellscape contributes to perceptions of pleasantness, such as in the work of Xiao, Tait and Kang (2018). The mapping of the smellscape can also directly contribute to multi-sensory urban and landscape design of urban greenspaces (Kang, Tait and Xiao, 2017). Smell walking and mapping can also be used in pedagogy, as part of student-led field investigations, focusing on the embodied and social practices through which we encounter places, but also on the methodological differences that stem from multi-sensory encounters (Phillips, 2015; Playful Mapping Collective, 2016).

So, a human-centred and graphic design-oriented creative mapping offers only one way in which smell walking and mapping might be deployed. The potential is there for a wider uptake, and for following best practice in deploying the method.

## Advice for others

Graphical ability, research skills and research questions strongly impact upon what might be best practice. However, in this section we focus on two key aspects: how to set up a successful smell walk, and how to design a smell map to convey perceptions of a smellscape to an appropriate audience. Kate McLean has provided a kit comprising guidance and inviting independent investigation by anyone using smell walks as a starting point for mapping the smellscape. This is supported by online documentation available at https://sensorymaps. com/wp-content/uploads/2015/10/Smellwalk_Intro_Kit_% C2%A9KateMcLean_2015.pdf As su and is accompanied by videos

## Box 10.1: Best practice in smell walking

| | |
|---|---|
| Phases and timing | Maximum forty-five minutes' walking time: nasal attention wanes<br>Start with smell catching<br>Then smell hunting<br>Then free smelling |
| Route | Anticipate appropriate variety of natural and synthetic smells to maintain interest. Provide a simple suggested route |
| Group size | Up to twelve people is ideal: if larger numbers then separate into sub-groups |
| Nose training and practice | Encourage discussion between group members after each stage is completed<br>Drink water to improve smell capability<br>Sniff own skin for relief to 'reset' nose |
| Smell notes | Introduce participants to deliver appropriate and consistent smell notes either in hard copy or in digital form<br>Record *location*: points but also lines and areas<br>Free text *naming* of smells<br>Numeric grading of perceived *intensity*<br>Numeric grading of perceived *duration*<br>Numeric grading of *affect*. Like / dislike<br>*Expectations* – expected or not<br>Free text association of *personal feelings* about smell |
| Post-walk discussion | Half an hour to discuss differences, trajectories and rhythms and to reflect on base notes of the smellscape with creative mapping exercise |

explaining the process of enacting a 'smellfie' (see https://vimeo.com/smellmap). This advice is summarised in Box 10.1.

Publicity is important for recruiting participants – a diverse group can work just as well as a narrowly defined demographic. Motivation is the most important factor in participation. Routes need careful selection, and should offer sufficient variety of natural and synthetic smells to keep the attention of participants, but walks should not last too long. Beyond forty-five minutes it becomes harder to maintain motivation to note smells, because of the unusual concentration required to attend to what our noses detect. Weather conditions strongly influence smellscapes: a windy day will disperse smells further from their sources; a humid and still day can enhance the richness of the smellscape; on a warm day walkers are likely to perceive different odours from those smelt during a cold walk. So, expect different outcomes on different days.

Setting up the walk is important. Material should be given out on which participants can record their reflections in the form of 'smell notes', and a mix of quantitative and qualitative evidence works best (see Box 10.1). In most cases this will involve manual note taking – but apps to automate procedures are likely to become more available. Be aware that use of an app focuses attention away from physically detecting smells. A map of the recommended route can also be provided for participants. Practical advice needs to be given, about risks, ethics and how to take smell notes. During the walk it is helpful to pay attention to three different kinds of smell:

- curious or unexpected smells that are short-lived, and which will be individually noted, such as perfume on a passer-by or woodwork being painted. In an analogy to perfumiers' use of smell, these volatile odours form the top notes of a smellscape;
- episodic elements of a smellscape reveal specific local areas of a town, such as the smell of fish from a market, or fried food from a takeaway – analogous to the middle notes; and
- background smells that form a context and a constant element in the smellscape, for example the residual smell of a brewery, or the dampness of a canal, which make up the base notes of the smell pyramid.

It is suggested that small groups work best – up to twelve people talking about the smells they encounter encourages creative social reflection and brings together different opinions about the smellscape. Individuals walking alone will miss smells, and larger group sizes can distract. Smell-walking practice is best enacted in different phases. Smell catching or passive smelling involves walking slowly through an area focusing on smell as the primary sense – breathing in deeply – and attending to the aromas that are encountered. This is a good strategy for starting a smell walk. A more active phase can then follow once participants have

**10.2** Smell walk participant holds her smell notes as she explores the Marais area of Paris, anticipating the potential smells of a recharging unit

got used to the process. Smell hunting involves seeking hidden smells, by using other senses to hunt them down, anticipating likely associations such as the smells around a litter bin, or taking action to make a smell, such as crushing leaves (Figure 10.2). Free smelling works well as the final phase of a smell walk, and keeps participants engaged in the process. A post-walk discussion offers a useful way to bring the experience to fruition, with talk starting from smell notes made during the walk. Smell sketching can also be a useful way for individuals to situate their own olfactory experience (for further discussion on sketching as a method see Heath and Chapman, this collection). Out of this shared group experience different individual perceptions of the smellscape

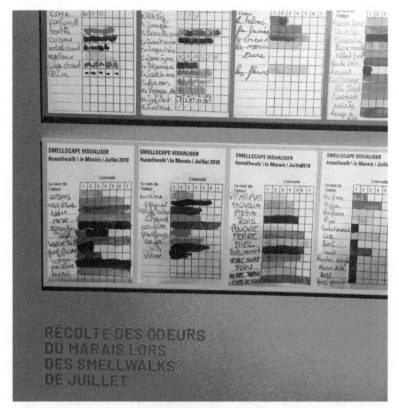

**10.3** Detail from 'Smell Harvest from the Marais during July Smellwalks' (2018)

emerge. The smellscape visualiser graphics shown in Figure 10.3 were completed by different smell walkers immediately following their smell walk and demonstrate this variety of individual perceptions of a shared route as well as similar smell experiences. Each walk is displayed as a horizontal set and the different colours deployed are a good way to creatively represent individual smell associations.

These smell-walking outcomes can be mapped by individual participants in a workshop or by the researcher coordinating the smell walks after the event. For a researcher with limited graphical skill it makes sense to work through the multiple visualisations documented at http://'maps. com/ so as to be aware of possibilities, but also to seek advice about

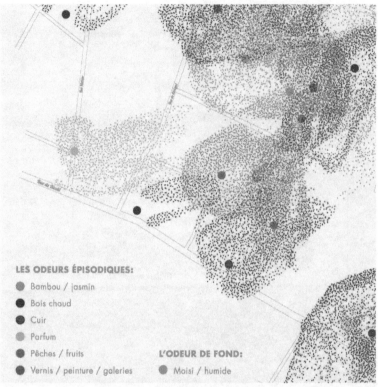

**10.4**　Detail from 'Smellmap: Le Marais' (2018)

graphic design in guides such as Perkins (2016) or Wood and Krygier
(2016). If in doubt keep the maps as simple as possible, using a graphic
variable such as colour hue to discriminate between different smells, and
making sure that an appropriate visual hierarchy is maintained with any
base information working as the ground to enhance interpretation of
the smells that serve as the figure. Figure 10.4 illustrates Kate McLean's
design practice and her clear use of the visual hierarchy of colour between
background and smells, as well as a systematic approach to icon design in
which a large dot indicates a smell source and smaller dots allude to scent
molecule dissipation in wind conditions noted on the days of the smell
walks. However, it is important to be very clear of the intended audience.
Think carefully about any mapping of change, and perhaps deploy jux-
taposition of multiple maps to convey impressions of mutability. Choose

a scale that is appropriate for the amount of detail. If exhibiting maps, make sure that the mapping clearly relates well to underpinning narratives of the research.

## Conclusions

By focusing attention onto our noses as against our eyes we can begin to notice the everyday information that they collect, and in so doing reassert the importance of senses beyond vision. Smell as something beyond cognition is a sense that speaks directly to a more embodied approach to mundane experience, and as such smell mapping can tell different stories about place from those narrated in methodologies more anchored to sound and vision. As such a more than representational appreciation of places and corporeal experience can usefully be informed by deploying smell mapping as a method.

In this chapter we have argued that the smell walk is a mobile method that offers a useful way of delivering smell mapping, generating a systematic and different appreciation of our everyday experiences. The smell walk, then, can generate different views of space; maps that focus on the intangible and ephemeral instead of the material and fixed (McLean, 2018). Making maps from the shared and contested experiences of smelly places can allow these qualities to be shared. A rigorous application of the methods described above shows the olfactory diversity that still survives and illustrates the importance of Porteous's (1985) argument for attending to the real-world qualities of the smellscape. It shows how smell can escape the specialist laboratories of the perfumier to become part of geographers' phenomenological methodological armoury. By following up on Henshaw's and McLean's work, and in particular the sources outlined in Box 10.2, a richer appreciation of everyday life becomes much more possible.

---

### Box 10.2: Further reading and useful resources

Henshaw, V. (2014) *Urban Smellscapes: Understanding and Designing City Smell Environments*, London: Routledge.

McLean, K. (2015) Smell walk introductory kit, www.sensorymaps.com/wp-content/.../10/Smellwalk_Intro_Kit_©KateMcLean_2015.pdf (accessed 27 September 2019).

The smellscape is taken for granted in our culture, but is itself a frequently unnoticed outcome of capitalist accumulation. As such, smell is a commodified part of a global system. Western cities are increasingly bland and inoffensive spaces in terms of their smells – a significant change from the richly offensive and diverse sensory experiences offered by these places in the past, and which still characterise slums and many parts of cities in the global South. So, a smell walk can become part of a political movement to reassert the importance of local diversity in our smellscapes, and the mapping of smells accumulated during smell walks can serve as a mechanism for telling different stories about these places, beyond the corporate blanding of global retail centres. By searching out olfactory difference and deploying maps to share this with others we can register the importance of a smell heritage that risks being marginalised. And by smell walking we can make our methodologies more like embodied real life.

## Bibliography

Classen, C., Howes, D. and Synnott, A. (1994) *Aroma: The Cultural History of Smell*, London: Taylor & Francis.

Corner, J. (1999) 'The agency of mapping: speculation, critique and invention', in D. Cosgrove (ed.) *Mappings*, London: Reaktion Books, 213–251.

Davis, L. and Thys-Şenocak, L. (2017) 'Heritage and scent: research and exhibition of Istanbul's changing smellscapes', *International Journal of Heritage Studies*, 23 (8): 723–741.

Drobnick, J. (2002) 'Toposmia: art, scent, and interrogations of spatiality', *Angelaki: Journal of Theoretical Humanities*, 7 (1): 31–47.

Drobnick, J. (2006) *The Smell Culture Reader*, Oxford and New York: Berg.

Henshaw, V. (2014) *Urban Smellscapes: Understanding and Designing City Smell Environments*, London: Routledge.

Henshaw, V., McLean, K., Medway, D., Perkins, C. and Warnaby, G. (2017) *Designing with Smell: Practices, Techniques and Challenges*, London: Routledge.

Kang, J., Tait, M. and Xiao, J. (2017) 'The design of urban smellscapes with fragrant plants and water features', in V. Henshaw, K. McLean, D. Medway, C. Perkins and G. Warnaby (eds) *Designing with Smell*, London: Routledge, 83–95.

Lockard, B. (2013) 'Sissel Tolaas, SmellScape KCK/KCMO', *Senses and Society*, 8 (2): 245–250.

Low, K. E. Y. (2008) *Scent and Scent-sibilities: Smell and Everyday Life Experiences*, Cambridge: Cambridge Scholars Publishing.

McLean, K. (2014) 'smellfie kit', available at https://sensorymaps.com/wp-content/uploads/2015/10/Smellwalk_Intro_Kit_%C2%A9KateMcLean_2015.pdf (accessed 19 February 2020).

McLean, K. (2017) 'Smellmap: Amsterdam – olfactory art and smell visualization', *Leonardo*, 50 (1): 92–93.

McLean, K. (2018) 'Mapping the invisible and ephemera', in A. J. Kent and P. Vujakovic (eds) *The Routledge Handbook of Mapping and Cartography*, London: Routledge, 509–515.

McLean, K. (2019) *Nose First: Practices of Smellwalking and Smellscape Mapping*. PhD thesis, Royal College of Art, London.

McLean, K., Lammes, S. and Perkins, C. (2018) 'Mapping the quixotic volatility of smellscapes: a trialogue-interview with Kate McLean', in S. Lammes, C. Perkins, A. Gekker, S. Hind, C. Wilmott and D. Evans (eds) *Time for Mapping*, Manchester: MUP, 50–90.

Perkins, C. (2009) 'Performative and embodied mapping', in N. Kitchin and R. Thrift (eds) *International Encyclopaedia of Human Geography*, London: Elsevier, 126–132.

Perkins, C. (2016) 'Mapping and graphicacy', in N. Clifford, M. Cope, S. French and G. Valentine (eds) *Key Methods in Geography* (3rd edn), London: Sage, 598–619.

Phillips, R. (2015) 'Playful and multi-sensory fieldwork: seeing, hearing and touching New York', *Journal of Geography in Higher Education*, 39 (4): 617–629.

Pink, S. (2015) *Doing Sensory Ethnography* (2nd edn), London: Sage.

Playful Mapping Collective (2016) *Playful Mapping: Playing with Maps in Contemporary Media Cultures*, Amsterdam: Institute of Network Cultures, http://networkcultures.org/wp-content/uploads/2016/12/PlayfulMappingInTheDigitalAge.pdf (accessed 27 September 2019).

Porteous, J. D. (1985) 'Smellscape', *Progress in Human Geography*, 9 (3): 356–378.

Quercia, D., Schifanella, R., Aiello, L. M. and McLean, K. (2015) 'Smelly maps: the digital life of urban smellscapes', *International AAAI Conference on Web and Social Media (ICWSM)*, Oxford, 26–29 May.

Rhys-Taylor, A. (2018) 'Coming to our senses: multiculturalism, urban sociology and "the other" senses', in S. Nichols and S. Dobson (eds) *Learning Cities: Multimodal Explorations and Placed Pedagogies*, Singapore: Springer Singapore, 23–36.

Riach, K. and Warren, S. (2015) 'Smell organization: bodies and corporeal porosity in office work', *Human Relations*, 68 (5): 789–809.

Wood, D. and Krygier, J. B. (2016) *Making Maps: A Visual Guide to Map Design for GIS* (3rd edn), New York: Guilford Press.

Xiao, J., Tait, M. and Kang, J. (2018) 'A perceptual model of smellscape pleasantness', *Cities*, 76: 105–115.

# 11

# Auto-ethnography: managing multiple embodiments in the life drawing class

Rebecca Collins

## Introduction

There has been growing interest in the role of sketching, drawing and other forms of artistic and/or creative practice as a research method within (and beyond) the social sciences (see also Heath and Chapman, this collection). As a geographer (and a lapsed art historian) my interest lies in how artistic, craft-based and creative practices can be used to investigate, express and (re)construct spatial experience and understanding (see, among others, Bain, 2004; Banfield, 2016; Hawkins, 2011, 2012). Such practices are often seen as particularly useful at engendering the slow contemplation and critical reflexivity demanded in order to immerse oneself in the field of inquiry, and, in turn, to enable embodied learning to inform understanding. While artistic and creative practices can be – and are – combined with a range of (primarily) qualitative research methods, much recent research has embedded them within ethnographic, or auto-ethnographic, work (e.g. O'Connor, 2007; Paton, 2013). In such projects researchers have been firmly, often deeply, embedded in their practice, either as long-standing practitioners of their chosen art or craft, or as curious new-comers (e.g. Banfield, 2016; Paton, 2013; Thomas, 2014).

In this chapter I consider how auto-ethnography, as a state of 'reflexive-thinking-being', employed here within a space of artistic activity (life drawing classes), has enabled me to explore geographies of bodies, nudity, sexuality and intimacy by moving – physically, conceptually and recursively – between moments of the mundane (engaging in my hobby) to instances of the spectacular (such as seeing my body featured in artists' work). As a life drawing practitioner of more than ten years, a life model of over six years and a critical feminist cultural geographer of nine years, these are my everyday identities. On the one hand, these simultaneous, intersecting identities experience and understand emplacement in the life class as an everyday occurrence; yet, on the other, they frame the looking at, and thinking about, nude bodies (mine and others) as far from the everyday experience – not to mention comfort zone – of most people. This embodied emplacement in the field site as a matter of course is fundamental to auto-ethnography. It also links directly to the centrality of the body as a research tool – not merely a place for the intellectual processing of ideas, but as a site and mediator of embodied experience fundamental to that which is researched (Bain and Nash, 2006; Crang, 2003; Longhurst, Ho and Johnston, 2008). My research demands my body is firmly situated at the centre of my inquiry. Consideration of how touch, smell, gesture, as well as different kinds of looking – all of which are fundamental to my work – is drawn into an analysis of how the act of (re)producing bodies, inside and outside the life class, mediates body–space relations.

Auto-ethnographic research – particularly that which is situated within a personal passion – thus presents invaluable opportunities in terms of deep, embodied knowing of a space or practice. However, it also presents considerable challenges. While embodying multiple identities might enable critical reflection in the field, it can also make it difficult to identify which version of oneself to prioritise in any given moment. As I sit holding a pose for artists to draw, am I model or researcher, and how does the choice I make shape my actions and interpretations? There is also the very great risk – shared by any researcher who opts to collapse the boundary between hobby and work – that in turning an analytical gaze on something I do for pleasure, I analyse the pleasure away (e.g. Luvaas, 2017; Rossing and Scott, 2016). In this chapter I relate how I seek to manage these opportunities and risks in an open-ended (slow[1]) research project situated in a life drawing class. I focus on the shifting roles and positionalities I embody in this project, rather than the related but also separate drawings and interviews that form part of it. I make reference to these insofar as they illustrate my concerns with auto-ethnography as a whole.

## Auto-ethnography

The appropriateness of the method(s) employed in any research project directly impacts the credibility of its outputs (Muncey, 2005). Since my research into how life classes challenge sexual(ised) body norms has been strongly driven by my bodily experiences as an other-than-heterosexual woman, it was essential to place that body at the centre of the inquiry. I was aware from the start that in order to fully embody not just the means of the project (attending life classes) but also its hoped-for impacts (instigating more conversations around bodies as other-than-sexual beings), I would need to be willing to directly confront persistent social taboos around nudity by not only being nude myself (something I was already comfortable with, having been life modelling for some years), but by talking to people about it, both inside and outside of the life drawing community – what I will henceforth term 'life drawing space'.[2] To do so has been to attempt to rehabilitate non-sexualised nudity, drawing it forward from the social margins where it has been pushed by public anxiety about sexually inflected nudity.

In essence, auto-ethnography involves 'knowing from within'. It uses personal experience as an analytical lens through which to understand (or challenge) wider cultural views, practices and experiences (Ellis, Adams and Bochner, 2011). In doing so, it frames the act of research as socially aware and political (Adams and Holman Jones, 2008; Bochner, 2001), and thus firmly contextually situated in terms of its drivers and impacts. One of the key motivators of auto-ethnographic inquiry is the desire to start a conversation around the focal topic (Ellis, Adams and Bochner, 2011). As such, it intersects conveniently with the role of art-based activism in drawing attention to impacts of power imbalances across space and culture (Luger, 2017). It is important to note that auto-ethnographers – whether artists, activists or otherwise – though making their own lives the subject of study, do not (usually) do so merely to learn about themselves, but to understand, and promote critical reflection on, larger cultural phenomena in which they are embedded (Luvaas, 2017). As such, the personal is used to draw attention to the nuances and complexities of the lived everyday. As Butz and Besio (2009: 1660) note, 'autoethnographies are necessarily trans-cultural communications, articulated in relation to self and a wider social field that includes an audience of "others"'. In other words, they aim to prompt both those within the community of study ('insiders') and those external to it ('outsiders') to critically consider the culture(s) inside and outside, and the interrelations between the two (Ellis, Adams and Bochner, 2011, citing Maso, 2001).

Inevitably, the auto-ethnographic researcher straddles the inside/outside boundary – indeed, the fact that we do so reflects a particularly privileged position. It also reflects a particular need for sensitive consideration of ethics (Labaree, 2002). In my own research, in which the ethnographic 'I' (Ellis, 2004) inhabits three roles (researcher, artist, model), it has been necessary to consider my relation to the people and spaces both inside and outside my field site of life drawing space (see Bain and Nash, 2006 for a comparable example), and to do so frequently, as my latest encounters prompt new reflections on past experiences (for further reflection on ethnographic encounters see Tipper, this collection). It has required me to consider how my shifting identities in life drawing space have not only affected me and my understandings, but also those with whom I share this space, and those whom I seek to engage outside it. Auto-ethnography also demands acknowledgement of the subjectivities that prompt the research in the first place, and that, as a result, make us inclined to interpret our experiences in particular ways. When, for instance, Bain and Nash (2006: 100) ask, 'how can the researcher take advantage of the body as an ethnographic research tool when the naked body is often readily disregarded as unreliable because it is a site of intense and unruly desire?', they reveal – intentionally or otherwise – their own subjectivities in relation to naked bodies they see first and foremost as sexual (perhaps because of the focus of their research on lesbian bath houses). In contrast, my aim in using auto-ethnography is to challenge this assumption about the naked body, both within and outside of research. And yet, in this respect, I too must acknowledge how my embodied subjectivities around nakedness, sex, sexuality and gender inevitably shape the narratives I craft. While my own historic, embodied experience is thus necessarily central to the analysis I present and claims I make, it exists in dialogue with the wider cultural norms and pressures in relation to sexualised and idealised bodies, and particularly claims made on and about female bodies, to which I seek to speak. As such, subjectivity is mobilised here as an epistemological resource (Butz and Besio, 2009).

For some auto-ethnographic research, including my own, it is necessary not only to centre the researcher-body in the inquiry, but also to present it within the field in a particular way (Bain and Nash, 2006). In a similar approach to Janet Banfield's working-with (as well as talking-with) artists in order to explore how best to 'know' artistic spaces of (re)production (2016), I position my body – as artist and model – within life drawing space in order to observe how artists respond to my, and others' bodies, and reflect on my own response to the bodies of (nude and clothed) others. Yet such explicit body placing in research has only in the last ten to fifteen years been recognised as possessed of insights rarely achievable through traditional qualitative techniques of observation and interview. Fifteen years ago Sarah Oreton (2004: 305) suggested that '[the] researcher's body, particularly the naked or semi-clothed body, is an under-utilized and under-theorized data collection tool'. The growth of interest across the social sciences in emotion, embodiment, intimacies and affect in the years since Oreton's observation has more firmly emplaced bodies at the centre of research (Butz and Besio, 2009), allowing qualitative researchers to bring a range of multi-sensory ways-of-knowing to bear on their research. While naked researcher-bodies remain scarce, other forms of (clothed) embodied experience (including sensory aspects such as touch and smell) have emerged as fundamental to understanding important cultural and spatial nuances. Longhurst, Ho and Johnston (2008), for instance, note that their embodied experiences in the field have sometimes told them more than interviews, and certainly *different* things from interviews (for further work on embodied experiences as method see Hall et al. and Perkins and McLean, this collection).

This combination of intense focus on the self in relation to others alongside embodied, affective, potentially multi-sensory spatial interactions creates a great deal of emotional work for the auto-ethnographer. Deep reflection on our relationships with others within and outside of the field site can involve acknowledging aspects of ourselves, or views we might be seeking to hold on to, that we might otherwise prefer to ignore (Ellis, 1999). It can also test our relationships, including with those emotionally close to us. Auto-ethnography thus demands an openness to personal change – albeit change that is reflexively considered in the context of the project. The depth of reflexivity required, along with the necessary introspection, also demands a willingness to embrace vulnerability (Ellis, 1999). Yet this, too, can – and often does – work in the service of research, as vulnerability may engender compassion and empathy (see also Ellis, Adams and Bochner, 2011; Ellis and Bochner, 2000). To this end, even research experiences that are unpleasant – physically or emotionally – should be acknowledged.

## Drawing on and with auto-ethnography

My research in life drawing space emerged entirely from biographical opportunism (Anderson, 2006; Scott, 2010). I was already drawing and modelling for pleasure, and I saw the opportunity (as a relentlessly omnivorous researcher) to reflect on these practices in relation to some of my intellectual interests. As a result, I have found myself, as I imagine many do, an accidental auto-ethnographer. As I rationalise the constituent parts of my project post hoc, I find that the other practices (what I might now frame as 'research methods') bound up in my auto-ethnography long pre-date my impulse to see them as data. And the truth is, I am yet to work out the implications of this. Alongside my intrinsic reflexive-thinking-being in life drawing space, I have images – both drawings I have done, and photographs of other artists' drawings and paintings of me. I have conversations – idle chit-chat with fellow artists and models as we wait for classes to start, over tea breaks and at the end of classes where the work produced is viewed. I have my research journal – certainly, now, a product of my decision to make my hobby a research project, but originally just a set of random scribblings noting things that had made me think. (Clearly a sign that a project was inevitable!) And, since formalising these scribblings, thoughts, idle chats and drawings, I have interviews – intentional conversations with friends and acquaintances from my own life drawing classes and the wider life drawing community, networked and approached via social media (Twitter in particular). These practices/methods intersect and overlap in all sorts of ways. Here I offer just three examples in order to illustrate how the ad hoc coming together of different facets of life drawing activity constitute the richness of this accidental auto-ethnography.

## i) Drawing and being

I can trace a transformative moment in my relationship with bodies to the night I drew Belinda. Belinda is in her late sixties. She is not a life artist, nor is she – generally speaking – a life model. She is the partner of Jonah, a long-standing life artist who, for a number of years, held informal life class 'salons' at his home. One evening, the scheduled model was unable to make it to the session. Belinda stepped in – as, I was later informed, she had on similar occasions in the past. She was one of the best models I have ever had the pleasure to draw. She held the short, warm-up, dynamic poses that demand considerable muscle strength with apparent ease, and required little, if any, direction to choose poses that were suitably varied for the artists. The transformative moment occurred in the long pose, which typically takes up the whole second half of a session (around an hour). She lay on her side on the sofa, facing out towards us. I was sitting near her feet – a wonderfully foreshortened pose. I drew with a biro that evening. I like biro for long poses. Its permanence is unforgiving, and as a result it demands slowness, tentativeness, a layering of soft marks and lines to build up form. The slowness enforced upon me by my choice of medium drew me into looking at Belinda's body with a deep attentiveness. I saw the muscular strength of her tanned legs stretched out towards me, and the softness of her breasts and stomach as gravity pulled them downwards. Working around her body with my biro, I saw a beauty in her form that initiated a step-change in my bodily compassion – towards myself and others.

Drawing Belinda, and many other models since, has evoked Nicole De Brabandere's observation that, through drawing, 'subjective haptic and visceral tendencies evolve, modulating the way that one moves, knows, and sees' (2016: 104) such that the emotional distance between artist and model is collapsed, in turn informing new modes of interaction 'off the page' (2016: 105). Drawing is thus not only central to my auto-ethnography because the project concerns life drawing; it is fundamental to prompting reflections on a wide range of embodied experience within and outside of this space. The impact of drawing medium, for instance, can profoundly shape how a model-body is perceived, interpreted and rendered, as well as how those analyses are reflected back at the artist (whether to be embraced or denied). (Even as I write this I wonder why I ever use anything but biro in a life class!) As I elaborate below in ii) Drawing and talking, life class renderings prompt conversation about the look, feel, mood and energy of bodies in a way that valorises bodily variety.

## ii) Drawing and talking

It is common, at the end of a life class, to have an 'exhibition' where artists are invited (sometimes expected) to share the work they have produced that session. This provides an opportunity for constructive critique, the giving and receiving of esteem through compliments on work, as well as the chance to look at the range of renderings that have emerged from a diverse mix of styles and media. Often in these moments artists can be heard apologising to the model – for giving her/him a 'deformed' foot, a head that is too small or, as one artist said about two drawings she had done of me, 'You're about two stone too heavy in the one on the left'. Overhearing, and being part of, these conversations about the drawings has created useful analytical space within my auto-ethnography. It has given me the opportunity to prompt fellow artists to elaborate on their self-critique – what exactly dis/satisfies them about their drawings, and why? How does that relate to how they see the model's body? It has informed my own practice, both as artist and model, as I experiment in my drawing with exaggerating form or using different media, and in modelling with poses that artists consider especially interesting or challenging. Ultimately my hope is that this produces interesting work – and work that artists are then keen to talk about with me. Talking about drawing has also prompted me to attempt critical distance on those critiques I see and hear – what are these artists saying about bodies and their drawings of them through their reflections on their own and others' work? These multiple intersections of drawing with talking illustrate the extent to which participation in life classes *demands* interaction with others, including through conversation. As such, talk about the experience of a life class is fundamental to the auto-ethnography itself.

## iii) Talking and being

The following text is an excerpt, slightly edited, from my research notes. I present it here to illustrate a recurring observation concerning the role of idle chat in life drawing space. I follow the excerpt with some additional reflections on this theme based on an interview, as well as informal conversation, with my friend and fellow model, Bev.

> Really nice evening in [village] for the [local] Art Society. It was facili-
> tated by Roy, so I had a sense it would be a good evening. Beautiful
> location. Quite a few of the Library group came – Henry, Marnie,
> Howard, and (unfortunately) John. My heart sank as he came in the
> door, but it did prompt some new reflections on life classes as places of
> social and intimate intersections. I was thinking about the awkwardness
> I feel when he's there – or the awkwardness his manner creates. I think
> in part it is to do with the fact that he seems to find interaction – at
> least with women – quite difficult. I never see him talking with the
> female members of the Library group. One of the things that relaxes the
> atmosphere in a life class is chat – between artists, and between artists
> and the model. Somehow the talk cloaks the scenario – the focus on a
> nude body – in 'normality'. An awkward interaction creates awkward-
> ness in a setting where both talk and nudity are co-normalised. There is
> something about talk in this context that builds a sense of safety through
> the intimacy that the 'normalisation through talk' helps to produce. A
> case in point – a lady called Shirley, who I'd never met before, came
> up to me at the end of the evening in [village] and said, 'I feel I know
> you now!' It was her first time life drawing (as it was for several others)
> and she said she is keen to do more having enjoyed this evening.

John's social awkwardness is a recurring theme in my research journal. It is clear that his presence affects my experience of life drawing space, perhaps all the more so since my efforts to engage him in conversation have not increased my sense of ease, nor, it seems, his. As a result it was surprising to me that he offered his time for an interview – albeit one that is yet to take place, as we have each had to cancel agreed meetings due to work commitments. Might this be read as an attempt to reach out socially, but within the structure of a formal meeting, which perhaps feels, to him, safer? Informal chat with others at the Library group, as well as my fellow model, Bev, suggests that my experience chimes with that of others. Perhaps John – who, for the record, is an excellent artist – is simply a socially nervous individual, more relaxed with his male peers than with women, or he feels better able to communicate in structured inter-actions like an interview. Regardless, the emergence of this instance of embodied awkwardness in a space in which I otherwise feel quite relaxed casts light on the theme of talk as a contextual normaliser of nudity. Further, it was talking with Bev about her similar reflections on this matter that helped prevent me over-thinking the nature of that awkwardness (over-thinking being the scourge of the auto-ethnographer, surely!). The combination of talk-in-space (i.e. stilted conversation with John, more relaxed conversation with other artists) and talk-about-space (i.e. sharing the experience with Bev) allowed me to make sense of my embodied experience through corroboration and rationalisation. Here I needed both talking and being together to prompt the analytical thought and subsequently make sense of it.

The intersections of these auto-ethnographic components are fundamental to my ability to manage the multiple roles I occupy in life drawing space. Drawing allows me to contemplate my own relationship to bodies, but also gives me a reference point for conversations about them with fellow artists. Modelling positions me in life drawing space in a way that sensitises me to interactions – such as the importance of idle talk – I may well have been oblivious to, had my experience of classes been only that of an artist. My identity as both artist and model positions me as a doubly credible insider, which has been valuable when I have approached artists and models with whom I am not personally acquainted via email or Twitter. Yet this double insider status potentially also makes me doubly fallible – twice as likely, perhaps, to become so bound up in these identities that my third identity – that of researcher – becomes harder to fully inhabit. Despite the challenges associated with these ongoing identity negotiations, and the need to balance drawing and talking with just being, this auto-ethnography has attuned me to how best to work the relationship between the mundane and the spectacular in the life class. I have to think, in researcher mode, about when to just give myself over to my hobby – when to Just. Go. And. Draw. – and when to highlight – to myself, a life class acquaintance or an interviewee – something striking that is worthy of thought and conversation. My judgement may not always be right, but at least if a spectacular moment arises when I was seeking mundanity, a sketchbook to scribble in is usually nearby.

## Advice for aspiring auto-ethnographers

So, you want to do auto-ethnography.

The first thing to consider is, are you sure? For all the benefits of auto-ethnography (and I do believe there are many, otherwise I would not still be doing this), it would be remiss of me not to restate Brent Luvaas's note of caution that 'processes of becoming cannot be fully undone. We cannot go back to the people we were before we did our fieldwork' (2017: 4). This might involve anything from simply 'falling out of love' with one's research topic, to a more fundamental 'onto-logical destabilization' (Rossing and Scott, 2016: 615), whereby one's very sense of self is questioned and renegotiated. Rossing and Scott (2016) also highlight the risk of 'intellectual disadvantage' that can result from 'going too deep' – known among anthropologists as 'going native'. As I highlight above, striking the right balance between immersed insider and critical outsider is not without its challenges. For me, the fact that life classes are necessarily a part-time, hobbyist pleasure has worked to my advantage. The need for gainful employ-ment that pays more than the low wages that characterise life model-ling means that I am emplaced in a critical academic mind-set far more often than I get to let my mind wander on a modelling job or as I sit at a drawing board. As such, it is worthwhile considering how critical space might be 'designed in' to your auto-ethnography.

A related issue is that of one's emotional orientation to the practice at the heart of the study. For Susie Scott (2010), in her auto-ethnography of swimming, her shift towards analytical observations of her practice, and that of others at the pool, meant her interpretations of many of those actions shifted. She began to consider notions of 'discipline', what it looked like to take swimming 'seriously' and what 'accom-plishment' in the pool looked like. There are both benefits and chal-lenges associated with such a perceptual shift. On the one hand, such deep reflection lends itself to the kind of analytical richness that can help avoid navel-gazing autobiography (Butz and Besio, 2009). On the other, what might, outside of academic analyses, be considered over-thinking may be to the detriment of one's own practice – a tense swimming stroke or a mannered drawing style, for instance. Each ethnographer must draw her own line here (pun fully intended).

Auto-ethnography can be hugely affirming of our self-identities and associated viewpoints, but we should also be aware of the potential to find ourselves questioning those identities and some of our most strongly held beliefs or views. After two and a half years researching life drawing space, and twenty-four interviews, my most recent inter-viewee, a contact made via Twitter, challenged one of my strongest-held views. He felt strongly that the growth in popularity of life drawing as a hen and stag party activity is hugely beneficial in terms of increasing acceptance of nude bodies and a range of body types. Not only did his view contrast with that of the majority of my other participants to date, but it also directly challenged one of my strongly felt drivers for instigating this project – the fact that, for me, life drawing space should be protected from associations with overtly hyper-sexualised cultural practices, such as hen and stag parties.[3] I still have some work to do to ensure I interpret and make sense of my interviewee's views accurately and ethically, and consider whether and/or how his perspective makes me rethink my own. In a sense this is a matter of ethics of interpretation – how can I most faithfully represent both my participants' perspectives, and my own, particularly when both may be subject to flux?

More generally, the ethics of how to acknowledge the contributions others make, knowingly or unknowingly, to an auto-ethnography requires careful consideration. In my research, I have been transparent with artists and models about my research in all the classes I attend, emphasising that it need not (and ideally should not) impact on how they engage with life drawing space, but that I am keen to hear any reflections they are happy to share. Outside of the spaces I frequent, I explicitly foreground my researcher identity to ensure those with whom I connect are aware of my aspiration to learn about their experiences. The inherent messiness of auto-ethnography can mean an unbounded 'leakiness' to managing ethics – how feasible is it to ethically manage the contribution of everyone with whom we might fleetingly interact in the context of our research? There is no easy answer, but I invite you to consider what ethical conduct would look like for *you* in the context of the interactions your project invites.

Finally, it is necessary to consider the impact of 'leaving the field', including whether or not you wish to. In doing so it is important to acknowledge the risk of becoming 'repulsed' (Luvaas, 2017) by our field site or practical focus if we fail to bid a timely retreat. My project is open ended. I still want to draw and model, and I want to maintain the friendships I have with a lot of fellow artists and models who have been my interviewees. Consider what this might look like for you. How embedded are you, or do you seek to be, in your field? What might be the repercussions of staying … or of leaving? Whichever we choose, there may be ethical implications for maintaining (or indeed ceasing) contact with those in the field (Ellis, Adams and Bochner, 2011). Is it more ethical to maintain a friendship with someone whose thoughts and actions you have deeply analysed, perhaps critically judged, or is it more ethical to thank them and walk away? As Ellis, Adams and Bochner (2011: 282) note, we 'have to be able to continue to live in the world of relationships in which [our] research is embedded after the research is completed'.

None of the challenges articulated in this chapter, including the ethics of fully or partially leaving the field, necessarily resolve themselves with time; indeed, many potentially become trickier to manage. It should be noted, though, that leaving the field can simply mean ending the research, not the practice. As my work on life classes develops, I anticipate moving my research away from the classes where I draw and model, and taking it into new contexts, including outreach workshops for community and college groups. I expect this will mean the project itself becomes less auto-ethnography and more of a qualitative mixed-methods inquiry. I may find my three identities (artist, model and academic) straddling two fields: my continued embodied practice as artist and model, but also a more conspicuous researcher-body outside of my everyday life drawing space.

## Conclusion

Auto-ethnography has enormous potential in a range of fields, indicated both by the wide range of methodological approaches and empirical studies that have recently been grouped together as auto-ethnography (Butz and Besio, 2009; Wall, 2006) and the growing number of studies which seek to place deep, embodied experience at

---

### Box 11.1: Tools, training and equipment

The tools, training and/or equipment for an auto-ethnography will depend very much on the subject of your work. As such, the only prerequisite I would advise is a research journal – electronic or paper, depending on your preference. If you intend to interview others in your field then some form of audio recording device, such as a Dictaphone, is very helpful.

For arts-based auto-ethnographies, the best training is to find a suitable class and throw yourself into it. Maybe go to more than one, if you have the resources. Depending on your specific practice, you may need to invest in basic tools, such as a drawing pad and pens/pencils/media of choice for a drawing class.

the heart of their research (whether or not they frame it explicitly as auto-ethnographic) (e.g. Banfield, 2016; O'Connor, 2007; Paton, 2013). The intersection of auto-ethnography and art/craft/creative practices holds particular potential methodologically, conceptually, empirically and culturally-politically. I hope to have demonstrated the capacity of auto-ethnography to achieve deep understanding of socio-cultures in such a way as to drive cultural change – or, at least, pose necessary questions of cultural norms.

In this chapter I have highlighted the challenges and opportunities of inhabiting multiple, sometimes simultaneous, and always shifting, identities. Having shared the nature of my focus on the emotional, subjective, multi-sensory body, I invite you to consider how you might use yours and to what use you might put its capabilities. Should you find yourself, as I have done, an accidental auto-ethnographer, you may need to engage in the same kind of post hoc rationalisation of 'what came before' in order to establish where to go next – or, indeed, where to let your study take you next. As part of this, consider what practices are nested within your auto-ethnography. Drawing, modelling and talking have, in my research, all proved valuable in and of themselves, but embedded in an auto-ethnography they are also much more than the sum of their parts. While there are a number of important considerations before, during and after an auto-ethnographic study, from the wisdom of collapsing the hobby/work boundary (if this is relevant for your inquiry), to the ethics of fully or partially leaving the field, the personal and analytical richness that has resulted from my decisions thus far has been profound. Managed thoughtfully, auto-ethnography has much to reveal.

---

### Box 11.2: Further reading

I recommend the following articles as a starting point if you are considering auto-ethnographic research:

Butz, D. and Besio, K. (2009) 'Autoethnography', *Geography Compass*, 3 (5): 1660–1674.

Ellis, C., Adams, T. E. and Bochner, A. P. (2011) 'Autoethnography: an overview', *Historical Social Research*, 36 (4): 273–290.

Luvaas, B. (2017) 'Unbecoming: the aftereffects of autoethnography', *Ethnography*. doi.org/10.1177/1466138117742674.

## Notes

1 Aside from the intrinsic benefits of slow scholarship (i.e. that it permits time to think) slowness is particularly beneficial, if not fundamentally necessary, to auto-ethnographic research because of its non-linear, ad hoc tendency (Ellis, 2004).

2 I use the term 'life drawing space' to describe both the space within an individual life class and the networks of life classes across which similar practices and understandings occur. It should be noted that such classes are highly culturally situated, both in location and in how their purpose and meaning are interpreted. Thus, while I seek to acknowledge connections between life classes across space, they should be understood as connections primarily among communities in the global North, and a liberal, middle-class sub-set at that.

3 I want to acknowledge that not all hen and stag parties today are characterised by hyper-sexualised activity. Nevertheless, it is a common trope and one that is potentially problematically amplified in relation to life drawing as a practice oriented around nudity, particularly for those with no knowledge of life classes who might assume a sexual imperative or undertone.

## References

Adams, T. E. and Holman Jones, S. (2008) 'Autoethnography is queer', in N. K. Denzin, Y. S. Lincoln and L. T. Smith (eds) *Handbook of Critical and Indigenous Methodologies*, Thousand Oaks, CA: Sage, 373–390.

Anderson, L. (2006) 'Analytic autoethnography', *Journal of Contemporary Ethnography*, 35 (4): 373–395.

Bain, A. L. (2004) 'Female artistic identity in place: the studio', *Social & Cultural Geography*, 5 (2): 171–193.

Bain, A. L. and Nash, C. J. (2006) 'Undressing the researcher: feminism, embodiment and sexuality at a queer bathhouse event', *Area*, 31 (8): 99–106.

Banfield, J. (2016) 'Knowing between: generating boundary understanding through discordant situations in geographic–artistic research', *Cultural Geographies*, 23 (3): 459–473.

Bochner, A. P. (2001) 'Narrative's virtues', *Qualitative Inquiry*, 7 (2): 131–157.

Butz, D. and Besio, K. (2009) 'Autoethnography', *Geography Compass*, 3 (5): 1660–1674.

Crang, M. (2003) 'Qualitative methods: touchy, feely, look-see?', *Progress in Human Geography*, 27 (4): 494–504.

De Brabandere, N. (2016) 'Experimenting with affect across drawing and choreography', *Body & Society*, 22 (3): 103–124.

Ellis, C. (1999) 'Heartful Autoethnography', *Qualitative Health Research*, 9 (5): 669–683.

Ellis, C. (2004) *The Ethnographic I: A Methodological Novel About Autoethnography*, Walnut Creek, CA: Alta-Mira.

Ellis, C. and Bochner, A. (2000) 'Autoethnography, personal narrative, reflexivity: researcher as subject', in Norman Denzin and Yvonna Lincoln (eds) *The Handbook of Qualitative Research* (2nd edn), London: Sage, 733–768.

Ellis, C., Adams, T. E. and Bochner, A. P. (2011) 'Autoethnography: an overview', *Historical Social Research*, 36 (4): 273–290.

Hawkins, H. (2011) 'Dialogues and doings: sketching the relationships between geography and art', *Geography Compass*, 5 (7): 464–478.

Hawkins, H. (2012) 'Geography and art. An expanding field: site, the body and practice', *Progress in Human Geography*, 37 (1): 52–71.

Labaree, T. V. (2002) 'The risk of "going observationalist": negotiating the hidden dilemmas of being an insider participant observer', *Qualitative Research*, 2 (1): 97–122.

Longhurst, R., Ho, E. and Johnston, L. (2008) 'Using "the body" as an "instrument of research": kimch'i and pavlova', *Area*, 40 (2): 208–217.

Luger, J. D. (2017) 'But I'm just an artist!? Intersections, identity, meaning, and context', *Antipode*, 49 (5): 1329–1348.

Luvaas, B. (2017) 'Unbecoming: the aftereffects of autoethnography', *Ethnography*, doi.org/10.1177/1466138117742674.

Maso, I. (2001) 'Phenomenology and ethnography'. In Handbook of ethnography, ed. Paul Atkinson, Amanda Coffey, Sara Delamont, John Lofland and Lyn Lofland, pp. 136–144. Thousand Oaks, CA: Sage.

Muncey, T. (2005) 'Doing autoethnography', *International Journal of Qualitative Methods*, 4 (1): 69–86.

O'Connor, E. (2007) 'Embodied knowledge in glassblowing: the experience of meaning and the struggle towards proficiency', *Sociological Review*, 55 (1): 126–141.

Oreton, S. (2004) '"Touch talk": the problems and paradoxes of embodied research', *International Journal of Social Research Methodology*, 7: 305–322.

Paton, D. (2013) 'The quarry as sculpture: the place of making', *Environment and Planning A*, 45 (5): 1070–1086.

Rossing, H. and Scott, S. (2016) 'Taking the fun out of it: the spoiling effects of researching something you love', *Qualitative Research*, 16 (6): 615–629.

Scott, S. (2010) 'How to look good (nearly) naked: the performative regulation of the swimmer's body', *Body & Society*, 16 (2): 143–168.

Thomas, N. J. (2014) 'Weaving at Coldharbour Mill: exploring ambivalence around the need to "make" when researching "making"', Royal Geographical Society with the Institute of British Geographers Annual Conference, 27–29 August 2014, London.

Wall, S. (2006) 'An autoethnography on learning about autoethnography', *International Journal of Qualitative Methods*, 5 (2): 146–160.

# Part III

## Mobilities and motion

# Part III

mobilities and motion

# 12

# Researching the run: methods for exploring mundane jographies

## Simon Cook

This chapter introduces and evaluates two methods of exploring running geographies, or jographies as I like to call them. Jographies are interested broadly in running practices, their spatialities, meanings, cultures and experiences (Cook, Shaw and Simpson, 2016a). The importance of investigating running in such ways is becoming ever more significant to contemporary society. Due to the accessible, convenient and physical nature of running, it is increasingly being positioned as a key practice in helping to resolve the public health epidemic of inactivity, as well as an example of mundane mobility. I consider running a unique way of inhabiting and being in the world. Considering it in this way focuses attention upon the textures and minutiae of the everyday: how it happens; how it feels; the senses, sensations and emotions bound up with running; the relationship between runners and places; and the meanings attached to running. Grasping these aspects of running permits deeper insight into why people take up and sustain running, and therefore what can be done to encourage more people to start running.

The questions posed by my interest in jographies have guided my research for the last few years, during which I have conducted three different projects exploring running widely as a mobile practice and more specifically as a mode of transport (see Cook, 2016, 2017; Cook, Shaw and Simpson, 2016b for more details). When these projects began, there was little in the way of methodological precedence for understanding running from social science/humanities perspectives. Auto-ethnography had been very successfully used by Allen-Collinson and Hockey (2001) in their research into running as serious leisure, but there was little guidance for engaging with the experiences of multiple, everyday runners. My research has, therefore, also involved an ongoing methodological experimentation in order to test out different methods for engaging with the mundane aspects of everyday running and the insights they offer into understanding the practice. In general, these experiments have been inspired by the recent advancements in mobile methods and I have been keen to test out their application to running (for another methodological approach focused on researching movement and bodies in action see Stoodley, this collection).

There have been two main methods I have experimented with – the go-along interview (GAI) and mobile video-ethnography (MVE) (for further information on go-alongs and mobile-video see chapters by Birtchnell et al., Stoodley, and Wilkinson, this collection). These methods could be considered as part of the jographer's toolbox; well, *this* jographer's toolbox at least. My aim in this chapter is to introduce these methods to you, explore the case made for each method and to evaluate their application within my own research, sharing some hints, tips and suggestions along the way. In order to do this, the chapter begins by exploring the background to the two methods, before explaining my use of them, and ending with the advice I have for others thinking about using similar methods.

## Methodological background

My methodological experiments with running have been influenced by the wider development of mobile methods. Mobile methods are an innovation of the mobilities turn, albeit a contested one (Merriman, 2014). This turn refers to the increasing attention to and importance of mobility that has developed within the social sciences, arts and humanities since 2000. The mobilities turn challenges the previous assumption that movement was a black box, something serving only to produce geographies/sociologies at either end of a journey, and something devoid of its own effects. The mobilities turn, however, argues that mobility is an incredibly important social agent and is essential to our experience and understanding of the world (Cresswell and Merriman, 2011). Mobility is recognised as fundamental in mediating our relationships with each other, space, time, places, objects and ourselves (Cook, 2018). Work within the mobilities turn has emphasised the practical action, embodiment, affect and context of mobilities, facilitating questions regarding the sensory, embodied, emotional, performative and fleeting experiences of movement (Büscher and Urry, 2009). The ability of traditional research methods to comprehend these textures of mobility has been questioned (Law and Urry, 2004), and associated with the mobilities turn is the rise of mobile methods, a suite of different methods which invariably attempt to 'keep up' with the practices being studied through tracing, tracking and moving-with. Inspired by the methodological developments of the mobilities turn, I have experimented with GAI and MVE as possible tools to access and engage with running practices in situ.

In the simplest sense, GAIs are interviews conducted on the move with participants. This often involves the researcher participating in the practice being studied and experiencing the places and spaces within which a practice may take place (Anderson, 2004). If seeking to engage with the mundane, GAIs offer a greater depth of insight compared with ordinary interviews due to the increased temporal and spatial proximity to the phenomena of interest. Much that falls within the mundane and everyday is taken-for-granted and can be difficult for participants to reflect upon and recall. However, interviewing participants about their thoughts, feelings, experiences and actions at the point at which they are taking place helps to overcome this barrier and can result in rich insights into these mundane experiences. The multi-sited nature of a GAI also means that the spaces and places encountered can act as stimuli, helping to conjure memories, prompt further reflection on issues discussed and provide useful/surprising distractions. The deeper understanding garnered through this is strengthened further by the increased levels of rapport that can be developed between researcher and participants. In GAI, the researcher and participants are engaging in a joint activity, which enters the participant's world. In these instances, participants become the experts, and a more familiar environment can increase their comfort, resulting in more evocative, unfiltered and honest insights being gained. The opportunities to engage more purely with the experiences of runners in a way which could account for the varied attachments they feel with places/spaces and in a manner which is comfortable for them are what interested me in using GAIs to investigate running.

While another method of moving with a participant, MVE often does not require the physical presence of a researcher at the moment of movement. Mobile video-ethnography is the use of videographic methods while on the move, capturing the events, occurrences, relations, interactions, places and practices of the mobile subject under study (Simpson, 2014). This can be a useful tool for researchers who have concerns about what impact their presence within the research site may have. Although cameras still affect a participant's thoughts, feelings and actions (Pink, 2014), this is a different influence from the presence of a researcher. Running is often a solitary practice within which intimate relationships and choreographies with place often develop (Hitchings and Latham, 2016). My interest in understanding and exploring these is likely to be affected more greatly by my presence and therefore the use of a camera may permit access to more 'accurate' or 'true' data in this regard. The use of MVE also permits researchers access to places or activities that it may not be possible or desirable to be in physically, which could definitely apply to running. Analysing material collected using MVE benefits hugely from the retention of context, which the video camera offers.

Although other research materials (such as interview transcripts, diary entries etc.) can enable the analysis and recalling of key moments, events and experiences, they are abstracts, isolated from the wider contexts within which they took place. Even the most detailed note taking is unlikely to be able to capture and retain the amount of contextual information a camera is able to. While arguably still a reduction in itself (more of that below), MVE is able to record the vast range of happenings that affect the experience under investigation, opening it up more clearly for researcher analysis.

Despite not being there, researchers can still see and hear what occurred and analyse it. Indeed, with its fixed and constant gaze, the camera often captures things of which the participant was unaware. MVE is claimed to provide the opportunity for deepening our understandings of practices by bringing into focus previously blurred aspects of mobilities that explore the minutiae and intricacies of such practices (Brown, Dilley and Marshall, 2008). These nuanced understandings are facilitated by 'seeing the doing': enabling the capture, replaying and slowing down of practices (Brown and Dilley, 2012). Again offering methods of exploring the taken-for-granted, the ability to use technology in such ways grants access to a level of detail which participants would struggle to discuss or even have an awareness of due to its scale or fleeting nature. As well as using the video as raw data, MVE can also be employed as a method in combination with interviews, with footage being used for elicitation and to prompt practitioner self-analysis, which is how I utilised this method.

## Using GAI and MVE

The previous section outlined the methodological background to my use of GAI and MVE to explore the mundane experiences of running. In this section, I will draw on my own experiences of using these methods in research to discuss the various ways I have innovated and applied them within my work. A heavy emphasis within this section will be on the logistical set-ups of these techniques. These methods are not homogeneous; for each practice and context the set-up can be very different (Laurier, 2014). To my knowledge, neither of these methods had been used before in running research, so much of my innovation has surrounded how to actually make these methods work in ways that did not disrupt the practices, did not place too much burden on participants, and yet were methodologically valuable for the researcher. The speed, physical exertion and delicate equilibrium of running made this quite challenging, for both researcher and participants, as any addition to the running body can have an exaggerated and intolerable effect. My set-ups have not been perfect but hopefully the advice I provide here can help anyone wanting to experiment with these methods further. I have further innovated by combining these two methods, something this section will end by exploring.

The first method I sought to harness for use in running research was GAIs. At the time, GAI had mostly been used within walking and cycling research. Although different types of mobility and movement present their own challenges for research methodology, walking and cycling are arguably easier practices within which to set up a go-along environment. Running not only requires more effort, but is also more physically immersive, which affords fewer options for equipment to be carried on the run. This lays down several challenges for using this method. The first (and arguably biggest) challenge for using GAI in running is the physical abilities needed to run alongside participants. I have always been a runner and, luckily, when I first experimented with GAI I was at my fittest. This meant that I could generally cope with the physical aspects of GAI. Since then, however, I have used GAI when I have not been quite so fit (to put it nicely) and needed to follow a training plan leading up to the data collection period. This is not a typical step in a research project and highlights an embodied issue in using some mobile methods, posing an access barrier and inequality issue in regards to who could use GAI and who could not. While such issues may also occur when researching other mobile forms (such as cycling – Spinney, 2006), they are rarely written in research outputs so not much is known about how researchers manage these. To combat some of these embodied issues, I also agreed with participants to undertake these GAIs at conversational pace. 'Conversational pace' is simply a pace at which all parties can hold a conversation while running without becoming breathless.

Audio recording was the next challenge to overcome in using GAIs for running, which is far from simple. Not only is there the issue of somehow carrying an audio recording device while running, but ensuring that it can pick up all parties without being dominated by the noise of wind or passing vehicles can also be difficult. So far, I have used two different set-ups for audio recording. One of my projects was based in Plymouth, UK. Plymouth is a relatively small and quiet English city, which afforded a simpler set-up. This involved strapping an audio recorder to my arm (I used a makeshift holster out of an old ankle support) and then ensuring this always remained between the two runners. This was mostly successful, although the swinging of the arm led to an inconsistent sound quality, and if ever the two runners separated then the participant was sometimes inaudible. I initially adopted this set-up for my next project using GAIs in London. It quickly became clear that this was not going to work in a busier city. Not only are there many more background noises/distractions, but the possibility of two runners staying side by side for the entirety of a run was almost zero.

After a bit of experimentation, I settled on a set-up that involved a separate microphone for each participant, meaning separation would not be a problem. This was a tie-clip microphone, attached to a runner's top, close to their mouth and plugged into individual audio recording devices stored in a pocket/backpack/bum-bag (depending on what suited the participant). Using a tie-clip microphone also meant that fewer background noises were picked up due to the directionality of the microphone. After the GAI, I combined the two audio files (one from participant, one from researcher) into one track. Performing a loud clap before the run began allowed for simpler synchronisation of the tracks – the clap appeared as a spike, which could then be aligned. This set-up was very successful and produced the highest-quality recording of the two I have used so far. What I have learnt to be invaluable in both of these set-ups, however, is the use of a windjammer (a fuzzy, spongy 'hat') for the microphones to reduce wind noise, and to ensure the hold/lock function is selected on the audio recorders. To my detriment, I found out how easily the motion of running can accidently knock the stop button before intended if the device is not locked!

The last big challenge I found with using GAIs for running was actually the act of interviewing. Many of the basics of interviewing can be difficult to accomplish while running. Even the fundamental element of talking can be tough at particular speeds or over particular topography. The interviews were very loosely structured. I had a broad list of themes that I hoped to cover in each interview but designed the interview order to be quite unruly and open to distractions, as many GAIs attempt to do (DeLyser and Sui, 2013). I really wanted the running, the places and the participant to guide the conversation; for what happened, what participants felt and what we passed by to lead the discussions. This led to an interview which often jumped between topics only to return to some again when they became pertinent once more, something characteristic of place-based and mobile interviewing (Evans and Jones, 2011; Holton and Riley, 2014). Listening carefully and being responsive to what the participants were saying was difficult at times. There is often an overwhelming torrent of stimuli to respond to, which needs to be done alongside trying to remember the rough interview schedule and concentrating on running itself. Physical and mental fatigue make this task even more difficult.

The free-form nature of the interview enables an openness to distractions and ideas that may have been outside the purview of a stricter interview schedule. It also proved very useful not to consider the interview as bounded; it often acted as the catalyst for ideas that ruminated for a few weeks or even months. Perhaps to be expected when discussing the mundane and other aspects of everyday life that we do not generally spend much time considering, these research interviews regularly catalysed a longer-term reanalysis of participants'

own practices. This led to follow-up communications from participants offering new ideas or clarifications. Once the interviews were
transcribed, I sent the transcriptions to the participants. This not only
ensured they had a record of what we spoke about as well as an
opportunity to revise, amend and add any points, but it also enabled
me to ask further questions or request clarifications I had not managed
to, or thought to, in the original GAI.

Overall, MVE has been a slightly simpler method to set up. The
biggest challenge involved attaching a camera to participants in a way
that was comfortable for them yet still provided a good view and a
stable shot. After a bit of experimentation with various different positions and straps, a head-camera seemed to offer the best option
(Brown, Dilley and Marshall, 2008). In my case, the camera was
attached to a headband and worn roughly in the centre of the fore-
head. Participants generally found this a tolerable set-up. Most spoke
of a brief adjustment period, after which they were no longer affected
by the camera. It posed a bigger problem in hot weather, however
(thermoception is an important element of running experience –
Allen-Collinson et al., 2018), and in one instance a participant did
opt to remove the camera after an hour or so. Participants also
remarked that the camera did not affect them as much socially as they
thought it might. Many forgot they were wearing one once in their
flow, and on one occasion a participant even took an impromptu visit
to the toilet mid-run. Machoism was perhaps the only common
impact of the camera, with participants saying that they ran quicker
than they may have otherwise, aware that someone else would be
watching. To record a run, participants were given the camera and
shown how to operate it. The choice of route was entirely of the
participant's choosing; I only asked that the recorded run be one they
would still have taken had they not been in the study – I wanted to
enter their running world and be taken on their journeys. Participants
would then complete a run wearing the head-camera and return it to
me. After this, I conducted rudimentary video analysis for the purposes of developing a specific interview schedule. This involved
simply playing back the footage at half-speed and noting the time and
a description of any events I wished to ask about (inspired by Spinney,
2011). A few days later, I met with each participant and conducted an
interview, which involved re-watching the video in full while pausing
and slowing down sections of particular interest. Participants were

asked to elaborate on what they were thinking, feeling, doing during the run and how the film evoked further insights (inspired by Simpson, 2014). These elicitation interviews proved really interesting, with participants often surprised by how many things they were unaware of, or thought were different, which led to some incredibly interesting discussions around running mundanities.

Beyond figuring out feasible ways of using GAI and MVE within running research, there is a further innovation I have made with these methods. In honesty, this innovation was more by luck than design. In my first project experimenting with these methods, I was keen to figure out what the different methods could bring to the interrogation of running practices. In doing so, I found these two to be very powerful in combination and it is something I have sought to replicate in other projects since. Both GAI and MVE get at different aspects of running practices and complement each other well. This is a combination that can be harnessed for other research projects too.

Combining GAI and MVE can offer researchers ways of meshing together different ways of knowing a practice, providing a means to attend to the micro and the macro, to what we are aware of and what we are not, and to explore how in-the-moment understandings, feelings and thoughts correlate with a more detailed scrutiny of what actually happened. This is nicely illustrated in my first experiments with these methods, where I took an interest in the mundane events of when runners pass pedestrians (and reported more fully in Cook, Shaw and Simpson, 2016a, 2016b). Through GAIs I was able to understand how runners felt about such encounters, and who they thought should take responsibility for ensuring they pass successfully. This managed to unearth the meanings, values and judgements runners ascribe to running/walking, and discovered how these entangle with embodied desires of running to indicate how these passing encounters should occur. However, combining this method with MVE enables a detailed scrutiny of these passing encounters. This not only demonstrated what actually happens when runners pass pedestrians and the various spatial strategies used, but also demonstrated a value–action gap between what runners say and what they do that was very interesting to explore further with participants. This reveals the value in combing GAI and MVE in helping to interrogate mundane practices from different angles, and is an innovation whose benefits could be applied more widely to other settings.

Both GAI and MVE are well developed and well used within the mobilities field and were some of the first methods innovated within mobile methods (D'Andrea, Ciolfi and Gray, 2011). My experiments with these represent the first time they have been used in combination, and to research running. As with all methods, both GAI and MVE increase the visibility of some things while decreasing the visibility of others. In combination, they offer a means to illuminate more aspects of practices and phenomena, offering researchers means of analysing mobile practices in a more holistic manner.

## Advice for others: evaluations

Having explored above how I actually employed these methods, I now wish to evaluate their effectiveness and provide some practical advice for anyone wanting to experiment with similar methods in the future. I have used the term 'experiment' throughout this chapter purposefully. These have been experiments with methods that came with the associated successes and failures you might expect. My 'best to date' presented here are by no means perfect and these are methods that can be tweaked and tailored to fit different research settings and scenarios. I certainly encourage such experimentation. As several options were experimented with before settling on what I have introduced here, I will outline the equipment and software I used, as at least it may give you a head start for your own experiments.

If I could only choose one of the two methods discussed in this chapter, it would be GAI. The rapport developed with the participant is quite incredible, which resulted in extremely insightful interviews. There was a real sense that I was being taken into their world and they were doing their utmost to explain it to me – it was an immersive, multi-sensory tour of their running practices. Accomplishing something together (a run in this case) undoubtedly helped to develop this rapport, especially as I was also an insider to the practice. Rather than feeling like a research interview, participants often commented that it just felt like talking to another runner as they normally would on a run. However, the design of the interaction between participant and researcher also helps to build this rapport.

Despite any efforts we make to avoid it, traditional interviews can feel a bit intimidating, alien or even clinical to participants, which can hinder some of the answers given. However, in GAI there is a method, which encourages a less filtered and more personal discussion of things that may traditionally be difficult to talk about. These conversations are further encouraged by the vast amount of stimuli offered by doing an activity together and moving through places. Many mobile methods seek to use place and practice in this way, acting to elicit more in-depth discussions around phenomena (Holton and Riley, 2014). These enable in-the-moment reactions and reflections to be offered, allowing potentially more authentic insights to be gained. The temporal and spatial proximity to the phenomena of interest not only removes layers of analysis through which remembering of an incident may be filtered, but it also enables participants to discuss in more depth and with more ease some of the aspects of mundane research which can be difficult to contemplate and articulate, such as feelings, experience and emotions. In GAIs, these benefits combine to offer a powerful method for considering and discussing mundane and mobile aspects of practices.

That said, GAIs can come with some logistical/technical problems which make them difficult to use in all instances. Achieving a comfortable set-up that results in audio files with enough quality can be difficult when needing to contend with multiple moving bodies and a constantly changing background context. The set-up I found most successful is provided in Box 12.1, but whatever you use, ensuring it is comfortable for you and the participant is essential. As with any technology, there is also a financial implication of using such equipment. While not too prohibitive, if your research budget is minimal, then GAIs may not be feasible. Beyond the logistics, actually conducting an interview on the run is difficult. First, personal fitness becomes an important factor in the viability of this method. A training plan may be required to help implement this method, and conversely injury may mean it becomes impossible to use GAIs. Even if you can make the start line, so to speak, having to remember an interview schedule (rather than having it to hand) and responding to what participants are saying while being open to passing stimuli and focusing on actually running, can often lead to things being missed or not explored fully. In such cases, post-interview communication can help to respond to these.

Despite this, many mundane phenomena fall below the radar of GAIs, which other methods may be better at catching. When interviewing on the move, there are many things to respond to and concentrate on, which inevitably results in many incidents not being

---

**Box 12.1: Tools, training and equipment**

Tools used for mobile video-ethnography
Runs were recorded using:

- Go-Pro™ session action camera;
- head band attachment for Go-Pro™.

Analysis of the video was aided using the following:

- VLC Media Player (free).

Equipment used for Go-Along Interviews
For each person the following equipment was used to record the interviews:

- Tie/Lapel Clip Microphone;
- Windjammer on the microphone;
- Audio-recording device to plug microphone into;
- Bum-bag to hold the audio-recording device in whilst running.

After recording, the two audio files were aligned using:

- Audacity digital audio editing software (free).

---

explored. Some may have passed by before the opportunity to speak about them arises and others may be too small in scale to be properly noticed. In such scenarios, methods capable of capturing mundanities in all their glory may be preferable. There is also the unknown question of what impact the presence of a researcher has on the interview and responses participants are giving. The immediacy of a GAI is argued to lead to more authentic answers due to the removal of multiple filtering processes involved in remembering an event. However, if the presence of a researcher is impacting that experience, is this immediacy still as useful? While overall I think the benefits of GAIs outweigh any influencing effects the researcher has, this is certainly something worth considering when analysing the material gained from GAIs.

Despite not being my favoured method of the two, there are many benefits MVE also brings to researching the mundane. Although not a method at the point of movement itself, MVE affords researchers a way of 'seeing there' by proxy (Laurier, 2010). The resulting video files, therefore, retain the context of the practices, which is extremely useful for researchers, and in particular can permit phenomena to be studied where it may not be physically possible or desirable to actually be there. The fixed position of the camera offers an unwavering, albeit limited, view of the events, places, happenings and phenomena of a practice. This is a view that does not blink, that does not struggle to remember, and that does not recall through various filters of memory and perspective. It provides researchers with a matter of fact account of what happened, which can then be analysed. This analysis is greatly aided by the ability to technologically manipulate the video file. The use of video software to freeze, zoom in, slow down, rewind and repeat enables a scrutiny of practices simply not possible in real-life, in-the-moment ethnography (Pink, 2014). MVE actually opens up movement for analysis in ways that would be impossible from simply 'being there' (Spinney, 2011). The use of video provides the chance to reveal unseen or unnoticed experiences of the run, producing a new understanding of the practice. It provides the possibility to go beyond the spectacular aspects of being on the move and to assess the importance of the smaller-scale and potentially unconscious or habitual happenings of running (Simpson, 2014). By 'stretching out' movements and allowing for more analytical detail than in observation alone (Spinney, 2011), it is possible to render visible some of the skills, movements and encounters that are often taken for granted, and in doing so understand running practices more deeply. This is incredibly useful in studying mundanity, and MVE invites attention to be focused on micro-movements more closely than in GAIs, offering extra detail and insights to researchers.

Despite the potential to reveal new levels of analysis and comprehension, MVE also comes with some limitations and practical difficulties that researchers wishing to use this method should be wary of. The biggest criticism often made of MVE, or indeed much video-based research, is that it privileges what can be seen as the basis for analysis. In providing an unwavering fixed gaze, full of detail and context, there is a muffling of other senses, as well as affective and felt relations, within MVE that can be significant in understanding practices. While sound is captured to some degree, many other senses are simply not possible to attend to by using video. For understanding the mundanities of running practices, MVE offers no opportunities to explore how the changing topography *feels* underfoot, how the dripping of sweat into the mouth *tastes*, how movement itself feels (*kinaesthesia*), how the parts of the body relate to one another (*proprioception*), or how heat affects the running experience (*thermoception*). As noted by Simpson (2011) and Spinney (2011), wariness should be apparent about claims that MVE can mine the embodied, sensory, emotional and kinaesthetic – they can certainly be hinted at and discussed but MVE will never fully encapsulate them. Spinney (2011) has remarked that when using video the researcher is basically creating a reduction – stripping away other ways of experiencing mobility and highlighting the body-in-action, making some aspects visible and others invisible in doing so. For such a highly textured and deeply embodied practice like running, this is a big disadvantage for the use of MVE.

Furthermore, the priority MVE does give to what can be seen is not complete. The fixed gaze of the camera fails to provide the full panorama of which the participants themselves will be aware. When re-watching the video in the post-run interviews, participants often comment on things that were happening off-screen, so to speak. While attaching the camera to the runner's head will show the changing direction of attention to the researcher, it does not track the focus of the eyes. MVE cannot show you what users were paying attention to and the significant aspects of their experience to them. While in some ways this is not a problem, as a major advantage of MVE is the ability to reveal things beyond cognition, there is a concern that such focus on the mundane is placing artificial importance on the minutiae at the expense of the phenomena participants hold integral to their practices and to understanding them.

Practically, there are other important considerations to make when using MVE. Most importantly within this is the question of what camera to use. Placing a camera on a runner can result in an uncomfortable experience and it is something that needs to be balanced with the quality of the video gained from MVE. The rhythm of a runner's body results in a video which appears to bob, something which can be quite painful to watch if the camera quality is too low, or if the camera is not fastened securely. High-quality, lightweight action cameras offer a good solution here (see Box 12.1) and although they are becoming cheaper, their cost could be a barrier for adopting MVE. However, the smaller and more lightweight cameras compromise battery-life, and on a few of the longer runs participants recorded (generally over ninety minutes), the camera died before the end of the run. Generally, a thorough trialling and testing of the equipment and set-up for MVE to optimise it for the practice you are studying is strongly advised.

Overall, I would advocate using both methods together. It is certainly an instance where the whole is more than the sum of its parts, and for those interested in the mundane and everyday, they offer a powerful suite of methods to interrogate any practice. The two methods complement each other's strengths and weaknesses, and provide two different perspectives on the same phenomena, resulting in very insightful research. However, the mobile nature of these methods raises challenges for researching in ethical and safe ways. For example, most ethical procedures and forms are generally based upon a static and single location in which any research encounter will be conducted, and I have found a mobile research site to be incongruous at times with such processes. Furthermore, a core principle of ethical research is informed consent. While I gained informed consent from those designated as participants, the same was not possible for those passed by, and therefore recorded, in the public spaces in which these runs took place. Arguably, these passing strangers were as integral to the research as the runners themselves, yet they have no idea they were even involved. Taking methods on the move poses challenges to ethical processes, and while these have not restricted my research so far, they have required greater consideration and may suggest that ethical approval processes need to catch up with the variety of methods being used in contemporary research.

## Conclusions

This chapter has introduced and interrogated the use of GAI and MVE as methods for researching the mobile mundane. My experiments with these methods developed from an interest in the mundanities of running practices and the recent development of mobile methods, which invites methodological innovation to find ways of keeping up with mobile phenomena. Throughout my research, GAI and MVE have been the methods I have used most often. In the case of running, GAIs involved joining people on their run, conducting an interview on the go, while MVE involved runners using a head-camera to record an unaccompanied run, which was then used as the basis for a post-run interview. Neither of these methods had been used within the context of running before, so many of my experiments with them concerned innovating with set-ups that were feasible and held methodological value, accounts of which are given throughout the chapter. Using GAI and MVE as methodological counterparts, however, was an accidental innovation on my part. Evaluating the methodological effectiveness of these methods demonstrated the complementing features they offer, providing a way for researchers to interrogate practices from multiple perspectives. GAIs offer excellent researcher–participant rapport and in-the-moment reflection to passing stimuli/experiences, improving participant's ability to talk about the mundane. However, there are still many aspects of jography which fall under the radar of cognition, and MVE can be used to make visible and analysable the minutiae of running practices. Together, they offer a powerful suite of methods to interrogate everyday mobile practices. That is not to say there are no limitations to these methods. The evaluation offered in the chapter demonstrated many logistical and ethical difficulties that accompany these methods, as well as the privileging each gives to particular aspects of everyday experiences at the expense of those they make less visible. Despite these, the strengths of the methods entail that further experimentation is warranted. There are many contexts within which the methods of doing with (GAI) and seeing with (MVE) can prove valuable additions to researchers of the mundane and I certainly urge further experimentation.

---

### Box 12.2: Further reading

Kinney, P. (2017) 'Walking interviews', *Social Research Update*, 67: 1–4.
Merriman, P. (2014) 'Rethinking mobile methods', *Mobilities*, 9 (2): 167–187.
Spinney, J. (2011) 'A chance to catch a breath: using mobile video ethnography in cycling research' *Mobilities*, 6 (2): 161–182.

---

## References

Allen-Collinson, J. and Hockey, J. (2001) 'Runners' tales: autoethnography, injury and narrative', *Auto/Biography*, IX (1–2): 95–106.
Allen-Collinson, J., Vaittinen, A., Jennings, G. and Owton, H. (2018) 'Exploring lived heat, "temperature work," and embodiment: novel auto/

ethnographic insights from physical cultures', *Journal of Contemporary Ethnography*, 47 (3): 283–305.

Anderson, J. (2004) 'Talking whilst walking: a geographical archaeology of knowledge', *Area*, 36 (3): 254–261.

Brown, K. M. and Dilley, R. (2012) 'Ways of knowing for "response-ability" in more-than-human encounters: the role of anticipatory knowledges in outdoor access with dogs', *Area*, 44 (1): 37–45.

Brown, K. M., Dilley, R. and Marshall, K. (2008) 'Using a head-mounted video camera to understand social worlds and experiences', *Sociological Research Online*, 13 (6): 1–10.

Büscher, M. and Urry, J. (2009) 'Mobile methods and the empirical', *European Journal of Social Theory*, 12 (1): 99–116.

Cook, S. (2016) 'Run-commuting', in S. Sultana and J. Weber (eds) *Minicars, Maglevs, and Mopeds: Modern Modes of Transportation Around the World*, Santa Barbara, CA: ABC-CLIO/Greenwood Press, 255–258.

Cook, S. (2017) 'Rushing, dashing, scrambling: the role of the train station in producing the reluctant runner', in J. Spinney, S. Reimer and P. Pinch (eds) *Mobilising Design*, Abingdon: Routledge, 62–75.

Cook, S. (2018) 'Geographies of mobility: a brief introduction', *Geography*, 103 (3): 137–145.

Cook, S., Shaw, J. and Simpson, P. (2016a) 'Jography: exploring meanings, experiences and spatialities of recreational road-running', *Mobilities*, 11 (5): 744–769.

Cook, S., Shaw, J. and Simpson, P. (2016b) 'Running order: urban public space, everyday citizenship and sporting subjectivities', in N. Koch (ed.) *Critical Geographies of Sport: Space, Power and Sport in Global Perspective*, Abingdon: Routledge, 157–172.

Cresswell, T. and Merriman, P. (2011) 'Introduction: geographies of mobilities – practices, spaces, subjects', in T. Cresswell and P. Merriman (eds) *Geographies of Mobilities: Practices, Spaces, Subjects*, Farnham: Ashgate, 1–18.

D'Andrea, A., Ciolfi, L. and Gray, B. (2011) 'Methodological challenges and innovations in mobilities research', *Mobilities*, 6 (2): 149–160.

DeLyser, D. and Sui, D. (2013) 'Crossing the qualitative–quantitative divide II: inventive approaches to big data, mobile methods, and rhythmanalysis', *Progress in Human Geography*, 37 (2): 293–305.

Evans, J. and Jones, P. (2011) 'The walking interview: methodology, mobility and place', *Applied Geography*, 31 (2): 849–858.

Hitchings, R. and Latham, A. (2016) 'Indoor versus outdoor running: understanding how recreational exercise comes to inhabit environments through practitioner talk', *Transactions of the Institute of British Geographers*, 41(4): 503–514.

Holton, M. and Riley, M. (2014) 'Talking on the move: place-based interviewing with undergraduate students' *Area*, 46 (1): 59–65.

Laurier, E. (2010) 'Being there/seeing there', in B. Fincham, M. McGuinness and L. Murray (eds) *Mobile Methodologies*, Basingstoke: Palgrave Macmillan, 103–177.

Laurier, E. (2014) 'Capturing motion: video set-ups for driving, cycling and walking', in P. Adey, D. Bissell, K. Hannam, P. Merriman and M. Sheller (eds) *The Routledge Handbook of Mobilities*, Abingdon: Routledge, 493–502.

Law, J. and Urry, J. (2004) 'Enacting the social', *Economy and Society*, 33 (3): 390–410.

Merriman, P. (2014) 'Rethinking mobile methods', *Mobilities*, 9 (2): 167–187.

Pink, S. (2014) *Doing Visual Ethnography*, London: Sage.

Simpson, P. (2011) '"So, as you can see …": some reflections on the utility of video methodologies in the study of embodied practices', *Area*, 43 (3): 343–352.

Simpson, P. (2014) 'Video', in P. Adey, D. Bissell, K. Hannam, P. Merriman and M. Sheller (eds) *The Routledge Handbook of Mobilities*, Abingdon: Routledge, 542–552.

Spinney, J. (2006) 'A place of sense: a kinaesthetic ethnography of cyclists on Mont Ventoux', *Environment and Planning D: Society and Space*, 24 (5): 709–732.

Spinney, J. (2011) 'A chance to catch a breath: using mobile video ethnography in cycling research', *Mobilities*, 6 (2): 161–182.

# 13

# Pedestrian practices: walking from the mundane to the marvellous

## Morag Rose

For many people walking is, perhaps, the very definition of a taken-for-granted mundane method. It gets us from A to B, to work, to school, to the shops, to the car. However, it can be much more, and in this chapter I will explore how walking can be used as a research tool. I will begin by outlining some of the literature on walking methods and then discuss my experiences of utilising some of them. Linking all these methods is a common understanding that walking is an embodied, sensual experience that provides a direct connection to the environment. It is particularly valuable when you want to study relationships with place, everyday experiences, or want to destabilise the conventional research relationship. Physical experience is, of course, different for everyone and it should be acknowledged that many intersections of identity will have an impact on an individual's walking. These will be considered, and I will also discuss limitations of walking methodology. I would like to be clear from the outset that my definition of walking includes mobility devices that enable movement, such as wheelchairs, scooters, sticks and orthotics (also see Birtchnell, Harada and Waitt, this collection).

My commitment to walking methods pre-dates, and permeates, my academic work, as I have been involved with psychogeographic collective, The LRM (Loiterers Resistance Movement) since 2006. I will discuss psychogeography later but in essence I am interested in how the environment influences our feelings. In psychogeographical walking, the 'derive' is a form of explicitly critical engagement, coming from a radical political perspective. We wander together to explore how regeneration policies impact the shape of the city and to experiment with creative, and playful, walking methods. More recently, for my PhD research, I walked with women to discuss their thoughts, feelings and experiences of Manchester.

This chapter shares fieldwork notes and practical tips to develop walking methods at a variety of scales:

1) lone wandering as way to understand everyday spaces;
2) one-to-one walking interviews, because walking and talking together facilitates rich conversations about the environment;
3) walking with groups of people who want to improve their neighbourhoods;
4) sensory walking which focuses on embodied encounters;
5) creative walking and psychogeography which uses ludic methods such as transposing maps, throwing dice or following themes to provoke new understandings of space. I have played games such as CCTV bingo to stimulate discussion and affective re-mapping. It's outside the scope of this work but sometimes walking itself becomes an artistic act or performance (see Walking Artists Network online).

This chapter shares my personal experiences of using walking methods. Of course many others have walked this way too, and I will also draw on their journeys.

## Walking as research tool

Walking can be used as a method in a variety of ways and an excellent collection edited by Bates and Rhys-Taylor (2017) provides an overview of recent work. Contributions include sociological accounts of Black History, walking with youth groups to understand their experiences of space, auto-ethnographic accounts of shopping centres, and community participation in walks to monitor air pollution. In his contribution, Back suggests that: 'walking is not just a technique for uncovering the mysteries of the city but also a form of pedagogy or a way to learn and think not just individually but also collectively' (2017: 20).

A growing number of researchers use walking interviews, which, as the name suggests, take interviews out into the landscape and onto the street. Walking and talking like this provides a method which 'combines participant observation and semi-structured interviewing, both of which foreground context in knowledge construction' (Warren, 2016: 11). Jones et al. (2008) review three case studies of walking interviews where a variety of techniques are used to spatially locate narrative. They find 'walking interviews are an ideal technique for exploring issues around people's relationship with space' (2008: 2). They report that participants are often more relaxed and forthcoming because mobility removes research from its traditional setting within an often-intimidating academy. This goes some way to breaking down hierarchies and making the research relationship more equal, so the participant feels able to determine direction and take inspiration from the environment. They conclude there is much potential for further work on the relationship between walking, perception, memory and space. Riley and Holton (2017) also provide compelling arguments for walking methods, particularly when place, dwelling and the environment are key themes. They highlight the methods' power to 'de-centre' an interview. For example, walking together breaks direct eye contact and allows for unexpected encounters.

However, rather than being a totally new technique walking interviews are perhaps best seen as a spin on familiar methods, allowing for greater allowance for environmental factors and the impact of memory. Evans and Jones (2011) find that walking interviews generate richer data, because interviewees are prompted by meanings and connections to the surrounding environment and are less likely to try to give the 'right' answer. There are several other studies which also resonate with this, each using slightly different ways to walk. Kusenbach (2003) used go-alongs, whereby the researcher shadows subjects, probing what they are doing in situ, concluding that the method helps establish a mutually comfortable relationship with participants where environmental factors provoke a naturalistic conversation (see chapters on go-alongs by Birtchnell, Harada and Waitt; Cook; Stoodley; and Wilkinson, in this collection). Anderson (2004) engaged in a talking while walking that he termed 'bimbles' with environmental campaigners in the countryside outside their protest camp. His bimbles demonstrated the impact of environment on memory and how (relatively) easy it can be to share stories when walking. Both Kusenbach and Anderson reaffirm my belief that being in, and moving through, a landscape is an excellent way to facilitate conversations.

I also take from them the importance of allowing participants to choose their own paths to enable conversations to be as natural as possible. Akerman (2014) affirms this, and goes so far as to suggest that in some cases walking interviews are the only way to gain insight. He walked with Tibetans living in New York who simply did not want to sit and listen to his 'barrage of questions' (2014: 3). Akerman felt walking gave his participants agency and generated empathy between them.

Walking also aids kinaesthetic learning through the engagement of multiple senses and an innate desire to 'show and tell', as explored by Pink (2015) as part of what she terms 'sensory ethnography'. Mobile methodologies like walking can create problems, especially around recording data. Jones et al. (2008) are critical of studies which do not attempt to physically map the places where participants make revelations, believing there needs to be a precise record of where something has been said so that this can be linked with the subject. This is of direct value to many of the projects they discuss, for example 'Rescue Geography', which aimed to curate a social history of spaces before they disappeared through regeneration. This methodology included a fixed route for each participant and/or GPS technology for precise geographical location.

Within this chapter I will now share my experiences of using a range of walking methods at different scales and discuss how I have dealt with the limitations.

## Lone walking

A lone walk can provide an opportunity to study the environment and get a sense of place. This kind of walking research tends to be auto-ethnographic in nature, and an excellent example is provided by Wylie (2005) (for further auto-ethnographic encounters see Collins, this volume); however, this work is deeply subjective and it can be difficult to extrapolate wider meaning. Lone wandering can be helpful to researchers for another reason, though. As Rebecca Solnit (2001: 10) says, 'I suspect that the mind, like the feet, works at about three miles an hour. If this is so, then modern life is moving faster than the speed of thought or thoughtfulness.' There are many writers and artists who claim walking as inspiration and method, from Charles Dickens and the Wordsworths to Virginia Woolf and Patti Smith.

You can try this method easily yourself, and this exercise can also prove helpful for developing wider skills as a researcher. It can work well within an environment you are very familiar with or can provide a way to explore somewhere new (however, do not forget to check the safety notes provided later on). Try to utilise what Mills (1959) calls 'the sociological imagination', where links are made between your personal experiences and wider social issues. This awareness helps with a critical engagement that can lead to an individual walk contributing to wider collective knowledges.

## Activity: shifting perspectives

So, an activity for readers to try. For twenty minutes, walk along looking up and paying attention to the skyline. What can rooftops tell you about where you are?

Occasionally stop, study where you are and observe how people are using this space. Also note who is not there; are there physical barriers or implicit messages that mean access is restricted? Thinking about the invisible can be very pertinent.

Now, turn around and retrace your steps. This time, look down. Study the ground beneath your feet, the textures and the detritus that you may pass over. Make sure you record what you have experienced. This may be photographs, fieldnotes, items collected, sketches or any other medium that you wish.

## One-to-one walking interviews

For my PhD research I wanted to learn about women's experiences of walking in Manchester, UK and how it shaped their relationship to the city. I chose walking interviews for the reasons discussed above; I wanted to provoke rich conversations with, about, and in, place (for further discussion on the importance of in-situ research see Stoodley, this collection). Walking through the landscape prompted reminiscences and comments, and anecdotally I felt conversations were often more candid and interesting than during conventional interviews. I did not want to follow a set path as I was interested in participants' individual experiences and therefore I asked them to show me where mattered to them. The majority of interviews started in Piccadilly Gardens, chosen as it is a central transport hub within the city, and a place that many people who live or visit Manchester are familiar with and thus also an easy conversation starter. The freeform approach I took did have a few disadvantages, largely around comparing data between participants due to the mapping of very different routes. However, I was seeking deep and rich qualitative information and was able to find common themes and concerns across diverse participants. I chose not to use GPS technology or take photographs as I felt they would be distracting both to myself and participants. I will discuss my preferred methods of recording later.

## Small group walkabouts

Walking methods can be useful in settings outside academia. Healthwatch Manchester 'ensures the public voice is heard by those who commission, design and deliver health and social care services' (Healthwatch Manchester, 2017) and are interested in the views and experiences of patients. They often employ participatory or novel methods to collect information, and anecdotal evidence meant they were concerned about the experiences of learning disabled people visiting hospitals. Community groups and individuals had told them about problems with accessible information and barriers making it difficult to navigate the support services available. Healthwatch Manchester therefore facilitated a series of what they call 'walk-throughs'. These were pre-arranged visits where small groups of learning disabled people visited various hospitals to undertake a guided observation of the services. They entered facilities, asked for directions and used wayfinder services which had been put in place to assist patient navigation. Afterwards they discussed their experiences. All the visitors had used services before, were volunteers and were accompanied by support staff. They were able to make a number of constructive suggestions for how to improve support, for example by making changes to signage and the speed at which people were expected to move. Chief Executive of Healthwatch Manchester, Neil Walbran says he valued walk-throughs because 'they provide a snap-shot of personal experiences and enable individual voices to be heard. Walkthroughs are not intended to be comprehensive or definitive reports. They value personal, subjective accounts rather than grand theory or statistical analysis' (Healthwatch Manchester, 2017).

## Sensory walks

Walking is multi-sensory and somatic; one of the great benefits of this walking method is the immersion in space and connection to bodily sensations. Sarah Pink explores this idea in her work on 'sensory ethnography', which includes a section on walking interviews. However, culturally we tend to prioritise the ocular and concentrate very much on what we can see. This is evident in the language we use in research, such as 'participant observation' and 'visual analysis'.

I have facilitated sense walks as part of an artistic micro-commission from The Cornerhouse Arts Centre, Manchester. I took participants on a pre-planned route which was designed to incorporate a range of ambiences and sensations. For example, we walked along a canal which had places that smelt very unpleasant and past tactile surfaces that participants were encouraged to touch. At particular points on the route we would stop and discuss our opinions about the place we were in. Some participants also chose to take photographs or field-notes which they later shared. It was difficult to collect everyone's stories when we were out and about and I did not have a budget for research assistants. Therefore, at the end of the walk we gathered together for a discussion in a de facto focus group. I wanted this to include creative methods as well and it also gave me a chance to include taste, which was a very difficult sense to incorporate into the walk; the idea of licking buildings or eating dirt was unethical and unappealing. I had an initial plan to invite participants to make a loaf of bread that tasted of Manchester but logistically this proved a challenge. Baking takes time, and it was also hard to find a suitable kitchen. Therefore I settled on a more symbolic gesture: creating edible artefacts which were not necessarily appetising but embodied the principle. I made several batches of edible modelling dough in a range of colours, and provided a selection of flavourings and decorations. These included extracts, spices, herbs, sweets and prepared fruits and vegetables. I asked everyone to build a model representing what they thought was the flavour of Manchester. Some chose to depict things they had encountered on the walk; others based their models on longer-term memories or more general impressions of the city. Offerings ranged from a Beetham Tower covered in candy hearts to a Vimto cordial canal. One participant made a smiling bee, covered in glitter and curry powder, that conjured up their childhood in the suburb of Rusholme. There is much scope for data analysis of these representations and they provide an example of creative methods which I am only able to allude to here due to lack of space.

## Activity: sound walk

What else might we learn if we try to focus on other senses? Here is an easy experiment for you to try.

Shhhhh! Walk in silence on your own or with others. Really concentrate on what you can hear as you walk, the different soundscapes; what does it tell you about the place you are in? How do the volume, pitch and quality of sound change as you move around? Can you hear bird song, human conversation, machinery, traffic? Victoria Henshaw (2013; see also Perkins and McLean, this collection) has produced guidelines for a smell walk and again we can learn much about a place by stopping and sniffing!

## Tours

The field trip is a familiar experience for school children everywhere and its ubiquity underlines the widespread belief that being out in an environment is helpful to study. Equally, guided walks, tours and heritage trails are a staple of the tourist experience. Generally they work best as an educational or outreach tool, but they can also be very entertaining. Participants may often be assumed to be passive but this is not always the case. Smith (2012) offers an entertaining critique of heritage tropes and offers alternative activities he calls 'Counter-Tourism'. Emphasis is usually on stationary points of interest and the walking in between is almost incidental, although Curtis (2008) discusses how children enjoy and learn from these gaps.

When constructing a tour, like writing a book chapter, choices are made about what to include and what to omit and there can be many reasons for this. I constructed The Ardwick Green Heritage Trail to celebrate an area just south of Manchester City Centre that has been generally overlooked in the majority of guides to the city. On the edge of the park are a number of voluntary organisations. I was working at GMCVO (Greater Manchester Centre for Voluntary Organisation) which is based in The St Thomas Centre, formerly St Thomas's Church, one of the oldest in Manchester. The area itself can lay claim to being the world's first suburb, as it became the home of wealthy merchants and mill owners during the Industrial Revolution. The trail features a number of buildings of historical and architectural interest as well as the traces of others that are now lost. It focuses particularly on the eponymous Green, a small park. Producing the trail utilised a range of sources. Colleagues held 'heritage tea parties' and other events to collect oral testimonies and many people shared personal memories and artefacts. We also consulted official archives and fictional accounts such as *The Manchester Man* novel (Banks, 1896), which includes detailed descriptions of the environment.

Drawing this together into a tour entailed drawing out themes, in a way similar to analysing interview or other qualitative data. There was a decision to focus on voluntary, community and cultural activity which clearly reflected both my own research interests at the time and my positionality within the voluntary sector. Tours were held as part of Heritage Open Days at GMCVO and they attracted a lot of interest from the general public. They included residents, both past and present, whose insights enriched future iterations of the project. The tours encouraged participation and were an excellent tool for collecting stories and disseminating information. However, I did encounter some issues. The area is bounded by busy, and loud, roads, which meant a lot of shouting was needed. Also, the popularity of the walks meant sometimes the crowds were quite large so we needed to begin ticketing the events to make sure they were safe and manageable. Funding was obtained to print maps that were distributed at local community hubs, again emphasising the collaborative nature of the project. Text space limited the amount of information that could be included, leading inevitably to debate about what was excluded.

## Creative walking

The walking methods discussed so far use familiar pedestrian practices; however, walking can also be transformed into a creative act. Heddon and Turner (2010) interview several women walking artists, and membership of the Walking Artists Network (online) illustrates the wealth and diversity of contemporary walking art.

The walking art I will focus on has evolved from psychogeography. This was first defined as 'The study of the precise laws and specific effects of the geographical environment, consciously organised or not, on the emotions and behaviours of individuals' (Debord, 1955). Psychogeography is more than a theory; it is also a practice based on walking, in particular the dérive, or drift, which is a wander guided by desires. The roots of psychogeography are inherently political: Debord and his colleagues in the SI (Situationist International) wanted to disrupt the flow of capitalism and find unmediated, uncommodified joy. Their walking was resistant because it was not designed to be productive or instrumental and they saw it as a challenge to the status quo. They walked to uncover the power structures which are hidden in urban design and they wanted to find another way, to draw their own maps. The dérive disrupts, disorients, reconfigures but it also enchants and is fun.

Academics have used psychogeography as way to engage university students in finding new ways to look at space. Bassett (2004) organised a field trip using psychogeographic techniques, intending to deepen his students' understanding through critical application of theories. Bassett felt his experiment, although limited by logistical constraints, was worthwhile as it provided students with an opportunity to apply theories to practical fieldwork and engage on the ground because it provided 'a way of getting students to open their eyes and ears to what is often taken for granted or ignored in negotiating urban space. It is a way of raising consciousness of urban places and rhythms' (2004: 398). The notion that the dérive can provide a new way of looking at and experiencing familiar territory is supported by Richardson (2013). She uses psychogeographical techniques with students to generate discussions across disciplines and suggests the biggest 'surprises' about place come when they dérive familiar streets or on campus, because places become 'transformed in the minds of the students into places for potential' (2013: 38).

As mentioned in my introduction, in 2006 I co-founded a psychogeographical collective called The Loiterers Resistance Movement. Open to everyone, the membership is fluid and includes artists, activists, academics and others curious about the city. On the first Sunday of every month we go for a free, communal dérive (see Rose, 2015 for more details). The LRM have been wandering the same areas for over a decade and in that time have become intimately acquainted with the terrain. As people wander in and out of the group they bring their own stories which embellish and sometimes destabilise the established narratives of the group. A substantial archive of images has been built up, often focusing on details which are frequently overlooked. For example, paying close attention to the everyday cityscape reveals traces of the past, glimpses of the future and mysterious artefacts that spark the imagination. On Lloyd Street, above an archway, for many years there was a stuffed animal, possibly a ferret or stoat, and no explanation was ever found for how the taxidermy got there. Stories were created and shared, some wildly implausible, but whenever we passed the vicinity someone would add another layer to the speculation. At some point around 2015 the building was refurbished and a barbeque restaurant moved in. One day our inanimate friend was gone as abruptly and mysteriously as he appeared. No doubt the reality will be prosaic although casual inquiries have yet to yield any explanation. We have also been able to highlight issues around privatisation, the loss of public space and the impact of regeneration.

## Activity: playing card walk

On these Sunday dérives a variety of tactics are used as a catalyst or prompt to guide our wander. One popular method repurposes a set of playing cards to divine the direction to follow. There are numerous variations; a personal favourite is as follows.

This walk works with any number of participants, but is best with between four and eight people. Start by shuffling the cards; the first person draws one and follows the instructions below. After completing their task the pack of cards is passed on to someone else to take a turn. Continue as long as you wish.

- number card = look for that quantity of a specific thing chosen by the card puller (e.g. six doorways, nine pigeons, three fire escapes);
- Jack = retrace your steps to where you last drew a card, observe what has changed, pull again;
- Queen = take the first left and walk for five minutes in the straightest line possible;
- King = take the second right and the first left;
- Joker = follow your nose for five minutes and go where you wish.

The cards introduce a random element which helps break everyday walking habits, encouraging playful exploration and helping to experience mundane landscapes in a new way.

## Diversity and access

It should be acknowledged that not all walking methodologies are equal or available to everyone. Some people may feel excluded, unable or unwelcome to walk in a specific place and the researcher should be aware of intersectional factors influencing an individual's capacity to participate in walks in a specific place. The physical environment is an obvious example, so someone with a wheelchair or pram may not take part in a walk that includes a lot of stairs. Other barriers may be more subtle and require cultural sensitivity or consideration of lifestyle choices.

I place my own research within an explicitly feminist geographical tradition. This is in part because I wanted to challenge a canon which is overwhelmingly male and which tends to assume the walker is explicitly male or ungendered with an assumption of maleness. This is problematic because of the very embodiedness of walking; bodies are all different and have different privileges. Gender – or presumed gender based on physical appearance – therefore has a fundamental impact on the experience of walking. Both my research and my own lived experience support the view that women and men walk in different ways and feel able to be in space in different ways. For example, Valentine (1990) discusses cognitive maps that women develop to feel safe in the city; Bates (2014) highlights the impact of everyday sexism; and Warren (2016) walks with Muslim women to understand their experiences. It would be disingenuous to claim a walking interview is an equal or truly participatory method but it certainly has qualities that can make it less formal and more conversational. It usually makes subjectivity and positionality explicit and helps dissolve hierarchies. Psychogeography also implies a critical perspective, and in my work there is often an overt radical influence (Rose, 2015).

## Planning your walk

When conducting walking research you need to develop a sort of dual awareness. This is a heightened version of the reflexivity needed by every qualitative or quantitative researcher. Part of you is paying attention to your participant, listening to what they say, watching for cues, prompting and making sure you give them enough space to talk about what they wish. However, another part of you must be constantly alert to your wider environment and how it may be changing. Are you blocking a pavement or at risk of trespassing? Is there a road coming up that you need to find a place to cross? You must be aware of emerging trip hazards, changes in weather or the movement of bystanders. You also need to remember to check your recording equipment is in order and/or you are making any notes necessary. This will come with practice and I would recommend conducting a few pilot expeditions to get a feel for what you need to do before embarking on your actual fieldwork (further considerations in mobile interviews are discussed in the chapters by Birtchnell, Harada and Waitt; Cook; and Stoodley, this collection).

Recording walking methods offers a particular challenge. Background noise can be a problem. For one-to-one interviews I use a small digital recorder with a windshield on it. This suffices, even in a busy city centre, but care must be taken to make sure the microphone is held in the correct position throughout. For back-up and multiple interviews, I use a small Dictaphone with a clip-on microphone which the interviewee wears, although this can be cumbersome and transcription is complicated by multiple recordings. I also keep a very detailed field diary which I complete as soon as possible after every interview. This includes information not easily picked up by the microphone, such as the weather, interaction with bystanders, body language and so on.

Personally, I don't take photographs or videos while conducting walking research as I find the equipment cumbersome to use and feel they interrupt the flow of the conversation. However, many people do advocate for their use (see Jones et al., 2008; Pink,2015). Conversely, even the hand-held microphone I favour can be seen as intrusive by some researchers (Akerman, 2014). I found it was surprisingly easily ignored by interviewees and offered a good compromise between recording quality and convenience. There were still some unexpected emergent logistical issues with recording. One walking interview I conducted was with someone considerably taller than me and holding the microphone up to her became very uncomfortable.

A decision needs to be made about how, and why, you choose to record the route of your walk as well as the content of conversations. For my PhD research I chose not to use GPS or similar. I occasionally spoke into the mic to confirm a location, and then wrote down the route as soon as possible afterwards. In retrospect, it may have been helpful to use one of the many popular apps designed to track movement, such as Strava, although the ethics of surveillance and data security must be considered. Many academics such as Jones et al. (2008) feel mapping data is an integral and important part of the research process. Nold (2009) explores a range of technologies of monitoring and tracking to produce emotion maps and documents the opportunities and threats these present.

## Stop!

Before you begin using walking methods you need to be aware that your research carries with it a specific set of risks which you may not encounter in other research settings. Some of these have already been discussed but it is important to reiterate them as keeping safe must be a primary concern.

Any kind of fieldwork requires a risk assessment to determine how to make it as safe as possible. If you are connected to an institution they will probably have their own procedures you must follow, and this section offers only a few basic guidelines. You must think carefully about the specific environment you will be working in and remember this process is not about stopping research but enabling it to do no harm, and I am sure that is a principle on which we can all agree. An example of a risk you will need to consider is traffic. This is an inevitable and dangerous element in most contemporary environments, though particularly for the urban walking methods discussed in this chapter. You can mitigate against the risk by, for example, only crossing roads at pedestrian crossings.

Weather can be another risk and make sure you are prepared for all weather conditions. This could mean applying suncream, or wearing waterproofs or warm clothes as needed. If the forecast is for extreme weather then your interview should be postponed. Wherever you are, a bottle of water is always helpful to have in your kit bag, along with recording equipment, spare batteries, field diary, purse and so on. Ensure your mobile phone is fully charged in case you need to contact anyone in an emergency. Although you may not have a preplanned route to share in advance, as with all fieldwork make sure you have informed somebody of who you are meeting, where you are starting from, and the approximate duration of your trip.

Be aware of your own physical limitations and emerging environmental risks. For example, during my fieldwork although I wanted participants to show me places that mattered to them, on two occasions I vetoed their choices. One woman wanted to explore a derelict building she was curious about, and although this would have been interesting and exciting I did not think it safe or appropriate. It would also have breached the ethical code and personal safety guidelines I was following. The other case was more difficult. A woman disclosed to me that she had a life-limiting illness that had an impact on her mobility. She wanted to walk along the canal with me as she was unable to do so alone in case she fell in. I did not feel physically able to keep her safe in this scenario and so we agreed a compromise, visiting a canal basin rather than the narrow and steep towpath she wanted to explore.

Remember to take care of yourself as well as your participants. I recommend that you avoid scheduling too many walks in a day in case you become tired and inattentive. The duration of a walking interview will of course vary according to both your subject and participant. Be alert to signs of fatigue. If you are facilitating a group walk, tour or dérive my experience suggests they should last a maximum of two hours – after this time somebody usually wants a break. Finish your walking interview somewhere that is convenient for your participant; it is unfair to leave them miles from their route back to where they wish to be.

Being in the field inevitably means you will be interacting with people who have not given consent to participate in your research. This is not generally a problem if you are simply moving through space; after all, we pass many people on the street every day and it would be unreasonable and unnecessary to hand an information sheet to everyone who shares public space with us. However, direct encounters should be avoided because you are unlikely to be able to ensure informed consent on the part of these passers by, and as ever a policy of doing no harm should be adopted. You need to also be mindful of issues such as causing an obstruction, encroaching on personal space and trespassing on private property. There is no law which prohibits taking photographs in public space, but ethics (and the majority of university policies) make clear that anonymity should be preserved. Without wishing to be alarmist you need to be aware of others in your environment for your own safety as well.

When interviewing women, in particular, I have attracted casual sexism and street harassment. This was uncomfortable and in some cases threatening; it also changed the course of the interviews I was conducting. It may also have caused distress to my participants. When this occurred I had several long discussions with colleagues and wondered what could be done to keep everyone safe. We concluded that this was a sad reflection on the everyday conditions women live within, and of course harassment is not directed just at women, it can be amplified by many intersectional factors. This was not sufficient to stop the research but action was taken to mitigate the risks and I developed a range of tactics to deal with these interruptions. These generally included ignoring the man, checking my interviewee was alright and making sure all our walks were in well-populated and well-lit areas.

## Conclusion

The walking artist Hamish Fulton believes 'A walk can exist like an invisible object in a complex world' (Fulton, online). This chapter demonstrates how the mundane act of walking can be transformed, going beyond the pedestrian to become a valuable addition to the researcher's toolkit. If you wish to use walking methods, considering the following will enable you to make the most of the opportunities they can provide.

- *Who?* Who will you be walking with? Do they have any specific access needs you should consider when planning your project? These may vary between individuals, so make sure you speak to participants before beginning your interview.
- *Where?* What environment? Are there particular risks? Will you pre-plan a route, shadow your participant or let them choose a route?
- *Why?* Why have you chosen a walking interview? Is it because you want to interrogate a particular landscape, elicit memories about a place, understand everyday mobility or something else?
- *How?* Will you be walking alone, with an individual or a group? Do you want to 'go-along' and shadow everyday routines or explore somewhere new? Will you plan the route in advance and structure your interview accordingly, or will each participant be able to choose their own path?
- *When?* Timing can be crucial to walking methods. Environmental factors such as weather and darkness have a temporal element which may impact on participants' welfare and their willingness to take part.

---

### Box 13.1: Tools, training and equipment

There is no specialist equipment required. You should dress appropriately for your environment and weather conditions; comfortable footwear is very important. I recommend taking a small bag with a water bottle, mobile phone, field diary and a map. Depending on how you wish to record the walk, you may also need a camera, audio recorder or art materials.

---

### Box 13.2: Further reading

Riley, M. and Holton, M. (2017) *Place-Based Interviewing: Creating and Conducting Walking Interviews*, Sage Research Methods Cases, http://methods.sagepub.com/case/place-based-interviewing-creating-and-conducting-walking-interviews (institutional log-in required).

Smith, P. (2012) *Counter-tourism: A Pocketbook: 50 Odd Things To Do in a Heritage Site (and Other Places)*, Charmouth: Triarchy Press.

Warren, S. (2016) 'Pluralising the walking interview: researching (im)mobilities with Muslim women', *Social & Cultural Geography*, 1–22. doi: 10.1080/14649365.2016.1228113.

---

## References

Akerman, S. (2014) *Walking With Exiles: Movement and Narration in Life History Research* Sage Research Methods Cases, http://methods.sagepub.com/case/walking-with-exiles-movement-and-narration-in-life-history-research (institutional log-in required).

Anderson, J. (2004) 'Talking whilst walking: a geographical archaeology of knowledge', *Area*, 36 (3): 254–261. doi: 0.1111/j.0004–0894.2004.00222.x.

Banks, I. (1896) *The Manchester Man – Illustrated*, Manchester: Abel Heywood and Son.

Bassett, K. (2004) 'Walking as an aesthetic practice and a critical tool: some psychogeographic experiments', *Journal of Geography in Higher Education*, 28 (3): 397–410. doi: 10.1080/0309826042000286965.

Bates, C. and Rhys-Taylor, A. (2017) *Walking through Social Research*, Abingdon: Routledge.

Bates, L. (2014) *Everyday Sexism*, London: Simon and Schuster.

Curtis, E. (2008) 'Walking out of the classroom: learning on the streets of Aberdeen', in T. Ingold and J. L. Vergunst (eds) *Ways of Walking: Ethnography and Practice on Foot*, Aldershot: Ashgate, 143–155.

Debord, G. (1955) Introduction to a critique of urban geography. In K. Knabb (Ed. & Trans.), Situationist international anthology revised and expanded Edition (pp. 8–12). Berkeley, CA: Bureau of Public Secrets.

Evans, J. and Jones, P. (2011) 'The walking interview: methodology, mobility and place', *Applied Geography*, 31 (2), 849–858. doi: 10.1016/j. apgeog.2010.09.005.

Fulton, H. (online) www.hamish-fulton.com/quotes.txt (accessed 20 November 2018).

Healthwatch Manchester (2017) 'Patient journeys – two sites (three services) review', www.healthwatchmanchester.co.uk/our-work/publications-and-reports/ (accessed 20 September 2018).

Heddon, D. and Turner, C. (2010) 'Walking women: interviews with artists on the move', *Performance Research*, 15 (4): 14–22. doi: 10.1080/ 13528165.2010.539873.

Henshaw, V. (2013) *Urban Smellscapes: Understanding and Designing City Smell Environments*, New York: Routledge.

Jones, P., Bunce, G., Evans, J., Gibbs, H. and Ricketts Hein, J. (2008) 'Exploring space and place with walking interviews', *Journal of Research Practice*, 4 (2): 131–144. doi: 10.1016/j.apgeog.2010.09.005.

Kusenbach, M. (2003) 'Street phenomenology: the go-along as ethnographic research tool', *Ethnography*, 4 (3: Special Issue: Phenomenology in Ethnography): 455–485. doi: 10.1177/146613810343007.

Nold, C. (ed.) (2009) *Emotional Cartography – Technologies of the Self*, http:// emotionalcartography.net/ (accessed 15 August 2018).

Mills, C. W. (1959) *The Sociological Imagination*, New York: Oxford University Press.

Richardson, T. (2013) Concrete, crows and calluses. Leeds, UK: Particulations Press.

Pink, S. (2015) *Doing Sensory Ethnography* (2nd edn), London: SAGE Publications.

Riley, M. and Holton, M. (2017) *Place-Based Interviewing: Creating and Conducting Walking Interviews*, Sage Research Methods Cases, http:// methods.sagepub.com/case/place-based-interviewing-creating-and-conducting-walking-interviews (institutional log-in required).

Rose, M/Ardwick Cultural Consortium/GMCVO/Manchester City Council (2014) *Ardwick Green Heritage Trail*, pamphlet, author's collection.

Rose, M. (2015) 'Confessions of an anarcho-flâneuse or psychogeography the Mancunian way', in T. Richardson (ed.) *Walking Inside Out: Contemporary British Psychogeography*, London: Rowan and Littlefield International, 147–162.

Smith, P. (2012) *Counter-tourism: A Pocketbook: 50 Odd Things To Do in a Heritage Site (and Other Places)*, Charmouth: Triarchy Press.

Solnit, R. (2001) *Wanderlust: A History of Walking*, London: Verso.

Valentine, G. (1990) 'Women and the designed environment: women's fear and the design of public space', *Built Environment (1978–) Women and the Designed Environment*, 16 (4): 288–303.

Walking Artists Network (online) www.walkingartistsnetwork.org/ (accessed 23 January 2019).

Warren, S. (2016) 'Pluralising the walking interview: researching (im)mobilities with Muslim women', *Social & Cultural Geography*, 18 (6): 1–22. doi: 10.1080/14649365.2016.1228113.

Wylie, J. (2005) 'A single day's walking: narrating self and landscape on the South West Coast Path', *Transactions of the Institute of British Geographers*, 30 (2): 234–247. doi: 10.1111/j.1475–5661.2005.00163.x.

# 14

# Mobile methods for mundane mobilities: studying mobility scooters in a context of spatial mobility injustice

Thomas Birtchnell, Theresa Harada and
Gordon Waitt

## Introduction

In this chapter, we consider mobile methods for studying a mundane transport phenomenon. We argue that a focus on the spatial dimensions of the electric mobility scooter – an assistive technology for people with physical mobility impairments and the elderly – offers a key optic in relation to the practicalities of mobile methodologies at large, and more broadly ideas of safe and sustainable transport that are the norm in the global North. Mobile methods, through drawing researchers into a performative mode of inquiry, offer a rich seam of data on counter-cultures and peripheral practices in transport regimes.

We consider mobile methods with transport goers in Australia facing disadvantage while undertaking the kinds of 'mundane' journeys most citizens take for granted. On a mobility scooter shopping, socialising, attending doctor's appointments and other humdrum activities become an everyday odyssey requiring subtle trip planning and the mustering of vim. We contend that this type of research and mode of inquiry into contra-modal travel will gain significance in the future given: i) the ageing of societies in the global North over the twenty-first century; and ii) the pressure for a transition away from fossil-fuel-powered automobiles to alternative modes of transport that are safer, smarter and more sustainable.

The chapter offers methodological novelty by narrating the freedoms and constraints of scooter riding as well as pointing to the implications for transport geography, policy and planning. We draw on experience from conducting a mixed-methods mobility project that combined video, semi-structured interviews, solicited diaries and accompanied journeys in Wollongong, Australia. Through this methodological approach we hoped to better understand the context of the participant by sharing the experience and acquiring a sample of the emotional state in situ. Such co-present immersion in taken-for-granted everyday experiences provides a platform for research to deliver more than narrative commentary on inequality and injustice. In this sense, the discussions herein speak to wider debates around methodology, mobility and everyday life.

The chapter focuses on mobile methods and mundanity in the following ways. First, we highlight how automatisation – that is, where motorists, pedestrians or passengers on public transport 'switch off' – in transport journeying can compromise the fine-grain details in conventional methods such as travel diaries. A method that is observational and participatory, such as the mobile mundane method we outline, obviates some of this concern. Secondly, we propose that mobile mundane methods offer a window into capturing prosaic issues critically. Observations that might usually be left by the wayside are rendered in fact meaningful and insightful in the consideration of the many elements within systems. Moreover, such minutiae, once critically imbued, afford abstraction and comparison to past and future systems.

The structure of the chapter is as follows. In the next section we avail the reader of the background of the research and its grounding in mobile methods. In section 3 we move to method as applied to the specific case study detailed in this research. Finally, we offer advice and conclusions.

## Background on the method

The sun is bright and the wind in our faces as we proceed cautiously along the patchwork footpath, our scooters shaking at times in a way sympathetic with the vacillating terrain. One moment the journey is smooth to match the recently laid asphalt, the next it is tortuously in concert with the friable admixture of loose stone and corroding bitumen. With the barely audible yelp in front by our consociate to indicate the impending depletion of the sidewalk's concrete surface in favour of grass our journey shifts tempo. Such a transition would be barely noticeable to a foot pedestrian, but to a mobility scooter operator a lawn-clothed nature-strip represents a dramatic obstacle, requiring a radical response. The mobility scooter in front comes to an abrupt stop in proximity to a troop of foot pedestrians patiently waiting to cross the road with the break in the flow of traffic. Their bemusement palpable, the peripatetic co-residents of the footpath shuffle aside as the mobility scooter edges outwards awkwardly onto the road and, in parallel with the verge, continues the journey, motorists' nervous faces in direct eyeline with the operator. Once the much-anticipated break in the traffic arises the mobility scooter pivots and darts across the road, again turning to run parallel to the verge, until a welcoming dip triggers another right-angle pivot. Stopping by a remnant telephone box we discuss with quantised breaths the manoeuvre and laugh at the mixture of fear and resignation emoting from our fleeting on-road companions.

As this vignette from one of our research diaries illustrates, what is mundane for one person is far from the case for another (also see Figure 14.1). Over the last decades scholars have made efforts to mobilise qualitative and quantitative fieldwork methods in order to engage with participants in situ and as they undertake social phenomena (Büscher and Urry, 2009). Such methods position people, regardless of their role in a project, as in motion in the 'field' and are in this sense ethnographic; being both observational and contextual (Hein, Evans and Jones, 2008).

Different modes of movement feature prominently in mobile methods (e.g. see Cook; Rose; Stoodley, this collection). The first foray was walking and the 'walk-along' with the researcher, conducting the interview while reflecting on the world around the participant and their spatial experiences of place (Jones et al., 2008). Here, regular routes offer rich data where the researcher can experience first hand how forms of mobility may operate to include or exclude. An obvious example here is the journey to school, where children who walk, skate, scooter or cycle may face danger from those whose parents drive them (Murray, 2009). In walking mobile methods different techniques manifest, including computer-based and on-site surveys and interviews (Kelly et al., 2011; Rose, this collection). Another facet of mobile methods is experiencing different cultural lifeworlds, such as those of Muslim women, through co-presence (Warren, 2017). Attenuation to urban rhythms is also another chief area of specialisation akin to the psychogeographical dérive (an unplanned journey through an urban space) of the Situationists in 1950s France (Tartia, 2018) (for further work on rhythm see Lyon, this collection).

**14.1** Mobility scooter user navigates road crossing in Wollongong, 2014

Our research drew on a sensory ethnography that combined semi-structured interviews with travel diaries and 'ride-alongs', which together or separately can form rich mobile methodologies. Sensory ethnographies emphasise the co-production of knowledge between the participants in their own familiar spaces and the researcher (Pink and Morgan, 2013). After Pink and Morgan (2013: 359), sensory ethnographies provide 'a route to understanding alternative ways of knowing about and with people and the environments of which they are a part', allowing the researcher to appraise the taken-for-granted routines of the participants. Mundane, everyday encounters are foregrounded when the researcher undertakes journey making alongside the participants. Consequently, insights are offered to how participants may resolve dilemmas while on-the-move, and researchers are encouraged to reflect on their embodied experiences in relation to those of the participants (for further work on reflexive embodied experiences of participants see Wilkinson, this collection).

We carried out twenty-four interviews, twelve travel diaries and eight 'ride-alongs' with twelve participants collected for a project on scooter mobility in the regional city of Wollongong, New South Wales, Australia; though sample size differed between projects depending on the research questions and focus. The built environment of Wollongong is shaped by the car, and everyday mobility is characterised by a high degree of car dependency. Participants were recruited through two strategies. In the first, participants were solicited via a pamphlet drop in a medical centre and two regional shopping centres. With the generous help of participants, we then recruited through snowballing. All participants experienced limited physical mobility. They included an amputee, stroke victims and those who suffered from chronic illness. All participants relied on a government benefit, only one worked (in a voluntary capacity) and all were aged from their early fifties to late eighties. Participants were differentiated by marriage status and gender: three single women, two married women, six single men and one married man. Two participants had access to a car and frequently travelled distances in excess of 50 km. The remainder travelled using a mobility scooter within a 5 km radius of their house. Most actively avoided walking and public transport (bus and train).

Three phases of fieldwork were conducted over nine months in 2014. The initial round of interviews focused on several themes: the purchasing of the vehicle; repair and servicing; journey planning; and compatibility, or lack of, with the built environment. Following the interview, the second phase of research was led by the participants, who kept a travel diary to record their trips for seven days. In the participant diaries the times and routes of the journeys were recorded and obstacles noted, alongside who or what they encountered. Provision was made for participants to draw an annotated sketch-map of their route and/or drawing to convey their experience. The travel diary entries became the basis for a follow-up round of conversations.

The third phase, the one most apt for this chapter, was approached through the 'ride-along'. Four participants dropped out of this stage. The ride-along secured insights not only to the unfolding journey, but also to how participants adjusted their house to accommodate the scooter and modified the scooter to accommodate personal needs. Eight participants were accompanied on a routine journey – four on foot and four on a mobility scooter – including a shopping centre, a café, a local club, a doctor's appointment, the beach and a fishing wharf. Permission was granted to photograph and video record these journeys. A follow-up interview was conducted to discuss what participants did and how they experienced the journey. This combination of methods allowed for an understanding of the technologies, competencies and skills of electric mobility scooter users and resulted in rich narratives. A narrative approach privileges how people give meaning to their everyday patterns of mobility and thus can shed light on how the use of mobility scooters presents personal and social benefits and challenges (Murray, 2009). The transcribed interviews and diaries were coded and analysed using a combination of content, discourse and narrative analysis as discussed by Waitt (2005) and Wiles, Rosenberg and Kearns (2005).

## Methodological insights

### Application of the ride-along

A principal feature of our treatment of the 'ride-along' is to highlight that mundanity does not equate to unimportance; quite the contrary, mobile methods afford a shared perspective that culminates in bringing to the fore the many instances of oversight in urban planning and the design of the built landscape. In the case of scooter users, ride-alongs allow participants to 'explain' to researchers their noteworthy moments, that is, those that stand out as significant to them. The methodology is useful for the researcher since it instantiates the everyday experiences of the participant rather than abstracting them into numbers or text that the researcher must probe for meaning (for a further 'go-along' methodology see Wilkinson, this collection).

In our study we aim to envision a socio-technical transition driven by 'maverick' – that is, unorthodox or independent-minded – people; users who develop fringe everyday routines that complicate built environments that do not match planning aspirations for equitable accessibility, for instance for the disabled or mobility impaired (Birchnell, Harada and Waitt, 2017). Ride-alongs assisted with this goal in revealing the everyday experiences of disadvantage through a fine-grain optic. It also gave the researcher (falsely or not) a sense of solidarity with the participant, that while perhaps destabilising scientific objectivity embellishes critical inquiry with experiential scaffolds.

The notion of mundanity here is useful for critical awareness of disputes that arise in efforts to undertake routines for those unable to meet the standards set for most users. In our study we formed a typology underlining three key features of transport mavericks: improvisation, capability and customisation. Using conventional interview and solicited diary methods did not provide in-depth insights into these more subtle and individuated consequences of scooter use. It was mobile methods that brought these to light.

## Improvisation

Most participants were so familiar with their own mobility scooter routines that it did not occur to them to describe in detail the minutiae of the daily challenges that they faced. For example, mobility scooters tend to contest the design principles of the conventional built environment since they are wider, heavier and more cumbersome at turns and terrains. This means that every journey entails impromptu strategies that arise in relation to the conditions they encounter despite their tacit knowledge of familiar pathways and places. For example, participants frequently narrated how over time they had refined their routine pathways to avoid known hazards and obstacles. This was often mentioned in a cursory way, yet emerged as a pivotal issue when undertaking the mobile methods. The researchers, being novice drivers of mobility scooters, did not have the tacit knowledge of the risks of scooter use.

The participants' tacit knowledge became apparent through the mobile methods. From the start of the journey, participants demonstrated an in-depth knowledge of where there were paved footpaths, cracked or patched bitumen footpaths with loose gravel, overhanging trees, footpaths deracinated by tree roots, ramps which did not accommodate their ascent and descent from the pavement, the hazards of travelling on grassed verges and the difficulties of crossing at designated pedestrian walkways at intersections. This knowledge was shared with the researcher as they journeyed to the shops, calling out to alert the researcher of hazards and dangers, and situating themselves as experts wishing to protect the researcher from harm. Participants demonstrated the best ways to avoid problems, encouraging the researcher to follow their path and to mimic their speed and manoeuvres. Thus, it emerged that the most obvious shortfall was how the provision of ramps to facilitate, for example, parents with prams or cyclists, were often not suitable for the larger shape and size of the mobility scooter and its limited manoeuvrability within the constrained public spaces at busy intersections. At pedestrian crossings it was sometimes impossible to cross without assistance.

> There's a ramp onto the footpath but they – where the traffic light is, with the button on I, it is too far up and I, and there's a telegraph pole right in the way and I just can't get to it ... I can't use the button on because I can't get access to it. (Garry, single, seventy-four years of age)

The tacit knowledge of such obstacles and barriers was accumulated over time through trial and error and indicated the regularity and mundanity of their routines to attend doctors' appointments, socialise or do the weekly shopping. Participants each drew on personalised mental maps which allowed them to competently traverse the terrain, actively avoiding known trouble spots and opting for routes which they deemed most 'comfortable'. While participants discussed these issues in an interview context, it was through the mobile methods that the researcher came to understand the comparative dangers that made up everyday journeys. An unforeseen element in this study's method, therefore, was the attitude to risk taking observed among the participants, who for the most part had habituated their exposure to danger or illegality throughout their journey. A combination of strategies was drawn upon to enable mobility scooter users to engage with exigent infrastructure routinely and in a way distinct from foot pedestrians and compensating for visual, cognitive or sensorial impairment (McIlvenny, 2018).

Equally unforeseen were the risks not only for the participants but also for the researcher, drivers and pedestrians. Not being adept at maintaining balance or road position on the mobility scooter presented dangers because of the risks of falling or collision. Likewise, through struggling to activate the walk signal at pedestrian crossings further dangers were identified: a lack of time to safely cross; and being brought into close proximity with turning vehicles because of the angle and placement of ramps which necessitated crossing the marked pedestrian zones (Figure 14.2). We argue that all mobile methods carry risks, some unforeseen, that must weighted against the benefits of their use.

## Capability

Beyond the many ad hoc strategies and solutions that mobility scooter users administer in their journeys is an underpinning of capability.

**14.2** John demonstrates how he must leave the marked zones for pedestrians at a crossing to be able to access the ramps, Albion Park, 2015

Using a mobility scooter allowed people to be in control of their lives to accomplish everyday tasks like grocery shopping, attending doctors' appointments and socialising. Mobility scooters were often a means to overcome the physical constraints of ageing, health or injury. For some, it meant that they were freed from obligation to other family members for transportation, and therefore did not impose a 'burden' on others. For many without family support, it was the only form of mobility that enabled them to leave the house to accomplish mundane tasks.

> Otherwise I couldn't get out. I can walk only about 100 yards and so I – If I didn't have that scooter I wouldn't be able to get out of the house at all. (Helga, single, eighty years of age)

Mobile methods were also advantageous for identifying differences in mobility scooter use along the lines of gender. While all spoke of the benefits of personal freedom and independence, this was most clearly demonstrated in how the participants responded to requests for a 'ride-along' journey. Travel patterns were gendered and intergenerational, with men usually relating greater self-confidence to travel further and on more high-risk routes, whereas women and older men expressed greater levels of anxiety about safety and the risks of breakdown. Mobility scooters require their users to exercise a degree of nous in mundane journeying. A major technical issue is the electric battery, which will atrophy if not regularly recharged, potentially stranding the occupant. As well, there is a learning curve in establishing the limits of the scooter in terms of its torque to climb hills or rapidity in braking. Having a mobility scooter meant that people assumed the technical responsibility for maintaining it in good working order. They were careful to charge the battery regularly, to check the pressure and condition of tyres, to ensure that the scooter was safely stored and was protected from wet weather. These practices fortified the belief that they could safely manage their own transport needs. Mobile methods, however, allowed the researcher to identify the way that different gendered beliefs about technical knowledge influenced how scooters were used. It was not only how participants spoke about the responsibilities for maintaining the scooter but was evidenced by the kinds of journeys that were made and their propensity for spontaneity.

## Customisation and storage of equipment

Mobile methods provided deep insights into the everyday forms and function of assisted mobility, such as how mobility scooters had been customised in several ways, and this can impact on the adoption of particular empirical techniques. In readying the vehicle for a ride-along, participants had to go through the motions of checking the scooter was suitably charged, they needed to move it from the place where it was stored, and to add any modifications that were necessary for the journey. Some refused to undertake a ride-along, citing insufficient battery charge, or the possibility of damage to the scooter through the chance of inclement weather. Others mused upon the state of the tyres and their desire to preserve them, meaning that they were not willing to risk damage and the consequent costs by making an unnecessary journey (i.e. for research purposes).

The request for ride-alongs was also useful as it illustrated the various storage solutions that were employed. Some created a safe storage inside the home (oftentimes in the lounge room close to the front door); in small social housing units, larger scooters were often

**14.3** Judy and her husband own two mobility scooters
and had installed a ramp and hoist to enable them
to store these on their raised veranda area,
Albion Park, 2015

the central feature of the living room with little room for other furniture; others stored the scooter in a garage, setting up a designated area
for charging and tyre inflation; most had crafted ramps to facilitate
access in and out of the house; and one couple had even installed a
hoist system so that the woman could lift the scooter onto a balcony
if her husband was not available to help negotiate the portable ramp
(Figure 14.3). Thus, it was the experience of preparing for a ride-along
that helped give more detail around the challenges faced by participants in how they had adapted their homes in subtle, and not so subtle
ways to accommodate their physical needs, lifestyles and dispositions.

## Types of journey

The mobile methods also prompted a consideration of the types
of journey that were undertaken. For example, all had altered or
modified the scooter in some way: adding mirrors and lights to
improve visibility; adding hooks, holders and poles to carry additional shopping or parcels; fashioning tubes to accommodate fishing
poles and umbrellas; affixing weights to shift the centre of gravity;

**14.4** Cecil's homemade trailer could easily be attached to the back of the mobility scooter to enable him to carry larger or heavier items, Corrimal, 2015

manufacturing trailer attachments to haul larger items; supplementing with toolkits and spare batteries; incorporating protective rain covers, and decorating with decals and ornamental flags. These modifications helped to personalise the scooter in much the same way as a car; how they adjusted the scooter reflected something of who they were and enabled them to accomplish tasks that were meaningful for them. Thus, journeying with Cecil revealed that he frequently had need of his hand-crafted trailer (Figure 14.4). Cecil was an aviculturist with large aviaries in the backyard of his home. He had discussed his love of birds, but there had been no mention of how this was related to his scooter use. In fact, he frequently purchased 20 kg bags of birdseed and transported them in his trailer, which attached to the mobility scooter. Other times, Cecil used the trailer to transport small pieces of furniture which could not easily be carried.

The personal relationships that people had with their scooters in many ways bore a resemblance to the way that car owners customise their vehicles to convey some aspect of identity. While size and portability were aspects that were individualised according to the physical weight and needs of the rider, often the style, colour and ornamentation were important considerations which reflected distinct dispositions. Sporting a red scooter with glitter decal letters which spelt out the name of her favourite rap singer enabled Linda to enjoy riding in the local neighbourhood while playing music loudly from her phone. Here, the scooter was not only implicated in maintaining an independent life but also in fashioning an identity.

## Advice for others

Mobile methods offer a better understanding of participants' lifeworld by mapping life on the move and enabling access to data that are irretrievable in conventional, often still, social science methods (Waitt and Harada, 2012). A crucial element in the efficacy of mobile methods bound to instances of social life is their evocation of familiar performances that can guide the data collection process non-verbally and through corporeal performance. Performativity here becomes an accompaniment to circumspect reflection. Notwithstanding these benefits, enacting mobile methods is often more challenging than other qualitative or quantitative methods given there are safety, logistical and physical aspects alongside conceptual ones.

For example, embarking on a journey on a mobility scooter involves habituating oneself to a different physical layout combining the human body and that of the vehicle. Due to the increase in size and speed of the mobility scooter there is a greater sense of being in the public gaze. With the main routeway being the footpath, this also creates a sense of disjunction between foot pedestrians and the scooter user. Being categorised as a pedestrian under the current legal and regulatory framework, scooter users often came into conflict with other pedestrians who were unaware of the impact of their behaviours. That said, mobility scooters can travel on the road where a footpath is not available, is being repaired or is unsafe due to damage, yet most recognised the dangers associated with road use. It was not only the danger of interacting with larger, faster-moving vehicles but also the stigma that kept them off roads in most cases. Verbal abuse also was common.

Mobile methods thus provided rich opportunities to witness how participants managed the dangers in terms of physical safety, but also to observe the way that certain mobility forms (e.g. two scooters together) attracted further attention. Significantly, participants reported that they usually travelled alone. Even couples with several scooters found that there was less negative attention when they travelled independently of each other. The ride-along with the researcher therefore seemed to position the mobility scooter as much more of an anomaly than a single rider due to increased visibility. This marks out scooter mobility from other forms of movement such as walking, running or cycling. Other pedestrians and road users stared, deliberately crossed the road or made mocking comments and gestures on occasion. Thus, alongside the risks of physical danger, there was also the impact of social pressure that may have had a further influence on feelings of acceptance and tolerance by the local community. While it is not the aim of participatory methods to cause distress to participants, in the case of the ride-along it should be noted that there is a chance that there could be some negative consequences for those who may already experience social exclusion due to the visibility of age, health or disability. Thus, it is advisable to discuss with participants which routes, times and destinations would likely be least stressful to them.

Moreover, unforeseen risks emerged through conducting the fieldwork. For example, while most mobility scooter users were ambivalent about using the road, they acknowledged that it was sometimes necessary. Quieter streets and back lanes were preferred. However, they often made up their own road rules when having to cross busy highways; travelling with and against the flow of traffic; pausing in the middle of roads where there were no pedestrian refuges; and speeding through roundabouts as if they had the 'right of way'. Many of these ad hoc practices were inherently dangerous considering the lack of protection offered from the mobility scooter construction design, yet overall most felt forced to use roads in this way. Thus, it is advisable to constantly reflect on the risks and benefits of conducting research, and to remind participants of the ethical responsibilities surrounding illegal practices.

## Conclusions

We conclude this chapter by summarising the main findings from the research and reflecting on how the 'ride-along' helped to uncover in-depth insights that would not have emerged using more conventional methods. First, the possibility of conducting a go-along in the first place can shed light on both method and findings. Where the participant owned one mobility scooter and agreed to the go-along it was difficult for the researcher to keep pace while walking. The regular speed of the scooter is faster than walking pace and this caused annoyance for some participants because they waited for the researcher to catch up and were focused on achieving their everyday tasks. There is little time for the researcher to photograph the obstacles and barriers pointed out by the participant because of this speed differential.

Secondly, where the participant owned more than one mobility scooter it was possible to accompany them on a second scooter. Moving together with participants through quotidian spaces helped to develop in-depth knowledges about everyday experiences. This highlighted the challenges of travelling via this technology, but also drew attention to the ethical and risk dimensions associated with increased visibility.

Thirdly, mobile methods provided additional insights into the taken-for-granted, specifically how participants negotiated common obstacles 'in the moment'. Unplanned obstacles that were encountered included cars parked over driveways, debris left on footpaths and garbage trucks stop-starting around the path of the mobility scooter. It highlighted the risks of interacting with fast-moving traffic as mobility scooters often made use of the road to avoid the obstacles and positioned mobility scooter users as 'risk takers'.

Fourthly, implications arise for equipment. In this project a hand-held lightweight video camera was used. The researcher recorded some sections of the participant's journey while stationary. Attaching the video camera to the mobility scooter was not a viable option. The uneven surfaces that were travelled and the high impact of traversing ramps, roads and footpaths made for poor video quality that could not be edited into key moments able to be reviewed with participants. Video recording life on-the-move requires careful consideration if the route or bodies (or both) are to be recorded, alongside how the recording device is to be immobilised while bodies are moving (see Stoodley, this collection).

Finally, mobile methods raise important ethical questions. Some people declined to participate in the go-along, deeming their everyday trips 'too boring'. Alongside an understanding of the mundane as unimportant, it may have been concerns that the presence of the researcher would attract unwanted attention, thus increasing the stigma that they already faced. Alternatively, it is possible that the presence of the researcher encouraged the participants to take additional risks as they demonstrated their skills of negotiating between road and footpath. Hence, participants may have 'performed' for the video recording, putting themselves at heightened risk of accident or injury. Moreover, there was a certain amount of unexpected risk for the researcher inexperienced at riding a mobility scooter. Conducting mobile methods underscores the importance of ethical guidelines and raises questions about the need for undertaking risk assessments and insurance liability for the institution sponsoring the research.

To conclude, our project suggests that each mode of transport offers its own methodological challenges (see Box 14.1). For example, those modes of transport that are motorised and embedded in practices of sociality, like driving, perhaps pose the fewest challenges in terms of the presence of the researcher's body. Most people are accustomed to driving and talking with a passenger. Challenges are posed to the researcher when the form of mobility is not embedded in sociality – like rail commuting – or requires levels of bodily fitness and special-ised competencies – like running, cycling, skateboarding or mobility scooters. For some forms of mobility that require physical endurance or involve the social norms of travelling alone, it may be optimal for the participant to audio record their reflections on the journey. Indeed, many road cyclists are already recording each journey on Strava and video cameras, particularly embedded in cultures of fitness training. Alive to these challenges, mobile methods offer distinct advantages that help the researcher unpack the taken-for-granted dimensions of journeys and map experiences of unplanned and unexpected events of each journey, often making the mundane anything but mundane.

---

### Box 14.1: Pros and cons of the method

| Pros | Cons |
|---|---|
| Offers an insight to the participant's everyday experiences and taken-for-granted worlds that may not be worth speaking about. | Disrupts objective abstraction. |
| Provides an experiential platform for critical inquiry. | Increases risk of 'going native'. |
| Demonstrates non-verbal/numerical nuances to research data. | Presents physical and legal challenges to researcher. |
| Diminishes the hierarchical position of the researcher over the participant in terms of status or power. | Risks trivialising participant's descriptions of meaningful events in the past. |

---

**Box 14.2: Tools, training and equipment**

Here is some equipment you would need to conduct mobility scooter interviews. Obviously other mobile forms of interview may require different equipment.

- mobility scooter;
- audio recorder (smartphone);
- video recorder (smartphone);
- helmet (depending on local laws);
- licence (depending on local laws);
- first aid kit;
- portable battery/charger;
- list of phone numbers for assistance;
- map/area guide.

---

**Box 14.3: Further reading**

Anderson, J. (2004) 'Talking whilst walking: a geographical archaeology of knowledge', *Area*, 36 (3): 254–261.

Harada, T. and Waitt, G. (2013) 'Researching transport choices: the possibilities of "mobile methodologies" to study life-on-the-move', *Geographical Research*, 51 (2): 145–152.

Middleton, J. (2010) 'Sense and the city: exploring the embodied geographies of urban walking', *Social and Cultural Geography*, 11( 6): 575–596.

## Bibliography

Birtchnell, T., Harada, T. and Waitt, G. (2017) 'On the verge of change: maverick innovation with mobility scooters', *Environmental Innovation and Societal Transitions*, 2 (2): 269–275.

Büscher, M. and Urry, J. ( 2009) 'Mobile methods and the empirical', *European Journal of Social Theory*, 12: 99–116.

Hein, J. R., Evans, J. and Jones, P. (2008) 'Mobile methodologies: theory, technology and practice', *Geography Compass*, 2: 1266–1285.

Jones, P., Bunce, G., Evans, J., Gibbs, H. and Ricketts Hein, J. (2008) 'Exploring space and place with walking interviews', *Journal of Research Practice*, 4: 1–9.

Kelly, C. E., Tight, M. R., Hodgson, F. C. and Page, M. W. (2011) 'A comparison of three methods for assessing the walkability of the pedestrian environment', *Journal of Transport Geography*, 19: 1500–1508.

McIlvenny, P. (2018) 'How did the mobility scooter cross the road? Coordinating with co-movers and other movers in traffic', *Language & Communication*, 65: 105–130.

Murray, L. (2009) 'Looking at and looking back: visualization in mobile research', *Qualitative Research*, 9: 469–488.

Pink, S. and Morgan, J. (2013) 'Short-term ethnography: intense routes to knowing', *Symbolic Interaction*, 36: 351–361.

Tartia, J. (2018) 'Examining the rhythms of "urban elements" on walking and driving routes in the city', *Mobilities*, 13 (6): 808–824.

Waitt, G. (2005) 'Doing discourse analysis', in I. Hay (ed.) *Qualitative Research in Human Geography*, Oxford: Oxford University Press, 161–191.

Waitt, G. and Harada, T. (2012) 'Driving, cities and changing climates', *Urban Studies*, 47 (15): 3307–3325.

Warren, S. (2017) 'Pluralising the walking interview: researching (im)mobilities with Muslim women', *Social & Cultural Geography*, 18: 786–807.

Wiles, J. L., Rosenberg, M. W. and Kearns, R. A. (2005) 'Narrative analysis as a strategy for understanding interview talk in geographic research', *Area*, 37: 89–99.

# 15

# Water-based methods: conducting (self) interviews at sea for a surfer's view of surfing

Lyndsey Stoodley

## Introduction

This chapter explores the watery and water-based method of (self) interviews at sea, through the example of surfing. An interview with a view, whereby participants are given a surfboard with a waterproof camera and question sheet attached to it. Allowing the researcher to investigate certain topics, while also observing the surfer in situ, this method has been used in an attempt to better understand everyday human–water relations or, more specifically, human surfer–water relations.

For surfers, who are most at home in their world of water, waves and wind, the littoral zone represents a special place. While surfing can be a hobby and a lifestyle, it is at sea where a seemingly impossible combination of geological, hydrological and meteorological features come together to create the necessary conditions for waves to break (Scarfe et al., 2003), enthralling surfers and spectators with their natural wonder.

Tales of the goings on in these surfing spaces are plentiful; storytelling (with its inherent exaggeration) and imagery have been powerful tools in the creation of surfing culture, industry and associated narratives (for a further discussion on telling stories see Widerberg, this collection). The stories and images focus largely on the grandiose retelling of the riding of the wave itself, or the 'search' to find these waves (see, for example, Booth, 2012). The intricacies of the experiences of surfers in this zone, however, which can be interpreted in both a physical and psychological respect, often go unheard and unseen. Though there is far more to surfing than the act of finding and riding the wave, little outside of these components has been explored in popular or academic literatures. The littoral zone therefore represents something of an opaque space, where experiences are isolated to the individual. Only a surfer knows the feeling, so the saying goes.

In this chapter I document the process of designing and conducting an embodied, immersive (self) interviewing method in an attempt to obtain responses as close to the moment of experience as possible, to better understand this feeling and the motivations it creates. Involving a camera and a question sheet attached to a surfboard, this method draws from work on mobile methodologies (Merriman, 2014; Spinney, 2011) and sensory ethnography (Pink, 2015), utilising technology to generate audio and visual data from the perspective of the surfer. The format invites the participant to take their time, paddle around and catch some waves if they come along. The questions probe on specific topics, while the place of the sea serves as both a venue and an active prompt. This provides insight into the conscious and subconscious movements and interactions of surfers as well as offering a unique chance for them to articulate thoughts and emotions in that moment. In this way, while focused on a specific example, the chapter speaks to wider discussions around mobile methods, water-based research and innovating with audio-visual data.

Beginning with some background on the field of surfing studies and how this method fits, the chapter then moves to look at how the method has been used, and to useful advice on its execution. Conclusions are then drawn, arguing that through engagement in these watery encounters, this method offers a novel, insightful contribution to our understanding of human–water relations and offers future approaches for studying everyday relationships with the sea.

## Turning to the sea

Our world is a water world. The oceans and seas are entwined, often invisibly but nonetheless importantly, with our everyday lives. (Anderson and Peters, 2014: 3)

Though our world is indeed a water world, geography has historically been firmly focused on the terrestrial, with the oceans and seas existing only at the margins, a 'landlocked field' (Lambert, Martins and Ogborn, 2006: 480). Water represents a stark departure from researching the land. No longer fixed, solid and stable, water is endlessly mobile, unstable and uncertain.

In spite of and because of this, a number of scholars have turned to the sea to utilise its 'potential to reorient our perspectives in multiple ways' (Lambert, Martins and Ogborn, 2006: 488) and address the evident bias towards the land. The beginnings of such a turn are largely attributed to Steinberg's 2001 work *The Social Construction of the Ocean*, in which he states that the 'ocean is not simply used *by* society, but is a space *of* society' (2001: 6). In her 2010 paper, Kimberley Peters built upon the reorientations presented by Lambert, Martins and Ogborn to explore both the emergence and the potential of ocean studies within social and cultural geographies. Peters (2010: 1262) suggests that one of the reasons that the sea has been under-researched is that 'it is a space today, which is outside of everyday consciousness because for many, everyday life is rarely played out at sea'. Everyday life is however impacted by the sea; weather systems, food and goods appear in our lives with little thought to their prior movements. We are all affected by the oceans, but for many this goes beyond the unconscious and uncared about influences, into the experiential.

The relationships that people have with the sea (and indeed 'nature' at large) are multifaceted, complex and full of contradictions. We hear about the therapeutic benefits that are possible from engagement, the associated dangers, the joy, the fear. Watery engagement can come in a multitude of forms; some on the surface, some immersed, some a mixture of the two. Numerous works have taken these encounters as an empirical base from which to study the importance of human–sea relationships, yet our grasp of human experience in seascapes remains largely undeveloped.

Anderson and Peters's 2014 edited collection *Water Worlds: Human Geographies of the Ocean* brings together a range of work which places the sea at its centre. Drawing on a variety of aspects, from kayaking to pirate radio, the editors argue that in conducting their research *from* the sea, it is possible to achieve 'a far more nuanced and complex perspective on the sea itself' (2014: 7). This method sought to engage in a literal interpretation of such thinking, to contribute to the growing field of surf studies which has emerged in recent years as a popular academic topic in both the social and natural sciences. Characterised as a coming together of land, sea, ritual and culture, surf research has necessarily been interdisciplinary, encompassing numerous fields. It is also international and highly varied in its scope. Edited collections such as *Sustainable Surfing* (Borne and Ponting, 2017) and *The Critical Surf Studies Reader* (Hough-Snee and Eastman, 2017) present good starting points from which to begin exploring the diversity of thinking in surfing literatures. Both provide examples of the differing interpretations of key themes, which include, among others, technology, identity, conceptualisations of surfing spaces and the surfing experience itself. The human experience of surfing has been widely represented in popular, sub-cultural and, increasingly, academic literatures (see, for example Anderson, 2012; Comer, 2010; Ford and Brown, 2006). What has come to be known as surf studies has broadened significantly and now represents a strong field that stretches beyond its niche. Though exceeding itself in many respects, surf studies remains agape with opportunities to learn more, particularly from within the mysterious and potentially mundane littoral zone.

Widely used research methods in studying surfing include surveys, interviews and a great deal of auto-ethnography as researchers attempt to make sense of their hobby and study area. The majority of this work has taken place on land, with fieldnotes and interviews being conducted after a surf session, or in a separate location altogether. Only a limited amount of empirical data on surfers' engagement with their surfing spaces has actually been conducted in situ. Evers (2015) has utilised a GoPro™ camera, similar to the one used in my research, to record and reflect upon his own personal surfing experiences. lisahunter (2019) provides another interesting example, using multiple cameras to record a sensory (auto)ethnography of a surfing session and applying a more than human lens which brings technology and non-human actors into the surfing assemblage. More often surveys are handed out at the beach, or distributed and completed online. While such conventional approaches have served a function and generated data, in understanding that the sea is 'other', different from land, it would appear that slightly different research methods could be more frequently engaged with. The immersion, the ephemerality and the mobility of watery spaces suggest that much can be learnt from mobile methodologies which have been widely used in a range of areas, and which encompass 'any attempt to physically or metaphorically follow people/objects/ideas in order to support analysis of the experience/

content/doing of, and inter-connections between, immobility/ mobility/flows/networks' (Spinney, 2015: 232).

This 'interview with a view' method draws heavily on the popular 'go-along' form of mobile method, which has been effectively used as an ethnographic tool across a range of activity-based studies (Kusenbach, 2003; Xie and Spinney, 2018; see chapters by Birtchnell, Harada and Waitt; Cook; and Wilkinson, this collection), though it differs in that instead of the researcher 'going along', a camera and question sheet are used to give participants the opportunity to conduct a self-interview. Self-interviews have been utilised predominantly in studies where the content is sensitive or highly personal, and often use computer software to facilitate recorded audio questioning and response inputting. The self-interview fulfils here a different purpose, where alternative technologies have been used to create a viable waterproof solution. In doing so, the surroundings and emotions of the participant can be observed in conjunction with their verbal responses, all of which are affected by the environment bearing on their senses. Self-interviews thus have wide application as a mobile method, where traditional techniques and modes of recording fail to capture the nuances of movement and motion as they are happening.

In the case of my research, taking place at sea, the interview participant is not only thinking about surfing, but is also seeing, hearing, feeling it. The smells and sounds of the coast, the temperature and movement of the water, the taste of salt in the air. In line with sensory ethnography methodology (after Pink, 2015, for example), the acknowledgement and recording of much of this sensory experience provide a comprehensive observational tool to further enhance the richness of the data collected.

Falling at the nexus of mobile methods, self-interviewing and sensory (auto)ethnography, this method provides a unique glimpse into the surfers' opinions and their surfing experience, and opens up an additional means through which these surfing spaces can be engaged with directly (see Collins, this collection for more information on auto-ethnographic methods).

## Self-interviewing at sea

As a surfer myself, I had been reflecting on my own experiences. Although it was the memories of the surfed wave which remained most clear, the relatively short amount of time actually spent on a wave dictates that the reality of a surfing session is actually much more mundane than one might think. Much of the time is spent paddling into position or sitting and waiting for waves to come through. In south Wales, where I surf, the stereotypical images of surfing good waves in sunny climes look largely unfamiliar. As we struggle in and out of wetsuits in car parks, attempting to maintain a degree of dignity while the cold wind whips towels around threateningly, the generic image of surfers wearing minimal swimwear, strolling casually towards the surf remains far away. Far-away destinations like California, and Australia are the places which align much more closely with the visual imagery of surfing than a grey, rainy day in Porthcawl, and it is these places which make up the empirical base for much of the surf literature which exists today (see, for example, Comley, 2016; Olive, 2016). In seeking an alternative, regional perspective, this method aimed to see and show a different side of surfing, and though the car park clothes-changing farce is perhaps amusing for bystanders, it is the watery experience that is of particular interest in this chapter.

While there is certainly a practical logic in conducting interviews on land, the walk up the beach insists that the session is now a past occurrence, a historical engagement. In taking place during the event, in situ, in the sea, this method draws on the environment and associated emotions as active prompts, and limits the opportunity for feelings to be distorted by memory. It was also developed in the summer, so offered a pleasant means through which the office could be temporarily relocated to the beach.

Though often a highly social experience, surfing is ultimately an individual pursuit. This means that to engage a surfer in any conversation in the water, let alone one that is not about the current conditions, can be tricky. When in a line-up (the position to catch waves), surfers squint towards the horizon as they watch for the next set of waves to roll in. There is a universal expectation that when a wave arrives, any conversation is dropped mid-sentence as one turns to paddle to catch it. I wanted to create a similar dynamic with these interviews, a state where the surfing comes first and thoughts of anything else are secondary; where the thrills and the frustrations of everyday surf sessions could be recorded and reflected upon.

It was decided that a self-interview would be the most appropriate way to gather responses in this environment, for multiple reasons.

First, a self-interview meant that I would not need to paddle alongside the participant, removing the risk of a disparity in fitness and skill levels and leaving them free to take their time and catch waves in the knowledge that nobody is watching them intently, waiting for an answer. Such a 'paddle along' method has not been used as yet, though it may in future. The space and time provided by the unrestricted self-interview would, it was hoped, allow for the disclosure of thoughtful responses which for some can be quite personal. For many surfers, surfing is a powerful and meaningful pursuit which goes beyond a simple designation as a sport or pastime. It can be an emotive subject, carrying a range of spiritual, religious, athletic, professional and personal significance (Farmer, 1992).

The other advantage of self-interviews is on a practical level. In a natural, outdoor setting, one in which crashing waves are desirable, the method is vulnerable to audio recording being overridden by the sounds of the sea. In isolating the interview to a single person, the microphone, which is integrated into the camera, is much better able to capture all of the answers, ensuring that ambient noises are recorded but are not dominant. Communication from board to board can be problematic in such an environment, so this enabled a more accurate recording without the need to bring in more specialist equipment.

The technology used, a GoPro™ camera and surfboard mount, was very important to the success of this technique (see also chapters by Cook and also Birtchnell, Harada and Gordon Waitt, this collection). Fixed to the nose (front) of my 8 ft surfboard, the camera was facing out to sea, and its wide-angle slight fish-eye perspective meant I could in essence see what the surfer could see. Though turning the camera to face the surfer would have provided the opportunity to record facial expressions, the length of the board meant that to do this, the camera would be very close to the participant (see Figures 15.1 and 15.2). This is something that I thought would be highly detrimental to the method: the notion of a camera 12 inches away from your face as you are paddling into and over waves and then stopping to talk is likely to be very off putting for potential participants. In removing this potentially intimidating prospect, the audio quality was also assured. In having the camera facing away from the participant, the microphone was ideally situated to capture the words being spoken.

As can be seen in Figure 15.3, the question sheet consisted simply of a printed A4 sheet which was laminated to protect it from the

**15.1** Funny faces: the author demonstrating why participants may be discouraged by a rear-facing camera

**15.2** That's better! Seeing what the surfer sees

water. To attach it to the board I used the equally sophisticated system of four strips of duct tape. This ensured the questions would stay in place, a few inches away from the camera. The question sheet consisted of an introductory paragraph, which set out the aims of the interview and guidelines for how to complete it. As a pilot study, and one which was being conducted at sea, I kept the tone very relaxed.

**15.3  Ready to go**

I hoped that it would be a fun activity to be involved with, not a chore to take precious time away from a surf session. I even included a silly question part of the way through (revealed later in the chapter) in a bid to highlight the fact that participants were out in the water, an unconventional interview space, and hopefully lighten the atmosphere further.

The questions themselves were drawn up in the first instance to help inform a study on surfers' compulsion to surf, exploring the relationships that they had with the surf spot and the environment

(Anderson and Stoodley, 2018). Though specific to this particular project, when exploring other topics related to surfing, it would be as simple as changing out the question sheet.

The structure of the questions used in this example was intended to allow the participant to relax into the interview, with questioning becoming slightly more complex as it progressed – a form which could again be transferred As time spent surfing is considered highly valuable, it is vital that the interview was relatively fast and efficient so that participants did not lose interest or become frustrated at their decision to volunteer their time. Questions were therefore limited in number, with the most important elements coming in the middle section, when it was hoped the surfer would be most comfortable but still fully engaged.

The first question asked about the participant's surfing background, and examples such as board type used, length of time surfing, level and favourite break were given to guide the response here. This was an effective way to open the dialogue as it allowed the participant to ease into the interview with a question that required little thought. It was helpful in enabling them to become accustomed to the unfamiliar board and set-up of the questions and camera. It also provides a good indication of the context of the interview, as can be seen in the excerpt below:

> Patsy: So I've been surfing for about ten years now, actually eleven years. I started surfing when I moved to Manorbier, this wonderful place where we are today and uh I was very lucky to have a lot of guidance from a local surf school and this woman called __ and ____ who ran the surf school so they gave us all the gear and everything at the beginning. My first surfboard was a 7'6 minimal, an allrounder but then my ex boyfriend got into longboarding and so did I and then I never looked back. So I go longboarding. I've got a 9'1 which I'm on today and I've got a 9'6 which I love as well. I tried to get on a shorter board too but I just love longboarding.
>
> [Conversation with another surfer about the camera]
>
> [Paddles for wave, doesn't catch it]
>
> Patsy: I like to think I'm somewhere in between intermediate and advanced, probably more towards intermediate. I don't know, maybe yeah in the middle. Surfing, I'm absolutely addicted to surf, I absolutely love it, I love being in the water, love being in the sea. Huge pleasure, it's just the best thing I've ever done and I don't think I'll ever stop. Stop when my body fails me [laughs]. (Interviewee 'Patsy', 12 August 2018)

From this initial question, attention can move to the more personalised aspects of the study. In this case, this meant probing on the motivations and meanings surrounding the surfing experience. Why do you surf? How do you feel a) when you are surfing and b) when you cannot go surfing? These are both elements which may seem straightforward, but as they deal with an individual's enthusiasms and emotions there is potential for responses to vary greatly. As one participant, Ivy, demonstrates after she catches a nice wave,

> Ivy: I definitely need to get a smaller board, cos that was amazing. Why do I surf? That feeling. That feeling I've just had then, of just being. The closest I can feel to being able to fly I think and the feeling is epic and when you catch that wave, cos you have to work so hard to get to the level that you can catch a wave that it's really satisfying. So when I'm surfing, yeah just super stoked. It's a bit corny but even when I can't surf, even when I'm not catching waves I just feel great being in the water. When I can't go surfing, it sucks. And I had a little girl three years ago and that's really curtailed my surfing and that's been, you know battling with those demons of I feel like really shit that I have to have responsibilities and not basically surf, it's just that balance isn't it, and finding that balance. So now when I get to go surfing I really value it. (12 August 2018)

The following question then aimed to utilise the (hopefully) new-found familiarity with the board and interview process to delve into location-specific components, taking advantage of the 'in situ' experiential interview form. This worked well and could be used to explore a range of topics related to that particular surf spot, or comparisons to it. These pilot interviews were conducted at popular surfing beaches in south and west Wales that were held in high esteem, even though they would not necessarily be considered as world- or even UK-class waves. I would anticipate that the conditions on the day will influence the response to such questions. If an onshore wind is howling, or somebody you do not know just blocked your way, you are likely to be less positive than if the sun is out and your friend has just seen you catch a good one and given you a cheer. These social cues are all recorded by the camera, so it is possible to interpret and analyse these events in concurrence with the spoken responses.

Following this, I chose to include a silly question. Simply saying 'wait, is that a fin over there?' This is of course unnecessary in terms of data collection, though it was found to effectively maintain and reinforce the informal, fun characteristics of the method. Had the interviews been in different locations, where the possibility of seeing a finned predator was real and therefore no laughing matter, this joke would not have been included. Wales however has an impeccable record when it comes to shark encounters, so it was quite clear that this was intended to be inane.

Returning to the subject, the next question explored once more aspects concerning the local beach. Though sightings of large fauna may be highly unlikely, from one of the beaches in this study you can see flumes of smoke coming from the nearby steel works and the water is a murky brown, thick with silt. The occasional plastic wrapper floats by. At the other, an eleventh-century castle nestles into the hills just up from the beach, and seals swim lazily in the bay. These environmental variants are the prompts which this method sought to exploit when asking these questions.

I included one final question on engagement with surfing more generally, and in the interviews completed to date it is clear that by this point the participants are ready to be finished with the process. Concise responses have been recorded and the interviewees have not hesitated in paddling back to me and their own boards.

The format of the questions was effective in engaging participants, and could be mirrored regardless of the surfing subject being explored. Easing the participant into the interview allows them to gain confidence, and the researcher to gain context. The place-specific questions draw upon the method's key strength of being conducted in situ, and the silly question keeps the process light. The final question should require a less taxing response to ensure that, as interest wavers, key information is not lost.

At the time of writing, this method has been used to complete eight interviews across two beaches. I had prepared to also trial this in northern California, but ocean conditions at the time of my visit were unsuitable, something which always needs to be considered. Had this gone ahead I had planned to use rubber suckers to attach a separate set of questions to a rented surfboard.

This method could be applied anywhere that surfing takes place, and also in other active situations, providing that suitable camera mounts and a surface on which to attach the question sheet are available. This specific method was of course designed around the activity of surfing, utilising the periods of lower activity in between waves. These breaks in the surf allow the surfer an opportunity to read and answer the questions without them being placed in any danger. To do the same while cycling, running or walking, for example, would likely be distracting. Such a task would generate an unreasonable level of risk to the participant, and perhaps in these instances the question sheet could be substituted for an audio track.

## Advice for other surfers

This has been a robust, fun method which has produced some very interesting insights into the surfing experience. A range of footage has been recorded which, in addition to responses to questions, shows interactions in the surf zone, and conscious and subconscious movements of participants. The recording of surfing experiences in the moment has exposed raw emotions of joy after catching a good wave, audible frustration from not catching waves, and occasionally fear, as the paddling speed can be seen to increase as the surfer scrambles to reach the point beyond which the waves are breaking. In seeing what the surfer sees, I have been able to better understand the particular experiences which are being discussed in that particular environment. These methods might achieve similar useful insights if used with other forms of mobility or motion, such as rowing, running or cycling (see Cook, this collection). While overall it has been a positive experiment, there are a number of shortcomings associated with such immersive interviews.

This method is, in essence, ableist in its current approach. The requirement for participants to read at sea presents a challenge in itself and excludes those with limited literacy skills or poor eyesight (as glasses cannot be worn while surfing). My surfboard, though more accessible than a high-performance board, would not be suitable for all, and would exclude the growing number of people who practise adaptive surfing. Modifications would need to be put in place to expand the concept to include these groups. For those who can participate there are still perceived and practical issues to deal with.

The set-up of the self-interview itself looks somewhat out of place in a surfing line-up; the question sheet and camera are not standard accessories and raise some attention in the water. I have had multiple comments of 'are they instructions?' or 'is that so you don't forget

---

### Box 15.1: Training, tools, equipment

A level of competency and confidence in surfing is required in order to paddle out and stay safe while an interview is taking place. Both the researcher and participant should be comfortable in the conditions.

It is not be recommended to attempt this method in big surf, nor at spots which are unfamiliar to the researcher.

Equipment used:

- surfboard and leg rope;
- GoPro™ camera & floaty casing;
- surfboard mount;
- laminated question sheet;
- duct tape.

---

what to do?' This is not a problem for me, but may be off-putting for participants if they perceive this to negatively affect them, particularly if the interview is being conducted at their local break where they have built up reputations. Surfing can, after all, be very image conscious (Ford and Brown, 2006). In addition to the equipment itself, a self-interview requires that the participant asks and answers questions on their own. Comments from participants suggest that this also made them feel uncomfortable to start with, as it was not totally clear why they appeared to be talking to themselves. Some of those who requested to participate decided not to complete the interview for these reasons, and some preferred not to because they were tired, or had not caught enough waves on their own board to want to try something new.

There could also be trust issues as surfboards were swapped. A surfboard is personal and valuable. To be asked to give it up, if only for a short time, can be a daunting prospect for a surfer. In order to gain the trust of participants I attempted to make it clear that I was capable of handling their board appropriately and paddled into positions beyond the point where I could catch a wave but remained in view. This ensured that the participant's board was in no danger of being damaged, and gave the impression that I was not doing this to have fun myself, but it was a serious attempt to conduct research and that the input and effort committed were appreciated. In the interviews conducted I knew or had been personally introduced to participants by other surfers which, to a degree, resolved this concern as trust was assumed through this connection. This limits the range of participants involved and to develop this method further a more refined recruitment process would likely be required.

To take off one leg rope and put on another can be difficult at sea. Fortunately, the swapping of boards proved to be an amusing event in most cases, relaxing the participant into the interview rather than raising any real issue. Though this could have been avoided by exchanging boards on the beach, to paddle out to the point where we try to catch the waves is energy and time consuming. Swapping beyond this point meant the participant was already nearly in position and could continue their surfing session with as little disruption as possible.

Along with the splashes, giggles and conversations which arose in the setting up of an interview, there was an abundance of ambient coastal sounds. Though a rich data source, this occasionally compromised the clarity of audio recordings. Transcription of interviews therefore proved to be relatively difficult, albeit not impossible. In listening repeatedly to the recordings I eventually lost only a small number of words in total which did not affect the overall meaning of what was being said.

The format of the self-interview itself carries inherent weaknesses. While the independence and freedom for participants are desirable, no probing or follow-on questions are possible, meaning that responses are final. In most instances this worked well, and I was pleasantly surprised with the quality of responses and the efforts that were made to contribute to this study. In one case however, in the first pilot session, I recruited my cousin, a drama student who had joined us for his first ever surfing lesson one summer's evening. He offered to complete an interview, keen to be involved in all of the events of the occasion, and paddled clumsily away chatting happily to the camera. The following is an excerpt from his interview and demonstrates comically the potential inadequacies of a self-interview at sea:

Matthew: Please talk about your surfing background e.g. how long you've surfed for.

I've surfed for about forty-five minutes to an hour.

Uhh board type: one that floats.

My level: sea level.

Favourite break: uhh I like lunchtime.

Why do you surf? Uhh cos I don't really want to drown.

How do I feel? I feel great thanks.

Oh, how do I feel when I'm surfing? Wet. Wet and umm wet.

When you can't go surfing, dry! I feel dry.

Other people: Matthew, paddle! Paddle!

[Matthew catches wave]

Surfer: Yes Matthew!

Matthew: Is this your local break? What connections do you have to this place?

Umm, the connections I have to this place are the fact that I'm here, I've been here on holiday. I come here most years for the Elvis convention. (19 June 2017)

To try to minimise some of these issues, in future I would recruit suitable participants before entering the water, and take more time to explain in greater detail what the interview is for and what is required for participation. I would also make clearer the process for exchanging boards, and reassure surfers that I would be on hand should any questions arise, or they would like to discuss anything on or off the record. It would be useful to conduct a follow-up land-based interview in order to probe further on the responses given at sea, to develop a more comprehensive picture of the ideas and opinions being portrayed.

## Conclusion

This chapter began with an introduction to this watery method, the 'interview with a view', which has incorporated elements of mobile methods and sensory (auto) ethnography into a self-interview format. Using high and low technologies, a waterproof camera and question sheet, it has been possible to gain an insight into the experiences and opinions of surfers from within the notoriously mysterious littoral zone, thus successfully meeting its aim of broadening our understandings of human (surfer)–water engagement. A range of audio and visual data has been collected in a way which has been entertaining and fulfilling for participants, and revealing for me as a researcher. There

---

**Box 15.2: Further reading**

Interview clips from my own research: http://blogs.cardiff.ac.uk/surfing-research/watery-methods/

Fincham, B., McGuinness, M. and Murray, L. (2010) *Mobile Methodologies*, Basingstoke: Palgrave Macmillan.

lisahunter, L. (2019) 'Sensory authoethnography: surfing approaches for understanding and communicating "seaspacetimes"', in L. lisahunter, M. Brown and K. Peters (eds) *Living with the Sea: Knowledge, Awareness and Action* (1st edn), Abingdon: Routledge, 100–113).

Pink, S. (2015) *Doing Sensory Ethnography*, London: Sage.

---

are a number of problems associated with this method, including its exclusivity, fundamental practicality and its potential for providing responses which lack sufficient depth. Such issues could be largely ironed out, with some adjustments making the interviews and surrounding experience more open, appealing and effective.

Though it may not be wholly transferable to other empirical areas of movement and mobility, the bringing together of various methodological approaches here demonstrates that opportunities for our knowledge-making toolkit to be expanded are plentiful. I argue therefore that there is scope for this method to be effective in contributing to the furthering of our understandings of immersion and interaction within this dynamic part of our watery world, and that this watery method provides an exciting way to collect a valuable array of rich multimedia data.

## Bibliography

Anderson, J. (2012) 'Relational places: the surfed wave as assemblage and convergence', *Environment and Planning D: Society and Space*, 30 (4): 570–587.

Anderson, J. and Peters, K. (2014) *Water Worlds: Human Geographies of the Ocean*, London: Ashgate.

Anderson, J. and Stoodley, L. (2018) 'Creative compulsions: performing surfing as art', in J. Anderson, L. Stoodley, L. Roberts and K. Phillips (eds) *Water, Creativity and Meaning: Multidisciplinary Understandings of Human–Water Relationships*, Abingdon and New York: Routledge, 103–123.

Booth, D. (2012) 'Seven (1 + 6) surfing stories: the practice of authoring', *Rethinking History*, 16 (4): 565–585.

Borne, G. and Ponting, J. (2017) *Sustainable Surfing*, Abingdon and New York: Routledge.

Comer, K. (2010) *Surfer Girls in the New World Order*, Durham, NC and London: Duke University Press.

Comley, C. (2016) 'We have to establish our territory: how women surfers "carve out" gendered spaces within surfing', *Sport in Society*, 19 (8–9): 1289–1298.

Evers, C. (2015) 'Researching action sport with a GoPro™ camera: an embodied and emotional mobile video tale of the sea, masculinity, and men-who-surf', in C. Evers and I. Wellard (eds) *Researching Embodied Sport: Exploring Movement Cultures*, London: Routledge, 145–162.

Farmer, R. (1992) 'Surfing: motivations, values, and culture', *Journal of Sport Behavior*, 15 (3): 241–257.

Ford, N. and Brown, D. (2006) *Surfing and Social Theory: Experience, Embodiment, and Narrative of the Dream Glide*, London: Routledge.

Hough-Snee, D. and Sotelo Eastman, A. (2017) *The Critical Surf Studies Reader*, Durham, NC and London: Duke University Press.

Kusenbach, M. (2003) 'Street phenomenology', *Ethnography*, 4 (3): 455–485.

Lambert, D., Martins, L. and Ogborn, M. (2006) 'Currents, visions and voyages: historical geographies of the sea', *Journal of Historical Geography*, 32 (3): 479–493.

lisahunter, L. (2019) 'Sensory authoethnography: surfing approaches for understanding and communicating "seaspacetimes"', in L. lisahunter, M. Brown and K. Peters (eds) *Living with the Sea: Knowledge, Awareness and Action* (1st edn), Abingdon: Routledge, 100–113.

Merriman, P. (2014) 'Rethinking mobile methods', *Mobilities*, 9 (2): 167–187.

Olive, R. (2016) 'Going surfing/doing research: learning how to negotiate cultural politics from women who surf', *Continuum*, 30(2): 171–182.

Peters, K. (2010) 'Future promises for contemporary social and cultural geographies of the sea', *Geography Compass*, 4 (9): 1260–1272.

Pink, S. (2015) *Doing Sensory Ethnography*, London: Sage.

Scarfe, B., Elwany, M., Mead, S. and Black, K. (2003) *The Science of Surfing Waves and Surfing Breaks – A Review*, San Diego, CA: UC San Diego, Scripps Institution of Oceanography, https://escholarship.org/uc/item/6h72j1fz (accessed 1 October 2019).

Spinney, J. (2011) 'A chance to catch a breath: using mobile video ethnography in cycling research', *Mobilities*, 6 (2): 161–182.

Spinney, J. (2015) 'Close encounters? Mobile methods (post)phenomenology and affect', *Cultural Geographies*, 22 (2): 231–246.

Steinberg, P. (2001) *The Social Construction of the Ocean*, Cambridge: Cambridge University Press.

Xie, L. and Spinney, J. (2018) 'I won't cycle on a route like this; I don't think I fully understood what isolation meant: a critical evaluation of the safety principles in Cycling Level of Service (CLoS) tools from a gender perspective', *Travel Behaviour and Society*, 13: 197–213.

# 16

# Mobile methods for exploring young people's everynight mobilities

Samantha Wilkinson

## Introduction

This chapter draws on the mobile methods I used when exploring forty young people's (aged 15–24) alcohol consumption practices and experiences in the suburban case study locations of Chorlton and Wythenshawe, Manchester, UK. This chapter is interested in bringing to the fore creative mundane methods that can be used to research the 'everynight lives' of young people. When everynight life has been considered in the literature, it has typically been in relation to sleep, sleeping and sleepiness (Kraftl and Horton, 2008; Williams, 2005). However, I am interested in the use of the term 'everynight' as deployed earlier by Malbon (1999) in his ethnography of clubbing and dancing bound up with the consumption of ecstasy, to denote the regular, routine and ordinary aspects of nights out for participants in his study.

When researching young people's everynight lives, I am particularly interested in their diverse im/mobilities (e.g. walking, dancing, taxi journeying), bound up with alcohol consumption, through unspectacular and ordinary spaces including home, streets, parks and car parks. While young people's everynight mobilities may be somewhat banal, this is not to say that these mobilities are not embodied, emotional and affective (Binnie et al., 2007). In getting to grips with the emotion, embodiment and affect inherent in young people's everynight lives, this chapter responds to Spinney's (2014) call for a broadening of the palette of methods utilised in the study of mobility.

In this chapter, I first discuss mobile participant observation and mobile phone methods, with a focus on how they have been used and developed by others in the existing literature. Following this, I highlight the benefits, and reflect on the difficulties, of three mobile methods I drew on when researching young people's everynight lives: 'go-along' participant observation (see also chapters by Birchnell, Harada and Waitt; Cook; Stoodley; and Rose, this collection); mobile phone interviews and text messaging. Before drawing this chapter to a close, I provide advice for others when using these methods, with particular focus on ethical considerations.

## Mobile participant observation and mobile phone methods

### Mobile participant observation

Participant observation enables researchers to 'immerse' themselves in settings (Hemming, 2008). In so doing, researchers are able to uncover the processes and meanings undergirding socio-spatial life, thus gaining an understanding of the richness and complexity of lived experience (Herbert, 2000). This method allows researchers to observe practices and experiences first hand, thereby enabling them to verify or refute the veracity of young participants' recollections, gained through other methods such as interviews (Johnson, 2013). Further, participant observation enables researchers to build up their familiarity with the spaces and places discussed by participants through other methods, which can aid their interpretation and analysis.

While movement between spaces is inherent to ethnography, Watts and Urry (2008) contend that it has only recently become a site for fieldwork. As Larsen (2014: 60) says: 'through ethnographic *participation* one needs to be on the move, to study it as it takes place *in situ* – on the street and in the city, *as and when* it is performed'. This highlights the importance of researchers adopting 'natural go-along' participant observation (Kusenbach, 2003: 455); this involves movement with people, following objects, and co-present immersion in mobilities (Sheller, 2010). As such, this method is well suited to explore the spatial practices of different groups of people (Kusenbach, 2003). 'Go-along' participant observation thus offers potential to access: 'some of the transcendent and reflexive aspects of lived experience *in situ*' (Kusenbach, 2003: 455) (for further discussion on in-situ research see chapters by Rose and also Stoodley, this collection).

There are some examples in which mobile participant observation has been utilised to explore everyday lives. For instance, Smith and Hall (2016) draw on ethnographic work undertaken with a team of 'outreach' professionals tasked to care for the street homeless in Cardiff, UK. The authors contend that the outreach professionals enact their duty of care through a repeated patrolling of the city centre, in the course of which they aim to encounter clients and engage them in the provision of immediate services, and in planning for support that may meet their needs in the longer term. The authors highlight that outreach workers must move through, and make use of, everyday city space, as they find it; they must also find their clients – searching them out repeatedly, wherever they might turn out to be. Similarly, Larsen (2014) discussed embodied, sensuous, mobile ethnography that can illuminate how routines, habits and affective capacities of cycling are both performed and cultivated. Larsen (2014) argues that mobile ethnography is useful for illuminating the embodied qualities of movement. The paper challenges *static* notions of the body by analysing how cyclists' affective capacities develop as they practice cycling (Larsen, 2014).

In addition, Collinson (2008) asserts that while there is a growing body of ethnographic studies within the sociology of sport, little attention has been directed to the practice of 'doing' sport. Collinson (2008) draws on data from a collaborative auto-ethnographic study of distance runners, to analyse the ways in which two runners jointly accomplish running-together. The article also analyses some of the *knowledge in action* that underpins the production of running-together, in relation to three key themes: ground and performance, safety concerns and 'the other', in the form of training partner(s), highlighting the importance of aural and visual components. The work of Smith and Hall (2016), Larsen (2014) and Collinson (2008) highlights the importance for participant observation to be fluid, flexible, relational and mobile, rather than static. That is, participant observers must observe and participate in, through and beyond spaces and places, rather than solely *in* them.

Having provided background on the method of 'go-along' participant observation, I now turn to explore how mobile phone methods have been used by other researchers in the existing literature.

## Mobile phone methods

Researchers often use mobile phones when conducting fieldwork, in order to contact participants. For instance, Pelckmans (2009) used mobile phones in his multi-sited fieldwork in Africa, noting that the devices enabled participants to connect with him anywhere, at any time. However, researchers have typically undervalued mobile phones as a source of data. There may be ethical reasons for the lack of uptake in mobile phone methods. For instance, Ess (2015) discusses smart-phones as devices that typically accompany people into their most intimate and private spaces, highlighting that individuals seem increasingly willing to share intimate and private information across these networks.

One way of using mobile phones is to ask young people to take photographs and videos using their phones. The use of a mobile phone is significant because, unlike disposable cameras, young people have more editing options and opportunities to review images, to potentially delete them and to retake them. With the bricolage features of editing and deleting photographs and videos on mobile phones, then, the resultant photographs and videos should be recognised as crafted products, as opposed to reflections of actuality. Text messaging is another possible means of using mobile phones to generate data. While other research methods, such as diaries, are often perceived to require literacy skills, texting requires a different type of literacy skill, enabling the inclusion of young people with a range of abilities. Further, social anxiety may cause some young people to prefer technological communication, rather than face-to-face communication (Pierce, 2009).

Text messaging has been used as a method in the existing literature involving young people. Mikkelsen and Christensen (2009), for instance, conducted research into 10–13-year-old children's mobility in Demark, deploying a rolling mobile phone survey. Each of the participating children was asked to answer questions five times a day, via text messages sent to mobile phones – 'an always-at-hand-media' (Mikkelsen and Christensen, 2009: 43). The interactive survey generated data about practices, activities and social relationships in real time, thereby enabling researchers to virtually follow the movements of participants (Mikkelsen and Christensen, 2009). In Mikkelsen and Christensen's (2009) study, all questions but one had fixed reply categories for the children to respond; notably, text messages have been under-deployed in an ethnographic sense in the existing literature to gain an insight into young people's lifeworlds. This is important, since the quantification of young people's mobilities does not go far enough in elucidating their everyday and / or everynight experiences.

Having explored how other researchers have used mobile phone methods in the existing literature, I now turn to discuss how I utilised mobile methods in practice, when researching young people's everynight lives, bound up with the consumption of alcohol.

## Mobile methods in my exploration of young people's everynight lives

Drawing on research conducted between September 2015 and September 2016 with 15–24-year-olds, in the suburban case study locations of Chorlton and Wythenshawe, Manchester, UK, this section brings to the fore how I utilised the methods of 'go-along' participant observation, mobile phone interviews and text messaging, respectively, when exploring young people's mundane mobilities and everynight lives.

### 'Go-along' participant observation in practice

I undertook 'go-along' participant observation over the period of twelve months in order to observe the drinking practices and experiences of young people, and the spaces and places in which such practices occur. This involved participant observation with seven different groups of young people and their friends. I went on twenty-one nights in/out in total, lasting a minimum of three hours and up to a maximum of twelve hours. I undertook approximately ninety-six hours of participant observation in total, in a diverse range of spaces, including streets, car parks, pubs, bars, clubs, casino and homes, and for a variety of occasions, from routine nights out to more celebratory occasions, such as an eighteenth birthday party. I consider that my age (twenty-three at the time of conducting the research), appearance, personality and drinking biography were key factors that enticed young people to invite me on their nights out. I cannot help but think that an older researcher, for instance, would not have been so openly invited to 'special occasions' such as eighteenth birthday parties.

Mobile participant observation allowed participants to 'lead' me through their drinking spaces and places, thus situating the research encounters in the spaces typically frequented by participants. By 'hanging out' with participants, to use Kusenbach's (2003: 463) phraseology, I was able to explore their streams of experiences as they moved through, and interacted with, their surroundings. By following young people in, and between, different mundane spaces, I acquired knowledge of their embodied practices – something not easily obtained through other methods. Further, I argue that 'going-along' with participants produced a shared rhythm of movement, which promoted conversation and the sharing of understandings (for further discussion on studying rhythms see Lyon, this collection).

While the 'go-alongs' were primarily 'walk-alongs', they involved an array of mobilities and mundane everyday activities, including running, dancing, taxi-ing and bus journeying. When conducting participant observation, I adopted an active role as 'participant', rather than solely observing participants in a detached, emotionless manner. I was not, however, a full participant. While participants often smoked drugs in my presence – predominantly cannabis – I refrained from joining in with this. I made a decision prior to entering the field that I would not consume any substances I would not normally take. I did, however, consume a very small amount of alcohol, perceiving that this enabled me to be somewhat of an insider. However, my consumption of alcohol was limited, in order to ensure that my observations were not impaired (see Wilkinson, 2015).

I had some participant observation 'prompts' that I looked over prior to a night in/out with participants, which helped refresh my mind of the kinds of things I had to look out for. I recorded some brief, important notes during the nights out/in with participants using the 'notes' function on my mobile phone. I typically did this when I went to the toilet; however, I did not have to be too discreet about utilising this function, as it just appeared as if I were texting and, as such, I was able to avoid the impression of supervision. While discretion was not necessary, since participants had provided consent for me to observe their drinking practices and experiences, I did not wish for participants to alter their behaviour through the course of the night if they felt I was analysing them. I wrote detailed fieldnotes regarding my participant observation sessions the morning following the night in/out with participants.

## Mobile phone interviews in practice

Mobile phone interviews typically lasted between thirty and forty-five minutes, and enabled young people to take me with them on a tour of their mobile phone photographs and videos, often navigating through a variety of mobile phone applications, for instance Instagram, Facebook, WhatsApp and Snapchat, and primarily their photograph and video albums. I did not have a list of prescribed questions to ask and, while I had some prompts, these generally were not needed, as young people were easily able to talk around their photographs and videos. In other words, their photographs and videos acted as an oral catalyst, sparking lively discussions.

I had planned to ask the participants in my study to send me photographs and videos on their nights out, via their mobile phones. Despite gaining ethical approval to do so, this approach was not suitable 'in practice' because of the costs involved with sending photograph and video messages. While many young people in my study held a mobile phone contract, which often allows unlimited text messages to be sent, often this does not include photograph or video messages, which in the UK are typically charged at 30–40 pence per message. I developed and refined the research design through listening to the experiences of a young person in my study; Heather (fifteen, Wythenshawe, interview) stated: 'there's a party on Friday. I'll video some of it through the night on my mobile, like video bits and I'll come in and show you.' This ties with Griffin et al.'s (2009) contention that the use of mobile phones to video and photograph episodes during young people's nights out is very common, and plays a fundamental role in the recounting of drinking stories after the event.

Nine young people in my study opted into the mobile phone interview method, eight of whom were young women. The gender gap may be explained by the fact that, in everyday life, it is common for young women to take more photographs than young men (Martínez-Alemán and Wartman, 2009). My positionality may have fed into this too, and may be a contributing factor as to why there was a lower uptake of the mobile phone methods by men; I reflect on this in the text messaging section below.

The mobile phone interviews I conducted 'with' young people in my study, in which they reflected on their nights in/out involving alcohol, illuminated the following benefits of using this method: first,

participant-generated photographs and videos provided me with 'ethnography by proxy' (Bloustein and Baker, 2003: 72) for otherwise
difficult-to-access spaces, such as homes of participants' friends and
relatives. Secondly, the use of mobile phones in this way offered participants an opportunity to 'show', rather than solely 'tell', aspects of their
identity that may have otherwise remained hidden. Thirdly, in line
with this, the interview acted as a means of triangulating what young
people *said* they did with what the photographs and videos *showed* they
did. Fourthly, mobile phones changed the materiality of interviewing
participants; the young people were, to some extent, 'in charge', while
I largely watched the scenes unfold. Added to this, as the young people
looked at the photographs and videos on their phones, the situation felt
relatively 'casual', enabling participants to talk freely, without continuous
eye contact with me. 'Thinking with' the photographs and videos, then,
enabled participants to discuss themes that were important to them,
in a manner that was meaningful to them. Further still, this method
is of great value for its virtual mobility potential; instead of going to
physical places, the phone virtually transported me as a researcher to
the mundane and ordinary spaces of young people's everynight lives.

## Text messaging in practice

Ten young people in my study opted into the text messaging method
(eight of whom were young women, and two young men). The difference in gender uptake to different methods is seldom mentioned in the
methods literature; however, it is worth reflecting on here. The lower
uptake of male participants to this method may have been because I
am a female researcher; I got the impression from one young man that
his girlfriend thought it was 'weird' that he was exchanging text messages with me (field diary, 9 May 2014). The one-to-one functionality
of mobile phones lends itself to romantic practices where young people
can flirt, and texting often provides new opportunities for young people
to create meaning and develop relationships with others (Ling et al.,
2014). It is worth considering that my positionality may have thus been
a reason why other young men may not have opted into this method.
    Many young people in my study had mobile phone contracts in
which they were able to send unlimited text messages with no associated costs. Other young people were on 'pay as you go' price plans,
which had 'bundles' of text messages included in the cost. Consequently, asking participants to send text messages did not 'price them

out' of taking part in my research. Below are some examples of text messages I received from participants:

> Just standin outside the offy[1] we have been here for ageeesss. Asked loads of people. no1 will go in!!! wanna go home. (Vera, fifteen, Wythenshawe, text message, 12 July 2014, 8.32pm)

> Having a quiet one with the ladies tonight at mine, few glasses of wine, not seen them in ages so will be good to catch up. (Evie, twenty-four, Chorlton, text message, 2 May 2014, 6.15pm)

> Trying to get served tonight. What shall I wear? Need to look old, but not too slaggy. Low top is always a hit right? (Olivia, seventeen, Wythenshawe, text message, 1 March 2014, 4.15pm)

The above examples of text messages received from participants illustrate that I used text messages as data in two predominant ways. First, conversations I had with the young people, via text messages, regarding nights out they invited me on were a valuable form of data. This provided insight into: what time they were planning on going out; what they were planning on wearing; what they were planning to drink; how they intended to source their alcohol; where they were intending to go; and whom they were intending to meet, for instance. Secondly, I asked participants to update me, via text messages, of their experiences and practices during their nights in/out involving alcohol, when I was not present. The use of text messaging was beneficial, as I was only able to undertake participant observation with one group of young people at a time. By still maintaining contact with other participants through text messaging, I did not completely 'miss out' on their drinking experiences as they were occurring.

An additional benefit of text messaging was its ability to allow insight into events that occurred without the interference of my presence. For instance, one club was notoriously cautious about letting groups of young men in. When I accompanied the young men during participant observations, they had no problem entering the club; when I was not with this group on another occasion, they texted me telling me that they were not permitted to enter. Take the text messaging exchange between myself and Tim below:

> Tim: Didn't get in to Montys [a club] tonight.
> SW[2]: Why is that?
> Tim: Too many boys and not enough girls the guy on the door said.
> (Tim, nineteen, Chorlton, text messaging, 2 January 2014, 11:59pm)

My presence during participant observations, as a female researcher, thus interrupted how the young men typically experienced their nights out, whereas text messaging was advantageous in enabling insight into the usual proceedings. Further, text messaging is a beneficial method because most other methods, such as diaries and interviews, require participants to remember and recall events. However, the date- and time-stamped text messages provided me with an 'experience snapshot' (Plowman and Stevenson, 2012: 539) of young people's alcohol-related mobilities. Overall, text messaging offered an informal, undemanding and unobtrusive means of understanding young people's everynight drinking practices and experiences, as they unfolded.

One of the limitations of this method is that often, as the young people were becoming increasingly involved in the night's activities and as their levels of drunkenness increased, they forgot to send texts, or the language in their texts became less decipherable. Further, there were occasions when young people told me their mobile phones ran out of battery, restricting me from understanding how their nights unfolded. Notwithstanding this, text messaging is a research technique in line with many young people's everyday/everynight practices. For young people in my study, text messaging is a culturally legible means of communication. More than this, text messages have the ability to provide insight into young people's situated practices and lived everynight realities.

## Advice for others

I would advise others considering using mobile methods, such as 'go-along' participant observation, mobile phone interviews and text messaging, to be attentive to ethical considerations, as I detail below.

During participant observations with young people who are consuming alcohol, I advise that a strategy must be deployed in order to retain informed consent. Deciding whether to include data acquired when participants appear drunk can be achieved by following up with participants on another occasion, when they are sober, to gauge whether they are comfortable with the inclusion of the observations of their inebriated behaviour. As this illustrates, rather than ethical practice being secured by a single act of informed consent, the approach to ethics should be situational and responsive. While ethical guidelines are useful, they are alone insufficient in ensuring that the researcher acts in an ethical manner. This is because they do not address 'ethics in practice' – that is, the day-to-day ethical quandaries arising through the process of *doing* research. Spaces and happenings are perpetually in process, and consequently ethical incidents constantly arise; this necessitates researchers to be ethically reflexive throughout the research process.

During participant observation, in order to ensure that the researcher does not encourage participants to drink more (in terms of quantity, cost or alcohol content) than they otherwise would, they should not purchase drinks for, or accept drinks from, participants. During participant observations, my original stance was that I would have a limited duty of care towards participants, offering help to those in vulnerable situations (e.g. if someone was clearly intoxicated and wishing to walk home alone), yet recognising that this help may not always be wanted or accepted. However, I found that friends were often very effective at looking after one another, and my assistance was never required.

I recommend that mobile phone interviews and text messaging are best adopted at a later stage in the research process, when the researcher has formed relationships with participants, built rapport and gained mutual trust. With regard to ethical considerations for mobile phone interviews, participants in my study provided intimate details of themselves and their friends' drinking behaviour through the photographs and videos. It is important to point out that it is often not possible for participants to gain formal consent from everyone that may be featured in their photographs and videos taken in public spaces. There are ethical issues with participant-generated photographs and videos, in that participants may capture other young people in their photographs and videos who have not consented to participate in the study and may be below the legal drinking age. Consequently, I suggest giving participants an easy-to-read information sheet detailing the types of things it is appropriate to take photographs of (e.g. spaces of drinking; movements through spaces; types of alcohol consumed), and other examples of things that you do not wish participants to capture (e.g. photographs / videos including close-shots of peers; and drug consumption).

Despite telling the young people in advance that I would not be disseminating their photographs and videos, several participants showed me their photographs and videos, asking: 'are we famous?' It seemed that they wanted to be identified, and to show and tell others that they had been involved in the research. However, it must be recognised that revealing photographic and videographic data would compromise the anonymity and privacy of the participants, which may have negative future implications, for instance when seeking employment. Consequently, as is commonly the case, while utilising visual means of researching, it is sometimes necessary to present the data as text. This approach recognises that photograph and video data can inform thinking and analysis in a backstage manner, without being publicly presented.

It could be argued that, through asking young people to photograph and video spaces on their alcohol-related nights out, the researcher is potentially placing them at risk (as Leyshon, 2002 recognised when encouraging his participants to video / photograph places within their villages). This risk can be minimised by asking the young people to take photographs and videos using their own mobile phones. Consequently, by not giving young people cameras / video cameras, you are not changing their habitual practices, which would arguably place them at greater risk. There is, nonetheless, a chance that the young people's mobile phones might be stolen; mobile phones are a significant site of victimisation (Pain et al., 2005). If young people are acknowledged as social actors, there is the argument that they have the necessary agency to avoid putting themselves at risk. While appreciating this, it is worthwhile briefing participants beforehand, reminding them not to take photographs or videos in any situations where they do not feel comfortable. Moreover, young people should be instructed to take photographs and videos only in places they usually go, in ways that they habitually would, while being mindful of the risks associated with roads and traffic. Despite these precautions, because photography and videography are a normal part of many young people's nights out, I found that participants in my study did not have any concerns about their safety when undertaking this method. I got the impression that they thought I was being overly cautious and perhaps 'mothering' them.

Another word of caution, when using text messaging to explore young people's drinking experiences, is that young people may send text messages in the mire of drunkenness that, when sober, they may no longer wish to be used as data. To overcome this ethical quandary, I recommend meeting with participants a few days after their nights out, presenting them with a printed copy of the text messages they sent, and asking them if they are (un)happy for this data to be used. No young people withdrew any text messages they sent me. As the text messages remained on young people's phones, they had physical evidence of the texts themselves. Many young people could recall sending me 'drunken' texts, and sent follow-up texts the next day. Young people found their drunken texts comical and were excited about them being used as data; again the 'are we going to be famous?' vibe prevailed. It should be made clear to young people at the outset that text messages exchanged with the researcher are not casual interactions. However, due to the significant amount of time a researcher spends with his/her participants over the course of a year, the problem of a blur between 'research friendship' and 'friendship' can be experienced. It is thus important to keep reviewing informed consent to remind participants that you are not only a friend, but you are also a researcher.

Box 16.1 details training / tools / equipment required by researchers wishing to undertake 'go-along' participant observation, mobile phone interviews and text messaging.

---

### Box 16.1: Tools, training and equipment

Tools for 'go-along' participant observation:

- university identification;
- mobile phone with credit;
- notebook;
- participant observation prompts.

Tools for mobile phones interviews:

- ensure participants have a mobile phone with a camera (either their own or lent one for the purposes of the study);
- guide for participants on what they should/should not take photographs and videos of;
- interview prompts;
- dictaphone.

Text messaging:

- ensure researcher has a research-specific mobile phone with credit (different number from their personal phone);
- ensure participants have a mobile phone with credit (either their own or lent one for the purposes of the study);
- guide for participants on what type of text messaging content the researcher is interested in.

## Conclusions

As I have argued throughout this chapter, in order to gain insight into young people's everynight drinking geographies and their alcohol-related mundane mobilities, mobile methods must be deployed. This chapter has elucidated three complementary methods that, when undertaking my research, I found fitted well with young people's lives, and how they document and share information; these are 'go-along' participant observation, mobile phone interviews and text messaging. By elucidating three novel mobile methods, this chapter has responded to Spinney's (2014) call for a broadening of the palette of methods used in the study of mobility.

This chapter highlights that mobile methods provide an original perspective on young people's everynight drinking experiences. To recap, 'go-along' participant observation produced a shared rhythm of movement that promoted conversation and the sharing of understandings. Moreover, mobile phone interviews proved to offer adaptive and creative means of understanding young people's drinking micro-geographies; they provided an ethnography by proxy, enabling me to virtually access the mundane spaces of young people's everynight lives. Further, I found text messaging beneficial in offering insight into the temporal unfolding of young people's alcohol consumption practices, experiences and mobilities; something that may be overlooked when using other forms of data collection.

Cumulatively, these mobile methods enabled me to gain insight into the mundane lived experiences of young people's alcohol consumption practices and experience. I have also emphasised that using mobile methods, when bound up with the consumption of alcohol, can be ethically problematic, and I have offered advice for other researchers in this respect. Due to their ability to offer novel insight into the spatio-temporal specificities of young people's everyday/night lives, mobile phone methods may be beneficial for other researchers aiming to gain insight into the mundane spaces, mobilities and rhythms experienced by different groups of young people. In Box 16.2, I signpost some key resources for readers, in order to found out more about mobile methods:

## Notes

1 'Offy' is an abbreviation a number of the participants in my study used to refer to the off-licence (a convenience store which sells alcohol).
2 Author's initials.

---

**Box 16.2: Further reading**

Resources for readers to find out more:

Buscher, M. and Urry, J. (2009) 'Mobile methods and the empirical', *European Journal of Social Theory*,12 (1): 99–116.

Wilkinson, S. (2016) 'Hold the phone! Culturally credible research "with" young people', *Children's Geographies*, 14 (2): 232–238.

---

## Bibliography

Binnie, J., Holloway, J., Milligton, S. and Young, C. (2007) 'Mundane geographies: alienation, potentialities, and practice', *Environment and Planning A*, 39: 515–520.

Bloustein, G. and Baker, S. (2003) 'On not talking to strangers: researching the micro worlds of girls through visual auto-ethnographic practice', *Social Analysis: The International Journal of Social and Cultural Practices*, 47 (3): 64–79.

Collinson, J.A. (2008) 'Running the routes together: corunning and knowledge in action', *Journal of Contemporary Ethnography*, 37 (1): 38–61.

Ess, C. (2015) 'New selves, new research ethics?', in H. Fossheim and H. Ingierd (eds) *Internet Research Ethics*, Oslo: Cappelen Damm Akademisk.

Griffin, C., Bengry-Howell, A., Hackley, C., Mistral, W. and Szmigin, I. (2009) '"Every time I do it I absolutely annihilate myself": loss of (self)-consciousness and loss of memory in young people's drinking narratives', *Sociology*, 43 (3): 457–476.

Hemming, P. J. (2008) 'Mixing qualitative research methods in children's geographies', *Area*, 40 (2): 152–162.

Herbert, S. (2000) 'For ethnography', *Progress in Human Geography*, 24 (4): 550–568.

Johnson, P. (2013) '"You think you're a rebel on a big bottle": teenage drinking, peers and performance authenticity', *Journal of Youth Studies*, 16 (6): 747–758.

Kraftl, P. and Horton, J. (2008) 'Spaces of everynight life: for geographies of sleep, sleeping and sleepiness', *Progress in Human Geography*, 32 (4): 509–524.

Kusenbach, M. (2003) 'Street phenomenology: the go-along as ethnographic research tool', *Ethnography*, 4 (3): 455–485.

Larsen, J. (2014) '(Auto)Ethnography and cycling', *International Journal of Social Research Methodology*, 17 (1): 59–71.

Leyshon, M. (2002) 'On being "in the field": practice, progress and problems in research with young people in rural areas', *Journal of Rural Studies*, 18 (2): 179–191.

Ling, R., Baron, N. S., Lenhart, A. and Campbell, S. W. (2014) '"Girls text really weird": gender, texting and identity among teens', *Journal of Children and Media*, 8 (4): 423–439.

Malbon, B. (1999) *Clubbing: Dancing, Ecstasy and Vitality*, London: Routledge.

Martínez-Alemán, A. M. and Wartman, K. L. (2009) *Online Student Networking on Campus: Understanding what Matters in Student Culture*, New York: Routledge.

Mikkelsen, M. R. and Christensen, P. (2009) 'Is children's independent mobility really independent? A study of children's mobility combining ethnography and GPS/mobile phone technologies', *Mobilities*, 4 (1): 37–58.

Pain, R. H, Grundy, S., Gill, S., Towner, E., Sparks, G. and Hughes, K. (2005) '"So long as I take my mobile": mobile phones, urban life and geographies of young people's safety', *International Journal of Urban and Regional Research*, 29 (4): 814–830.

Pelckmans, L. (2009) 'Phoning anthropologists: the mobile phone's (re-) shaping of anthropological research', in M. de Bruijn, F. Nyamnjoh and I. Brinkman (eds) *Mobile Phones: The New Talking Drums of Everyday Africa*, Cameroon: Langaa and African Studies, 23–49.

Pierce, T. (2009) 'Social anxiety and technology: face-to-face communication versus technological communication among teens', *Computers in Human Behavior*, 25 (6): 1367–1372.

Plowman, L. and Stevenson, O. (2012) 'Using mobile phone diaries to explore children's everyday lives', *Childhood*, 19 (4): 539–553.

Sheller, M. (2010) 'Foreword', in M. Fincham, B. McGuinness and L. Murray (eds) *Mobile Methodologies*, Basingstoke: Palgrave Macmillan, vii–x.

Smith, R. J. and Hall, T. (2016) 'Pedestrian circulations: urban ethnography, the mobilities paradigm and outreach work', *Mobilities*, 11 (4): 498–508.

Spinney, J. (2014) 'Close encounters? Mobile methods (post)phenomenology and affect', *Cultural Geographies*, 22 (2): 231–246.

Watts, L. and Urry, J. (2008) 'Moving methods, travelling times', *Environment and Planning D: Society and Space*, 26 (5): 860–874.

Wilkinson, S. (2015) *Young People, Alcohol and Urban Life*. PhD thesis, University of Manchester.

Williams, S. (2005) *Sleep and Society: Sociological Ventures into the (Un)Known*, London: Routledge.

# Index